Fingerprints

Fingerprints

A COLLECTION OF
MYSTERY STORIES BY
THE CRIME WRITERS OF CANADA

edited by

Beverley Beetham-Endersby

Irwin Publishing
TORONTO CANADA

Canadian Cataloguing in Publication Data

Crime Writers of Canada
Fingerprints

ISBN 0-7725-1504-2

1. Detective and mystery stories, Canadian (English).* I. Title.

PS8323.D4C7 1984 C813'.0872'08 C84-099023-5
PR9197.35.D4C7 1984

Designed by Lisa Guthro for Robert Garbutt Productions
Typeset by Compeer Typographical Services Ltd.
Printed in Canada by Tri-Graphic Printing Limited

1 2 3 4 5 6 7 8 TRI 91 90 89 88 87 86 85 84

Published by Irwin Publishing Inc.

Contents

Foreword

Crime Writers of Canada was founded two years ago to celebrate the achievements of writers in the genre and to provide a forum for those who conjure murder and mayhem from their typewriters and word processors.

We have some eighty members from across the country, including both published authors and those with a professional interest in crime writing. This year Crime Writers of Canada inaugurated an annual Awards Banquet to honour the recipient of the Arthur Ellis Award (Arthur Ellis was the pseudonym for all Canada's hangmen). The first winner was Eric Wright for his novel *The Night the Gods Smiled* and the Chairman's Award was presented to Derrick Murdoch for his services to the craft of crime writing through his weekly column in the *Globe & Mail.*

This volume is the first collection of what we trust will be an ongoing enterprise—a sampler, if you will, of the literary range and imagination of our members. Each of these stories is as individual as a fingerprint. We hope you will enjoy them and that they will act as an introduction to the full-length works of the Crime Writers of Canada.

TONY ASPLER
CWC Chairman, 1982–84

Fingerprints

McGowney's Miracle

MARGARET MILLAR

Born in Kitchener, Ontario, Margaret Millar published her first novel, The Invisible Worm, *in 1941 and is now completing her 25th work of fiction. One of the great practitioners in the field of mystery and psychological suspense, she has had her work translated into more than a dozen foreign languages. A past president of the Mystery Writers of America, she received that organization's most prestigious honour — the Grand Master Award — in 1983 for lifetime achievement. She has also been awarded an Edgar Award for the Best Mystery of the Year for her classic* Beast in View.

WHEN I FINALLY found him, it was by accident. He was waiting for a cable car on Powell Street, a dignified little man about sixty, in a black topcoat and a grey fedora. He stood apart from the crowd, aloof but friendly, his hands clasped just below his chest, like a minister about to bless a batch of heathen. I knew he wasn't a minister.

A sheet of fog hung over San Francisco, blurring the lights and muffling the clang of the cable cars.

I stepped up behind McGowney and said, "Good evening."

There was no recognition in his eyes, no hesitation in his voice. "Why, good evening, sir." He turned with a little smile. "It is kind of you to greet a stranger so pleasantly."

For a moment, I was almost ready to believe I'd made a mistake. There are on record many cases of perfect doubles, and what's more, I hadn't seen McGowney since the beginning of July. But there was one important thing McGowney couldn't conceal: his voice still carried the throaty accents of the funeral parlour.

He tipped his hat and began walking briskly up Powell Street toward the hill, his topcoat flapping around his skinny legs like broken wings.

In the middle of the block, he turned to see if I was following him. I was. He walked on, shaking his head from side to side as if genuinely puzzled by my interest in him. At the next corner, he stopped in front of a department store and waited for me, leaning against the window, his hands in his pockets.

When I approached, he looked up at me frowning. "I don't know why you're following me, young man, but—"

"Why don't you ask me, McGowney?"

But he didn't ask. He just repeated his own name, "McGowney," in a surprised voice, as if he hadn't heard it for a long time.

I said, "I'm Eric Meecham, Mrs. Keating's lawyer. We've met before."

"I've met a great many people. Some I recall, some I do not."

"I'm sure you recall Mrs. Keating. You conducted her funeral last July."

"Of course, of course. A great lady, a very great lady. Her demise saddened the hearts of all who had the privilege of her acquaintance, all who tasted the sweetness of her smile — "

"Come off it, McGowney. Mrs. Keating was a sharp-tongued virago without a friend in this world."

He turned away from me, but I could see the reflection of his face in the window, strained and anxious.

"You're a long way from home, McGowney."

"This is my home now."

"You left Arbana very suddenly."

"To me it was not sudden. I had been planning to leave for twenty years, and when the time came, I left. It was summer then, but all I could think of was the winter coming on and everything dying. I had had enough of death."

"Mrs. Keating was your last—client?"

"She was."

"Her coffin was exhumed last week."

A cable car charged up the hill like a drunken rocking horse, its sides bulging with passengers. Without warning, McGowney darted out into the street and sprinted up the hill after the car. In spite of his age, he could have made it, but the car was so crowded there wasn't a single space for him to get a handhold. He stopped running and stood motionless in the centre of the street, staring after the car as it plunged and reared up the hill.

Oblivious to the honks and shouts of motorists, he walked slowly back to the curb where I was waiting.

"You can't run away, McGowney."

He glanced at me wearily, without speaking. Then he took out a half-soiled handkerchief and wiped the moisture from his forehead.

"The exhumation can't be much of a surprise to you," I said. "You wrote me the anonymous letter suggesting it. It was postmarked Berkeley. That's why I'm here in this area."

"I wrote you no letter," he said.

"The information it contained could have come only from you."

"No. Somebody else knew as much about it as I did."

"Who?"

"My—wife."

"Your wife." It was the most unexpected answer he could have given me. Mrs. McGowney had died, along with her only daughter, in the flu epidemic after World War I. The story is the kind that still goes the rounds in a town like Arbana, even after thirty-five years: McGowney, unemployed after his discharge from the Army, had had no funds to pay for the double funeral, and when the undertaker offered him an apprenticeship to work off the debt, McGowney accepted. It was common knowledge that after his wife's death he never so much as looked at another woman, except, of course, in line of duty.

I said, "So you've married again."

"Yes."

"When?"

"Six months ago."

"Right after you left Arbana."

"Yes."

"You didn't lose much time starting a new life for yourself."

"I couldn't afford to. I'm not young."

"Did you marry a local woman?"

"Yes."

I didn't realize until later that he had taken "local" to mean Arbana, not San Francisco as I had intended.

I said, "You think your wife wrote me that anonymous letter?"

"Yes."

The street lights went on, and I realized it was getting late and cold. McGowney pulled up his coat collar and put on a pair of ill-fitting white cotton gloves. I had seen him wearing gloves like that before; they were as much a part of his professional equipment as his throaty voice and his vast store of sentimental aphorisms.

He caught me staring at the gloves and said, with a trace of apology, "Money is a little tight these days. My wife is knitting me a pair of woollen gloves for my birthday."

"You're not working?"

"No."

"It shouldn't be hard for a man of your experience to find a job in your particular field." I was pretty sure he hadn't even applied for one. During the past few days, I had contacted nearly every mortician within the Bay area; McGowney had not been to any of them.

"I don't want a job in my particular field," McGowney said.

"It's the only thing you're trained for."

"Yes. But I no longer believe in death."

He spoke with simple earnestness, as if he had said, I no longer play blackjack, or I no longer eat salted peanuts.

Death, blackjack, or salted peanuts—I was not prepared to argue with McGowney about any of them, so I said, "My car's in the garage at the Canterbury Hotel. We'll walk over and get it, and I'll drive you home."

We started toward Sutter Street. The stream of shoppers had been augmented by a flow of white-collar workers, but all the people and the noise and the confusion left McGowney untouched. He moved sedately along beside me, smiling a little to himself, like a man who has developed the faculty of walking out on the world from time to time and going to live on some remote and happy island of his own. I wondered where McGowney's island was and who lived there with him.

I knew only one thing for sure: on McGowney's island there was no death.

He said suddenly, "It must have been very difficult."

"What was?"

"The exhumation. The ground gets so hard back East in the wintertime. I presume you didn't attend, Mr. Meecham?"

"You presume wrong."

"My, that's no place for an amateur."

For my money, it was no place for anyone. The cemetery had been white with snow that had fallen during the night. Dawn had been breaking, if you could call that meagre, grudging light a dawn. The simple granite headstone had read, ELEANOR REGINA KEATING, OCTOBER 3, 1899—JUNE 30, 1953. A BLESSED ONE FROM US IS GONE, A VOICE WE LOVED IS STILL.

The blessed one had been gone, all right. Two hours later, when the coffin was pulled up and opened, the smell that rose from it was not the smell of death, but the smell of newspapers rotted with dampness and stones grey-greened with mildew.

I said, "You know what we found, don't you, McGowney?"

"Naturally. I directed the funeral."

"You accept sole responsibility for burying an empty coffin?"

"Not sole responsibility, no."

"Who was in with you? And why?"

He merely shook his head.

As we waited for a traffic light, I studied McGowney's face, trying to estimate the degree of his sanity. There seemed to be no logic behind his actions. Mrs. Keating had died quite unmysteriously of a heart attack and had been buried, according to her instructions to me, in a closed coffin. The doctor who had signed the death certificate was indisputably honest. He had happened to be in Mrs. Keating's house at the time, attending to her older daughter, Mary, who had had a cold. He had examined Mrs. Keating, pronounced her dead, and sent for McGowney. Two days later I had escorted Mary, still sniffling (whether from grief or the same cold, I don't know), to the funeral. McGowney, as usual, said and did all the correct things.

Except one. He neglected to put Mrs. Keating's body in the coffin.

Time had passed. No one had particularly mourned Mrs. Keating. She had been an unhappy woman, mentally and morally superior to her husband, who had been killed during a drinking spree in New Orleans, and to her two daughters, who resembled their father. I had been Mrs. Keating's lawyer for three years. I had enjoyed talking to her; she had had a quick mind and a sharp sense of humour. But as in the case of many wealthy people who have been cheated of the privilege of work and the satisfactions it brings, she had been a bored and lonely woman who carried despair on her shoulder like a pet parakeet and fed it from time to time on scraps from her bitter memories.

Right after Mrs. Keating's funeral, McGowney had sold his business and left town. No one in Arbana had connected the two events until the anonymous letter arrived from Berkeley shortly before Mrs. Keating's will was awaiting admission into probate. The letter, addressed to me, had suggested the exhumation and stated the will must be declared invalid since there was no proof of death. I could think of no reason why McGowney's new wife wrote the letter, unless she had tired of him and had chosen a roundabout method of getting rid of him.

The traffic light changed and McGowney and I crossed the street and waited under the hotel marquee while the doorman sent for my car.

I didn't look at McGowney, but I could feel him watching me intently.

"You think I'm mad, eh, Meecham?"

It wasn't a question I was prepared to answer. I tried to look noncommittal.

"I don't pretend to be entirely normal, Meecham. Do you?"

"I try."

McGowney's hand, in its ill-fitting glove, reached over and touched my arm, and I forced myself not to slap it away. It perched on my coat sleeve like a wounded pigeon. "But suppose you had an abnormal experience."

"Like you?"

"Like me. It was a shock, a great shock, even though I had always had the feeling that someday it would happen. I was on the watch for it every time I had a new case. It was always in my mind. You might even say I *willed* it."

Two trickles of sweat oozed down behind my ears into my collar. "What did you will, McGowney?"

"I willed her to live again."

I became aware the doorman was signalling to me. My car was at the curb with the engine running.

I climbed in behind the wheel, and McGowney followed me into the car with obvious reluctance, as if he was already regretting what he'd told me.

"You don't believe me," he said, as we pulled away from the curb.

"I'm a lawyer. I deal in facts."

"A fact is what happens, isn't it?"

"Close enough."

"Well, this happened."

"She came back to life?"

"Yes."

"By the power of your will alone?"

He stirred restlessly in the seat beside me. "I gave her oxygen and adrenalin."

"Have you done this with other clients of yours?"

"Many times, yes."

"Is this procedure usual among members of your profession?"

"For me it was usual," McGowney said earnestly. "I've always wanted to be a doctor. I was in the Medical Corps during the war, and I picked up a little knowledge here and there."

"Enough to perform miracles?"

"It was not my knowledge that brought her back to life. It was my will. She had lost the will to live, but I had enough for both of us."

If it is true only a thin line separates sanity and madness, McGowney crossed and recrossed that line a dozen times within an hour, jumping over it and back again, like a child skipping rope.

"You understand now, Meecham? She had lost all desire. I saw it happening to her. We never spoke—I doubt she even knew my name—but for years I watched her pass my office on her morning walk. I saw the change come over her, the dullness of her eyes and the way she walked. I knew she was going to die. One day when she was passing by, I went out to tell her, to warn her. But when she saw me, she ran. I think she realized what I was going to say."

He was telling the truth, according to his lights. Mrs. Keating had mentioned the incident to me last spring. I recalled her words: "A funny thing occurred this morning, Meecham. As I was walking past the undertaking parlour, that odd little man rushed out and almost scared the life out of me. . . ."

In view of what subsequently happened, this was a giant among ironies. As we drove toward the Bay Bridge and Berkeley, McGowney told me his story.

It was midday at the end of June, and the little backroom McGowney used as a lab was hot and humid after a morning rain.

Mrs. Keating woke up as if from a long and troubled sleep. Her hands twitched, her mouth moved in distress, a pulse began to beat in her temple. Tears squeezed out from between her closed lids and slithered past the tips of her ears into the folds of her hair.

McGowney bent over her, quivering with excitement. "Mrs. Keating! Mrs. Keating, you are alive!"

"Oh—God."

"A miracle has just happened!"

"Leave me alone. I'm tired."

"You are alive, you are *alive!*"

Slowly she opened her eyes and looked up at him. "You officious little wretch, what have you done?"

McGowney stepped back, stunned and shaken. "But—but you are alive. It's happened. My miracle has happened."

"Alive. Miracle." She mouthed the words as if they were lumps of alum. "You meddling idiot."

"I—But I—"

"Pour me a glass of water. My throat is parched."

He was trembling so violently he could hardly get the water out of the cooler. This was his miracle. He had hoped and waited for it all his life, and now it had exploded in his face like an April-fool cigar.

He gave her the water and sat down heavily in a chair, watching her while she drank very slowly, as if in her short recess from life her muscles had already begun to forget their function.

"Why did you do it?" Mrs. Keating crushed the paper cup in her fist as if it were McGowney himself. "Who asked you for a miracle, anyway?"

"But I—Well, the fact is—"

"The fact is, you're a blooming meddler, that's what the fact is, McGowney."

"Yes, ma'am."

"Now what are you going to do?"

"Well, I—I hadn't thought."

"Then you'd better start right now."

"Yes, ma'am." He stared down at the floor, his head hot with misery, his limbs cold with disappointment. "First, I had better call the doctor."

"You'll call no one, McGowney."

"But your family—they'll want to know right away that—"

"They are not going to know."

"But—"

"No one is going to know, McGowney. No one at all. Is that clear?"

"Yes."

"Now sit down and be quiet and let me think."

He sat down and was quiet. He had no desire to move or to speak. Never had he felt so futile and depressed.

"I suppose," Mrs. Keating said grimly, "you expect me to be grateful to you."

McGowney shook his head.

"If you do, you must be crazy." She paused and looked at him thoughtfully. "You *are* a little crazy, aren't you, McGowney?"

"There are those who think so," he said, with some truth. "I don't agree."

"You wouldn't."

"Can't afford to, ma'am."

The windows of the room were closed and no street sounds penetrated the heavy frosted glass, but from the corridor outside the door came the sudden tap of footsteps on tile.

McGowney bolted across the room and locked the door and stood against it.

"Mr. McGowney? You in there?"

McGowney looked at Mrs. Keating. Her face had turned chalky, and she had one hand clasped to her throat.

"Mr. McGowney?"

"Yes, Jim."

"You're wanted on the telephone."

"I—can't come right now, Jim. Take a message."

"She wants to talk to you personally. It's the Keating girl, about the time and cost of the funeral arrangements."

"Tell her I'll call her back later."

"All right." There was a pause. "You feeling okay, Mr. McGowney?"

"Yes."

"You sound kind of funny."

"I'm fine, Jim. Absolutely first-rate."

"Okay. Just thought I'd ask."

The footsteps tapped back down the tile corridor.

"Mary loses no time." Mrs. Keating spoke through dry, stiff lips. "She wants me safely underground so she can marry her electrician. Well, your duty is clear, McGowney."

"What is it?"

"Put me there."

McGowney stood propped against the door like a wooden soldier. "You mean, b-b-bury you?"

"Me, or a reasonable facsimile."

"That I couldn't do, Mrs. Keating. It wouldn't be ethical."

"It's every bit as ethical as performing unsolicited miracles."

"You don't understand the problems."

"Such as?"

"For one thing, your family and friends. They'll want to see you lying in—What I mean is, it's customary to put the body on view."

"I can handle that part of it all right."

"How?"

"Get me a pen and some paper."

McGowney didn't argue, because he knew he was at fault. It was his miracle; he'd have to take the consequences.

Mrs. Keating predated the letter by three weeks, and wrote the following:

> To whom it may concern, not that it should concern anybody except myself:
>
> I am giving these instructions to Mr. McGowney concerning my funeral arrangements. Inasmuch as I have valued privacy during my life, I want no intrusion on it after my death. I am instructing Mr. McGowney to close my coffin immediately and to see it stays closed, in spite of any mawkish pleas from my survivors.
>
> Eleanor Regina Keating

She folded the paper twice and handed it to McGowney. "You are to show this to Mary and Joan and to Mr. Meecham, my lawyer." She paused, looking very pleased with herself. "Well. This is getting to be quite exciting, eh, McGowney?"

"Quite," McGowney said listlessly.

"As a matter of fact, it's given me an appetite. I don't suppose there's a kitchen connected with this place?"

"No."

"Then you'd better get me something from the corner drugstore. A couple of tuna-salad sandwiches, on wheat, with plenty of coffee. Lunch," she added with a satiric little smile, "will have to be on you. I forgot my handbag."

"Money," McGowney said. "*Money.*"

"What about it?"

"What will happen to your money?"

"I made a will some time ago."

"But *you,* what will you live on?"

"Perhaps," Mrs. Keating said dryly, "you'd better perform another miracle."

When he returned from the drugstore with her lunch, Mrs. Keating ate and drank with obvious enjoyment. She offered McGowney a part of the second sandwich, but he was too disheartened to eat. His miracle, which had started out as a great golden bubble, had turned into an iron ball chained to his leg.

Somehow he got through the day. Leaving Mrs. Keating in the lab with some old magazines and a bag of apples, McGowney went about his business. He talked to Mary and Joan Keating in person and to Meecham on the telephone. He gave his assistant, Jim Wagner, the rest of the afternoon off, and when Jim had gone, he filled Mrs. Keating's coffin (the de luxe white-and-bronze model Mary had chosen out of the catalogue) with rocks packed in newspapers, until it was precisely the right weight.

McGowney was a small man, unaccustomed to physical exertion, and by the time he had finished, his body was throbbing with weariness.

It was at this point Mary Keating telephoned to say she and Joan had been thinking the matter over, and since Mrs. Keating had always inclined toward thrift, it was decided she would never rest at ease in such an ostentatious affair as the white and bronze. The plain grey would be far more appropriate, as well as cheaper.

"You should," McGowney said coldly, "have let me know sooner."

"We just decided a second ago."

"It's too late to change now."

"I don't see why."

"There are—certain technicalities."

"Well, really, Mr. McGowney. If you're not willing to put yourself out a little, maybe we should take our business somewhere else."

"No! You can't do that—I mean, it wouldn't be proper, Miss Keating."

"It's a free country."

"Wait a minute. Suppose I give you a special price on the white and bronze."

"How special?"

"Say, twenty-five per cent off?"

There was a whispered conference at the other end of the line, and then Mary said, "It's still a lot of money."

"Thirty-five?"

"Well, that seems more *like*," Mary said, and hung up.

The door of McGowney's office opened, and Mrs. Keating crossed the room, wearing a grim little smile.

McGowney looked at her helplessly. "You shouldn't be out here, ma'am. You'd better go back and—"

"I heard the telephone ring, and I thought it might be Mary."

"It wasn't."

"Yes, it was, McGowney. I heard every word."

"Well." McGowney cleared his throat. "Well. You shouldn't have listened."

"Oh, I'm not surprised. Or hurt. You needn't be sorry for me. I haven't felt so good in years. You know why?"

"No, ma'am."

"Because I don't have to go home. I'm free. Free as a bird." She reached over and touched his coat sleeve. "I don't have to go home, do I?"

"I guess not."

"You'll never tell anyone."

"No."

"You're a very good man, McGowney."

"I have never thought I wasn't," McGowney said simply.

When darkness fell, McGowney got his car out of the garage and brought it around to the ambulance entrance behind his office.

"You'd better hide in the back seat," he said, "until we get out of town."

"Where are we going?"

"I thought I'd drive you into Detroit, and from there you can catch a bus or a train."

"To where?"

"To anywhere. You're free as a bird."

She got into the back seat, shivering in spite of the mildness of the night, and McGowney covered her with a blanket.

"McGowney."

"Yes, ma'am?"

"I felt freer when I was locked in your little lab."

"You're a bit frightened now, that's all. Freedom is a mighty big thing."

He turned the car toward the highway. Half an hour later, when the city's lights had disappeared, he stopped the car and Mrs. Keating got into the front seat with the blanket wrapped around her shoulders, Indian style. In the gleam of oncoming headlights, her face looked a little troubled. McGowney felt duty-bound to cheer her up, since he was responsible for her being there in the first place.

"There are," he said firmly, "wonderful places to be seen."

"Are there?"

"California, that's the spot I'd pick. Flowers all year round, never an end to them." He hesitated. "I've saved a bit throughout the years. I always thought someday I'd sell the business and retire to California."

"What's to prevent you?"

"I couldn't face the idea of, well, of being alone out there without friends or a family of some kind. Have you ever been to California?"

"I spent a couple of summers in San Francisco."

"Did you like it?"

"Very much."

"I'd like it, too, I'm sure of that." He cleared his throat. "Being alone, though, that I wouldn't like. Are you warm enough?"

"Yes, thanks."

"Birds—well, birds don't have such a happy time of it that I can see."

"No?"

"All that freedom and not knowing what to do with it except fly around. A life like that wouldn't suit a mature woman like yourself, Mrs. Keating."

"Perhaps not."

"What I mean is—"

"I know what you mean, McGowney."

"You—you do?"

"Of course."

McGowney flushed. "It's—well, it's very unexpected, isn't it?"

"Not to me."

"But I never even thought of it until half an hour ago."

"I did. Women are more foresighted in these matters."

McGowney was silent a moment. "This hasn't been a very romantic proposal. I ought to say something a bit on the sentimental side."

"Go ahead."

He gripped the steering wheel hard. "I think I love you, ma'am."

"You didn't have to say that," she replied sharply. "I'm not a foolish young girl to be taken in by words. At my age, I don't expect love. I don't want to—"

"But you are loved," McGowney declared.

"I don't believe it."

"Eventually you will."

"Is this another of your miracles, McGowney?"

"This is the important one."

It was the first time in Mrs. Keating's life she had been told she was loved. She sat beside McGowney in awed silence, her hands folded on her lap, like a little girl in Sunday school.

McGowney left her at a hotel in Detroit and went home to hold her funeral.

Two weeks later they were married by a justice of the peace in a little town outside Chicago. On the long and leisurely trip West in McGowney's car, neither of them talked much about the past or worried about the future. McGowney had sold his business, but he'd been in too much of a hurry to wait for a decent price, and so his funds were limited. But he never mentioned this to his bride.

By the time they reached San Francisco, they had gone through quite a lot of McGowney's capital. A large portion of the remainder went toward the purchase of the little house in Berkeley.

By late fall, they were almost broke, and McGowney got a job as a shoe clerk in a department store. A week later along with his first pay cheque, he received his notice of dismissal.

That night at dinner, he told Eleanor about it, pretending it was all a joke, and inventing a couple of anecdotes to make her laugh.

She listened, grave and unamused. "So that's what you've been doing all week. Selling shoes."

"Yes."

"You didn't tell me we needed money that badly."

"We'll be all right, I can easily get another job."

"Doing what?"

"What I've always done."

She reached across the table and touched his hand. "You don't want to be a mortician again."

"I don't mind."

"You always hated it."

"I *don't mind,* I tell you."

She rose decisively.

"Eleanor, what are you going to do?"

"Write a letter," she said with a sigh.

"Eleanor, don't do anything drastic."

"We have had a lot of happiness. It couldn't last forever. Don't be greedy."

The meaning of her words pierced McGowney's brain. "You're going to let someone know you're alive?"

"No. I couldn't face that, not just yet. I'm merely going to show them I'm not dead so they can't divide up my estate."

"But why?"

"As my husband, you're entitled to a share of it if anything happens to me."

"Nothing will ever happen to you. We agreed about that, didn't we?"

"Yes, McGowney. We agreed."

"We no longer believe in death."

"I will address the letter to Meecham," she said.

"So she wrote the letter." McGowney's voice was weary. "For my sake. You know the rest, Meecham."

"Not quite," I said.

"What else do you want to know?"

"The ending."

"The ending." McGowney stirred in the seat beside me and let out his breath in a sigh. "I don't believe in endings."

I turned right at the next traffic light, as McGowney directed. A sign on the lamppost said, LINDEN AVENUE.

Three blocks south was a small green-and-white house, its eaves dripping with fog.

I parked my car in front of it and got out, pleasantly excited at the idea of seeing Mrs. Keating again. McGowney sat motionless, staring straight ahead of him, until I opened the car door.

"Come on, McGowney."

"Eh? Oh. All right. All right."

He stepped out on the sidewalk so awkwardly he almost fell.

I took his arm. "Is anything wrong?"

"No."

We went up the porch steps.

"There are no lights on," McGowney said. "Eleanor must be at the store. Or over at the neighbours'. We have some very nice neighbours."

The front door was not locked. We went inside, and McGowney turned on the lights in the hall and the sitting room to the right.

The woman I had known as Mrs. Keating was sitting in a wing chair in front of the fireplace, her head bent forward as if she was in deep thought. Her knitting had fallen on the floor, and I saw it was a half-finished glove in bright colours. McGowney's birthday present.

In silence, McGowney reached down and picked up the glove and put it on a table. Then he touched his wife gently on the forehead. I knew from the way his hand flinched that her skin was as cold as the ashes in the grate.

I said, "I'll get a doctor."

"No."

"She's dead?"

He didn't bother to answer. He was looking down at his wife with a coaxing expression. "Eleanor dear, you must wake up. We have a visitor."

"McGowney, for God's sake—"

"I think you'd better leave now, Mr. Meecham," he said in a firm, clear voice. "I have work to do."

He took off his coat and rolled up his sleeves.

My Vacation in the Numbers Racket

HOWARD ENGEL

Born in Toronto, but raised in St. Catharines, Ontario, Howard Engel has been for many years a CBC Radio producer. He now lives in downtown Toronto and is a founding member of the Crime Writers of Canada. His first Cooperman mysteries, The Suicide Murders, The Ransom Game *and* Murder on Location, *won him wide acclaim and have been published internationally. His fourth Benny Cooperman novel is called* Murder Sees the Light. *In the novels, Benny's mother has usually made cameo appearances. Here she comes into her own.*

DEAR BENNY,

I was thinking of you all alone in that hotel room of yours with the frost making leaf-prints on your window, so I thought I'd see if I couldn't get this cassette machine working long enough to send you a letter. I think I've pushed the right button, but I don't think I've got the courage to try playing it back in case I wipe what I think I've recorded.

You'll be surprised to hear that your father and I are in Sarasota. You thought we were still in Miami, where I meant to send you a postcard, but things just happened too fast to send postcards. Right from the beginning this winter hasn't been like any other winter we've ever spent in Florida. I'll try to tell you what happened if I can still remember.

One thing I remember, and I'll start there, is the Red Cap. That's a place your father and I went with Shirl. Do you remember Shirl? She's that blonde that if it wasn't for me I think your father might have been nuts about back a few years. She used to work in his store, and then she started doing her hair up and moved to the millinery shop in the Leonard Hotel. That's where she used to hang out until she met Dave Steiner. He was the first man she ever met who had his shirts made to order. Dave might be a little shady in his business life but he was always generous where Shirl was concerned. We have been visiting them every winter for a few days since we started going to Miami. Which brings me back to the Red Cap, the lounge on the edge of Miami where Shirl and Dave used to take us. It's a kind of bar, but a real joint, if you know what I mean. Even for down there it's a joint. They call it the Red Cap, and it's sort of a Last Chance

Saloon because it's open all night and it's so far away from everything. It's located right in the middle of these big, big. . . . What-do-you-call-'ems? You know, storage tanks for gas? A huge field of them. And right across the road from the bar is the whole electric whatchamacallit for the whole city of Miami. A power station, not a sub-station or anything like that. And this joint just sits there in the middle of all that gas and electricity with its peeling sign winking on and off like it was something to be proud of.

They have a piano player there, some drunk that comes in all the time. They told me he used to be somebody but you could have fooled me. He leaned into the keyboard like he was protecting it with his body. I don't think I ever saw him look up, not even when the girl replaced his empty glass with a full one. He wasn't the only musician. When they finish their club dates, jazz musicians drop around on their way home. There was always some sort of jam session going on if you came in late enough.

The night I met Stone Eyes was the night it all started to happen. Dave and your father were out looking after some business together and were going to pick us up at the Red Cap. Shirl parked her convertible in back and we walked into that neon haze around the front door. So just before she starts telling jokes with the owner, Shirl tells me not to talk to anybody she doesn't introduce me to first. It's a safety precaution, I know that. But you know me; I'm always the little juvenile delinquent. And so I started talking to this tall guy sitting at the bar. He had eyes that looked like they were made of stone. I'd never in my life seen eyes like that. They looked like they were really made of stone. Anyway, I know you're going to say that we were all pretty stoned and sure, we were, because it was after four in the morning and Dave and Manny were busy like I told you.

So anyway, I look around and everywhere there's something chipped or faded or falling apart: plastic liquor signs that light up, even neon in the windows writing the name of an American beer backwards. It's a really low place and the people in it . . . let's say that it's not where you expect to find ladies with pearls and twin sets, if you know what I mean. This is 159th Street after all: the last chance. You get all types here, millionaires and crooks. They say the mayor or a former mayor used to come here all the time. One time Shirl told me that the guy she'd just introduced me to owned half of Miami. Now, Benny, you know what I think of Miami. If it wasn't for the Canadian winter, they could give it to Castro. When you look at them all sitting there talking over their drinks you can't tell the crooks from the millionaires. And you know me. I couldn't care less which is which. Every crook Shirl ever introduced me to treated me like a lady. Anyway, I always talk to men in bars. You know, I tell them I'm from Canada and that I'm visiting friends in Miami and very soon we're talking. And so I was talking to this tall man in the grey suit with the eyes I was telling you about.

That night the orchestra was not great. In fact it was terrible. I was only listening with half an ear until it started playing "Windmills of My Mind". The guy with the eyes was humming into his drink. I leaned over and said to him, "That's from *Don Quixote*, isn't it?"

"What?" he asks.

"The music: 'Windmills of My Mind'. From the musical."

"Oh," he says, and I look into those stone eyes of his.

"That's Cervantes."

"Naw, that's Voltaire. *Candide*," he says, "I'd know it anywhere. You're thinking of *The Man of La Mancha*. That goes different. It's a better book. Longer, but better. They both got a lotta giggles in 'em." And I can't get over it; in a place like that to be having an intellectual conversation with the man with the stone eyes. So, anyway, I don't agree with him about the music, naturally, but I ask him where he went to university. He looks surprised and smiles and says that he didn't even finish high school. Well, I don't tell him that I dropped out in junior fourth, but I compliment him on his reading.

"Ask me any question," he says.

"Is this a game or something?"

"Naw. Just quiz me about stuff. Try me on the Bible. I specialize on the Bible."

"Who was Malachi?"

"It means 'messenger' and he was the last of the Minor Prophets. He wrote a whole book. That was easy. Try me again."

"Who was Lazarus?"

"Trick question, huh?"

"What do you mean?"

"'Cause there were two of them. One in the parable of the Rich Man and the other one gets raised from the dead. Right?"

"How am I supposed to know? I just asked the first thing that came into my head." I asked him where he got his education and he started laughing.

"I did twenty years of reading in one stretch when I was in prison."

Well, I could have fallen right off my stool — like the time I broke my coccyx and Charlie Wilson from General Motors picked me up and called a doctor. I guess he could see my surprise. I think I let my mouth go slack.

"You got lots of time for reading in prison," he said. "I guess I've smoked more Bibles than most people have read."

I looked him over, but there was nothing of the jailbird about him except that his hair was cut shorter than you see nowadays. But that doesn't mean anything. His clothes were as good as your father's. So, I try to stop staring at him and ask him what he'd done to get sent to prison for twenty years.

"Name it, " he said. My mouth was open again and I snapped it shut. "I guess I've done just about everything one time and another," he said. Then he told me that one of the things he'd done was kill his wife. So there I am sitting and laughing and talking about *Candide*, *Don Quixote*, and the Bible with a wife-killer. I go into a trance and when I hear what he's saying again he's talking about guns. ". . . too much respect for them to carry one. I hate wearing one under my coat in the heat. And you can get into a lot of trouble with guns. I'm all for gun control, you know. I heard about one old-timer with bad kidneys from Louisiana. His relatives riled him up so bad he took a few warning shots at them with a handgun. When it went off it severed the tube from his dialysis machine and he bled to death. I know another guy who thought he saw a prowler at the foot of his bed and shot his own pecker off. You'll have to forgive my language." I tried to show him that it was all right this time, but that I wasn't used to that kind of talk.

Just then the girl behind the bar with blue spots showing through her pancake make-up comes over with a drink for me. I tell her that I didn't order it and she tells me that *he* ordered it for me. I explain that I couldn't accept it, and she leans over the bar and tells me that in the three years this guy has been coming in here every night regular, this is the first time he'd ever bought anyone a drink. So, being me, I naturally accepted. He'd spent twenty years in prison for killing his wife and God knows what else he's done, and who ends up on the bar stool next to him? Me! Oh, I know, I'm terrible. But I can still picture those stone eyes of his and remember talking about Cervantes and Voltaire. Isn't that the limit? I mean, look: he could have gotten very ugly with me, you know. You accept a drink from some of these guys and they think they own you. One rye and water and you're bought and paid for.

So, anyway, your father and Dave came back around then. They saw me sitting at the bar and I waved to your father and said: "Manny, come over here, I want you to meet a friend of mine." Dave saw who I was talking to and went over to the table where Shirl was still talking to the owner. Manny and Stone Eyes shook hands but didn't exchange names. After that we left. I think I have a feeling that Stone Eyes knew Dave from someplace. I'm not sure. I know that Dave has never done time. Somebody else would have asked my educated ex-con all about his life in prison but not me. He would have expected that, and I always do the unexpected.

So anyway, after that we go back to Shirl's and Dave's place, which is right there off 159th Street, and have a few more drinks and a few laughs. It's a nice place with patio and pool, and Shirl has fixed it up real cute with lamps she's made from kits you can buy for making coloured plastic lampshades. That's about as artistic as she gets. I tried to get her interested in art once when she lived in Grantham, but she thought that the man taking the class was queer. Generally, if they don't have hair on their knuckles, she thinks they're queer. So we have a drink and a few laughs, like I say, because we were trying to cheer her up, take her out of herself after everything she'd gone through, what with the robbery and then the probation thing. Don't get me wrong, Benny, she didn't get probation for a robbery that *she'd* committed. I know they have some pretty strange friends, but apart from the numbers, they're very careful, Shirl and Dave. She isn't really any different from the girl who used to work in your dad's store in Grantham. You should meet Shirl again. She always liked you. Your father says that Shirl and Dave are very careful about the numbers, too. Shirl didn't tell anybody she was mixed up in it. The first few winters we came to Miami we didn't know anything about it. It was only after we heard about her being out on probation, we got to wondering about the big apartment, the pool, and everything. And she had to tell us when we asked her what it was she was on probation for. Then we remembered about the suitcase every Thursday and Saturday, how she was always taking it to a different motel to count out money and tally lists of numbers.

Well, your father, who as you very well know would never hurt a fly, was fascinated by this. He remembered how he'd carried the suitcase for Shirl on a couple of occasions and how sometimes he'd help her add up the accounts. To him it was no different from doing his books at the store. But I didn't want any part of it. I wondered whether it was the Mafia, but Shirl said it was an independent group. But she gave the Mafia its due. If you want anything done in Miami, including protection, you have to get it from the Mafia. The police, she said, are just a joke. Why when we arrived in Miami this year, what with Shirl being depressed and everything, I have to give her Mafia connections their due. At the airport your father couldn't rent a car anywhere. We phoned Shirl and she said she'd look after it.

Inside of half an hour we had a rent-a-car, and not only that, but the guy turned back the speedometer about two hundred miles so that in the end we had the car for the whole two weeks and it only cost your father eighty dollars. If it wasn't for the saving and a few other things I'm going to tell you about, I'd be putting all this down in ballpoint in a letter instead of on a cassette. You know how I hate writing letters. Your father writes a beautiful letter, but you and your brother take after me. Remember how the camp counsellor used to threaten you with no swimming if you didn't write home?

Now I don't want you to get me wrong. Your father and mother have not turned to a life of crime. God forbid. And you may not remember but Shirl is just about the most giving and wonderful person on earth. She's the best friend a girl could have and she's always thought the world of your father. But, to tell the truth, she has run into a lot of unsavoury characters. Even Dave. I once saw Dave shake her, right up against the wall of the patio of her apartment, and demand to have half of the money they got from Lou for not mentioning his name at the trial. Lou has always been good to Shirl. He's the guy who looks after the apartment and her other expenses. I think he was at one time sweet on Shirl. I wouldn't be surprised. Lou gave them fifty thousand for taking the rap for him.

When they got the fifty, Shirl and Dave went through it so fast you'd think that they knew it was going to be discontinued. They spent it like it was sea water. And they both used to live pretty high on the hog even in the old days. It took them less than four weeks to rip through that bank roll. They bought a second colour TV with all sorts of Atari games. They got a Polaroid camera, you know, all that stuff. And Shirl got a new mink coat. In that climate! Two mink coats! The old one wasn't three years old and she didn't even have to trade it in.

I don't want you to get us wrong, Benny. The first time we went to Miami, as I was saying, we didn't dream about the numbers. I mean when I think of all the clues there were: Dave and Shirl were always so careful about being followed, driving around the block to see if there was anybody parked by the apartment. That sort of thing. And, of course, not only did your father help out with the tallying, he even went around with Dave to all those black bars collecting bets and then delivering the money afterwards. How can I defend us to you, Benny? We had no training for getting involved, that's all. Your father has kept books all his life, so naturally he became a little suspicious when he saw books with no names in them. In case you're shocked, let me tell you that we were too. Only we just woke up and found ourselves right in the middle of it.

Oh, they've had the numbers in Florida for years. This bunch was run by a gang from Detroit. The numbers were on short slips of paper, about two inches by four, in bunches held together by elastics. It's all on the up and up. There's no way you can cheat on it because the numbers are a combination of who won the first race at Jamaica or the last race at Santa Anita, or something like that. It's all in the open, and if you win, you know it, and if you don't, you're down two, three bucks. For a two-dollar win, you can get maybe two hundred or more if it's a special combination win. It's like slot machines or the lotteries. Most of the time you lose, but if you win, Lou and his bunch can go down a couple of hundred thousand. Dave said once a few years ago Lou was borrowing cab fare one day and he owned the company a week later. Naturally, most of the time they don't lose, but they don't cheat at it. I mean you can't fix all those horse races, can you? For a racket, it's as honest as you can make it.

The robbery and Shirl and Dave taking the rap for Lou when the apartment was raided happened last summer. As she said, we missed the fireworks. We missed the court case, too. All the excitement. When we got back to Miami things were a lot different, more creepy. Dave gave me the willies. Manny liked Dave, but me, well, to be honest, I never much liked the look of him. He was like most of Shirl's men: big, dark fellows. Mediterranean types. They always looked like they were carrying guns under their jackets, but most of them weren't carrying anything more than maybe fifty pounds overweight.

Anyway, after the court case, Shirl and Dave got off. I don't know why they didn't deport Shirl. I don't understand how she stays there. It's this lawyer they've got. I can see why she wouldn't want to leave that place of hers; it's really a beautiful place. And she's got a toy poodle, Maggie, a wonderfully cute, dear little fellow. I adore Maggie, and you know about me and dogs as a rule: we can't stand one another. They know it and I know it. It's never been a problem. But I was telling you about the apartment. Wasn't I? The apartment? It's a palace, that's all. Five bedrooms, patio, pool, and a view over, well, I'm telling you that it wouldn't make it very hard for Manny and me to pack up and move down here and that's for sure. And if you want something, anything, Shirl or Dave or Lou knows somebody who can get it. Oh, it's just marvellous.

Where was I? Oh, the apartment. That's really one for the books. You have to see it. Anyway, the point I was making is that after the robbery, they, Shirl I should say, just let it go to rack and ruin. She lost heart, poor girl. Well, I guess, after all she went through, I mean. It must have been hell. A woman can get frightened of things a man doesn't have to worry about in a situation like that. Oh, the kid went through hell. And Dave? Not a scratch. He wasn't even there. I never trusted Dave. He looks like those movie torpedoes, and he acts like that's the way he wants to look. Tough, he-man. Not that Shirl ever went for the choirboy type. Like I said, she always went for the dark, brawny type with size eighteen necks. And most of them had a mean streak. Not like that boy from out Pelham Road she married out of Commercial. He had a real sweetness about him, but Shirl put him on the worry wagon with a vengeance. She preferred the flashy type; she couldn't help it. When they were loaded, Shirl's men always spent freely. They like Cadillacs in the drive and convertibles, if you please. One, two, make it three. Like Shirl and her minks. Same thing.

The numbers were always collected and counted in a new place every time. Shirl first got to use the apartment because it was used as one of the places. Then they didn't want to have anything in the apartment overnight. Wasn't it a big surprise that the Feds knew about the first time in months that there was stuff linking them to the numbers in the place. That can't have been just bad luck. It's like what it says in the mystery stories I read all night, somebody "shopped" them. Now, not only did they lose the money they were holding, but they are having to fight the tax people, you know, Internal Revenue, who want to count the numbers money as income, and undeclared income at that. I mean they had hundreds of thousands with them and none of it was theirs. There must have been a leak of some kind, because Lou and his cousin before him had been running numbers there without anything happening for years and years.

After the trial came the robbery. Shirl thinks there was something fishy about that too, and I don't blame her. When we came back this winter, Shirl was a different woman. She'd lost her—what's the word? Specialness? The thing that made men turn and look at her. You know I've known Shirl for years and we've been very close. We've gone through rough times together. So there was no fooling Manny and me when we got off that plane.

Shirl thinks the world of your father, Benny, and God bless him, he's not one for sitting around when there's work to be done. Anything before talk. That's your father. So, right away he starts cleaning up the place. She'd let it go downhill quite a bit, though who could blame her after what that kid has been through. I looked after Maggie, the poodle. Manny loves gardening. Me, I have a black thumb, can't make anything grow except that ivy I've been trying to kill off in the kitchen. Wouldn't you know it: if I wanted it to live, it would have died off years ago. But your father has a talent, as you know, and he started in on her place, trimming the hedge and cutting back the rubber plant, and cleaning the dead plants out of the place.

Manny bought some annuals. They have annuals all year round down here. He made a proper garden for the patio like we have at home. Oh, your father's wonderful at that sort of thing, while I sit back with a rye and water. Ha! That's my style. Especially when it comes to work. Shirl adores Manny. Always has. Not that she'd try anything. Much more likely that he'd look too far into those baby-blue eyes of hers and fall in. I trust your father, but he's only human. Everybody loves Manny. Everybody. There's something sweet about him. You can smell it on his skin. Me? Well, they think I'm pretty special too, but oh, they all love your father.

Well, he cleaned out the pool, scrubbed it, vacuumed it, and replaced the burnt-out lights in the bottom. When at last the place started to look like something again, Shirl started coming out of herself. You know how she can sound tough, but she didn't have to act that way with us. Not ever. We were always special for her and she never put on a show for us. One night she turned on the night lights in the pool and we all went for a swim. She still looked beautiful in that turquoise light, although she wouldn't wear a bikini any more. When we were all dried off and having a drink I had enough courage to ask her to talk about the robbery.

It was after four in the morning when she came home, parked her Cadillac in the drive, and let herself into the apartment. Dave wasn't with her. When she opened the door, they were inside waiting for her. They grabbed her from behind by the throat and mouth. She only saw stockinged faces and screamed into rubber gloves. They blindfolded her, put adhesive tape over her mouth, and tied her to a chair. She said they talked of raping her right at the start, but she made them understand that she had a heart condition, so they left her alone. Here's an interesting thing: they knew she was wearing a diamond pendant under her turtleneck sweater. Can you beat that? They knew all about her. They even knew about the second mink coat. They knew which was her car. They took their time collecting everything in the place that was fenceable. I learned that word from Ellery Queen. They made themselves Nescafé and went through every pillow, mattress, upholstered chair in the place with their knives. They even cut up the backs of her pictures. The poor kid! Shirl could hear the birds and the sounds of starting cars next door when they left. She knew that it was getting light on

159th Street. Before they left, they poured acid from the swimming pool shed into the pool. Then they left in her car. They found the Caddy a few days later. The cops, I mean, but they won't find the rest of her stuff. Even the cops told her not to hold her breath until that happened.

The rings! She had a seven-hundred-dollar Pucci and a diamond cut like—well, it was the only one of its kind. But the thing that got her was the swimming pool. Shirl couldn't talk about it too much. It was Dave who told us about the acid in the pool. He said that Shirl was broken up into little pieces when he got home after her call to him in New York. "She was a wreck for about a month, weren't you honey?" he said. "I nearly didn't have the heart to tell her about the pool, but she kept bugging me about why I had it drained. Didn't you, sweetheart? I tried lying to her, but that wasn't no good, so I had to tell her. And that got her started all over again. But she's all right now, huh? How's my little girl?" She was sick about that. If she had tried to go swimming, her skin would have been eaten right off by the acid. It makes you sick just thinking about it. It's funny, they didn't break up the place any in a malicious way, except for what I told you already, but they did that to the pool. I don't understand people doing a horrible thing like that.

The next day, I think it was, the three of us, Shirl, Manny, and I, went shopping. Dave was off on business of some kind. I wanted to get some postcards to let you get a taste of the balmy south to pin to your bulletin board. I knew you were looking after our plants and your brother says he likes to hear from us regularly. Not that either of you'd ever think to drop us a line. So we went into this arcade and were browsing around when suddenly Shirl looks at me, really scared, and says, "I've got to get out of here. I'll see you later." And off she goes into the crowd and out the other end of the arcade. Well, you could have knocked me over with a lemonade. I looked at your father and he looked at me and for a minute we didn't know what to do. Like, it took us a minute to realize that Shirl had left so fast.

Anyway, I bought about half a dozen cards, got some stamps

from the machine, and was writing out one to your brother when Manny gives me a nudge. When I look up, he nods at two men standing about ten feet away. They are watching us. One is a dumpy guy in a sports jacket and the other is wearing a pale blue nylon windbreaker with a zipper. There was no mistake about it. They were watching us. As soon as they saw that we saw them, the tall one in the windbreaker comes over and asks where Shirl is. How do you like that? I tell him it's none of his business.

"You don't understand," he says, "we're friends of hers. Is Dave with her?" He tried to look friendly and the chubby guy was nodding and tried to look agreeable.

"Well, you just missed her, " I said, a little apprehensively. "She had some things to do."

"Well, that's too bad. At least we can give you a lift back to where you're staying."

"That won't be necessary," I said. "Thank you very much."

"We're driving right past 159th Street," the other one added.

"We're just shopping, " Manny said, and added, "For the love of Mike!" to show that he was serious.

"I'm afraid I'm going to have to insist," said the first guy, trying to take my arm. He smelled of talcum powder like a baby. "Our car's parked right outside."

Well, I looked at Manny and your father looked at me, and there didn't seem to be anything we could do about it. They both wore smiles and seemed friendly enough. While the short one looked like a thug in the movies, I had to remind myself we weren't in the movies. Things like that don't happen to a couple having a holiday in Miami, for goodness sake. So we went with them to the car which was double-parked at the front of the arcade. There was a man at the wheel and the motor was running.

If I was worried at all, I felt better as soon as I saw that the driver was old Stone Eyes from the Red Cap. The guy I was telling you about? He did a real double-take when he saw me. But he didn't smile or say anything. He just got out of the car and came around to open my door. Manny and I sat in the back with the one in the windbreaker and Stone Eyes and the heavy-set one rode in front. For a while nobody said anything. Manny watched the streets run by the car windows and I kept my eyes on the backs of the necks in the front seat. What was I going to do? I'd never be able to remember where they were taking us. All the streets in Miami look alike to me. Or so I thought. After a while I could see these big gas drums, so I could roughly guess where we were. Stone Eyes ran into an empty parking lot and leaned back and said: "What do you say we all have a little drink?"

The waiter with the broom tried to say that the place was closed, but the men just walked right over him. The place looked different in the daylight. There were no shadowy places. Empty, it looked twice as big. Stone Eyes looked at Manny, but he said to me, "Look, why don't you sit at the bar for a sec. I'll join you after I have a word with my associates." He and the other two sat in a booth and started in on what sounded like the middle of a conversation. After about five minutes, he ambles over and sits next to us at the bar. I was sipping a rye and water and so was Manny. The waiter brought him a drink without even asking.

"My friends and I are a little curious about your plans here in Miami. I mean are you down here on a vacation, a visit, or what? They're a little concerned that maybe you're not on a vacation at all, that maybe you're planning to settle down here and I don't mean in a retirement condominium. It's a friendly argument we're having. A little speculation about where you fit into our little circle of friends. We could go on speculating, sure, but a few words from you can settle the whole thing. What do you say?" I could see the other two leaning this way from their booth, trying to hear as much as they could without getting up, but not making a big thing about not appearing to be listening at all. Manny looked pained, the way he gets when I use the garlic powder from the old house and we've run out of Gelusil. But as usual, it's your mother who opens her big mouth.

"We've been down here for about two weeks. Planning to

stay three. You're not from the Department of Tourism or something. So, why the interest?" Of course I knew they weren't tourist inspectors, but I just come out with things. You know me. Stone Eyes thought about this for a minute while he took a slow sip from his drink.

"So, you're going back to Canada in a week, right?"

"That's right."

"And you're not in business down here, right?"

"Of course not."

"Good. Okay, that's all I got to know. Be right back." And over he goes to his pals again for another confab. Manny was looking at his fingernails. He gave me a weak grin. Stone Eyes came back to the bar. Your father just had time to say:

"It's going to be all right. You'll see." Stone Eyes looked at both of us, then reached for his drink. He didn't say anything until the glass was empty. He rubbed his mouth with a red bandanna he carried in his pocket.

"Okay, as soon as you're ready, I'll drive you home." He still didn't smile. I don't think I ever saw him do that. But this time his non-smile was as close to a smile as I ever saw him get. "One thing," he said as I was getting off my stool, "my associates would appreciate it if you didn't mix into Dave's and Shirl's business any more." I started to protest, but Manny had me by the upper arm before I could utter a syllable. "You know how things are in business," Stone Eyes continued, "people are superstitious about outsiders. You follow me? It's like our friend Candide. He got his nose busted a few times putting it into the wrong places. I don't mean this unfriendly. It's just that my friends don't understand people the way I do." We were now going out the door of the Red Cap, and Stone Eyes held the door for your father and me. He took me to one side in the parking lot: "Look, what you do is this," he said, "you go back to Canada in a week, even sooner wouldn't hurt things none, and you don't say anything about what you've seen. That's all." He looked at me really hard with worry in those cold eyes, then he said, "Come on. I'll drop you at the house."

The ride back to Shirl's was much more relaxed. The short

one was telling what his ten-year-old son told him about oil spills in the Gulf of Mexico. All three of them said something about the destruction caused by oil spills. Stone Eyes blamed it on lax shipping registry laws and referred to the Law of the Sea Conference that was going on someplace, and then the blue windbreaker got onto acid rain as we came to a stop in front of Shirl's. The other guy said that he was very impressed with the interest young people have in ecology. "Kids are really great the way they want to protect and preserve stuff." That was the end of it. We got out and said goodbye.

So, we let ourselves into the apartment. We didn't notice anything wrong, but when Shirl got back an hour later and when we told her what happened, she really went into orbit. I mean first of all she gets the shakes when she sees that Dave's stuff is gone from the closet. She checks the dressers and starts to cry. She asks us to describe the men we met and in less than no time we are packing ourselves into a limousine and on our way to the airport. Can you beat that? One minute I'm sitting in the sun with a tall, cool drink on the patio, the next I'm packing and Shirl's trying to smile and not fooling anybody. Shirl went with us to the airline terminal and gave us both a big hug as we got into the limo. The last we saw of her she was wiping tears from those huge blue eyes and slamming the door of her Caddy.

Now isn't that the darndest thing you ever heard? Of course I figured it all out on the flight to Sarasota. Shirl knew that Dave was in on the robbery because he knew about the acid in the swimming pool. How can you tell there's acid in a pool unless you told somebody to put it there? He pulled the robbery to put Lou off the scent. He must have been creaming the top off his numbers money. A lot of them try that. People get greedy, that's all. So Lou hired those thugs to shake things up to see if any change rolled out of our pockets that didn't belong to us. It all started looking like something in a paperback mystery novel. Isn't there a private eye down here who lives on a houseboat? John D. something. The whole two weeks sounds like a case he might have got involved in.

Anyway, your father and I are both well. You can pick us up at the airport on Tuesday, Flight 604 from Sarasota. And, Benny, don't forget to water my plants.

Love,
Mother

The Cure

ERIC WRIGHT

Eric Wright was born in England and has lived in Canada for the past thirty-two years. He has a B.A. from the University of Manitoba and an M.A. from the University of Toronto. He lives in Toronto with his wife and two daughters and teaches English at Ryerson. As well as writing numerous short pieces for various magazines, he has written three novels featuring Inspector Charlie Salter of the Metropolitan Toronto Police: The Night the Gods Smiled *(1983),* Smoke Detector *(1984), and* Death in the Old Country *(forthcoming in 1985).* The Night the Gods Smiled *won the 1983 City of Toronto Book Award, the John Creasey Award for the best first novel published in England, and the Arthur Ellis Award from the Crime Writers of Canada.*

WHEN BETHELL DECIDED to rob his old friend, Sligo, his motive was to teach Sligo a lesson, unsettle him a bit. He had suffered from Sligo for twenty years, seventeen of them as his next-door neighbour. When Sligo moved away, Bethell thought, peace at last, but their wives were friends and Bethell's wife found Sligo a good sort, so he continued to see nearly as much of Sligo as ever. (Sometimes, though, when Bethell raged about him in the bedroom after the two couples had spent an evening together, his wife would say, "For God's sake. Don't see him if he bothers you so much.")

Just why Sligo bothered Bethell was hard for Bethell to explain, because it had its roots in a relationship between the two men that was apparent only to Bethell. It was an attitude that Sligo took to Bethell, an assumption of a mentorial relationship on Sligo's part which Bethell found irritating from the very early days when he otherwise welcomed Sligo's friendship. When Bethell first moved into his house and began repairing the little stone wall that edged his front yard, Sligo appeared from next door and took over. "You haven't had too much experience of this kind of thing, have you?" he said with a chuckle. It was true; Bethell had no experience at all of dry-stone-walling, but he had borrowed a book from the library and he was looking forward to finding out if he could do it. That incident set the pattern. When Sligo saw how incompetent Bethell was, he never let him alone. Whenever Bethell appeared in his backyard with a two-by-four and a hammer, Sligo was over the fence in a moment, ready to straighten him out.

Sligo's protection and advice spread from house repairs into every corner of Bethell's life. Bethell had no garage, so Sligo cleaned out the rubbish in his own two-car garage and told Bethell to park there in the future. He visited the St. Lawrence Market and brought back food on Bethell's behalf, specials he knew Bethell should have at those prices. When there was a sale of wine at the liquor store he bought extra for Bethell, and Bethell ground his teeth and thanked him. Sligo tasted the soup on Bethell's stove and added salt, talked man-to-man with Bethell's children, rearranged the logs on Bethell's fire, and dispensed advice like a relative by marriage.

The quality of Sligo's advice and help was as mixed as the next man's. He was far from infallible, but he rarely admitted doubt in the first place or error when something went wrong, finding, when pressed, some fault in the way Bethell had executed the advice. Like Odysseus, he was never at a loss, so that when some question or problem cropped up concerning an area outside his experience he would (or so it seemed to Bethell) bluff and fake an answer, or claim to know the expert in the field whom he would consult next day. Perhaps the worst of it was that Bethell's wife would often forget how much he resented Sligo. When Bethell had a problem, as often as not she would say, "Why don't you ask Sligo? He might know."

And Bethell *knew* that Sligo lied to preserve his role. For example, he told Bethell how much he had paid to get his house painted, a real bargain, but the painter, whom Bethell hired also, told him the true figure was twice as much, and when Bethell faced Sligo with this in front of their wives, Sligo said that the painter had exaggerated so that he could overcharge Bethell. Bethell looked hard at Sligo's wife during this exchange, but she didn't blink an eyelash, so she was in on it, too.

On another occasion, Bethel was in the market for an old icebox for his cottage, an item he had remembered seeing in rural dumps all over Ontario in the last twenty years and which he expected to pick up for the cost of removing it. When he started to look around he was appalled to discover that he had come too late to the market and iceboxes were now antiques going for around three hundred dollars. Sligo had refused to let Bethell buy one at this price and told Bethell to leave it to him. Bethell got a lot of satisfaction during the next few weeks out of asking Sligo how the search was going, and Sligo had had to agree that iceboxes weren't as easy to find as he had thought. Nevertheless he insisted that he would come up with one, and then, one Saturday afternoon, he came home with a beauty in excellent condition which he had picked up "at a farm auction near Belleville" for fifty dollars. Bethell didn't believe him, but would Sligo have paid money out of his own pocket just to keep his reputation intact? Bethell thought so.

It was no comfort to Bethell that his own wife reported back to him that Sligo thought Bethell was a dear, sweet guy, all the more so for being so unworldly. Bethell was a civil servant, and Sligo was a jobber of some kind; he lived in the real world, as he told Bethell, unlike Bethell who never had to worry about his cash flow.

Bethell was aware, mainly from concerned remarks of his wife, that he was taking Sligo too much to heart and he took the chance to talk about Sligo to a psychological counsellor whom he was consulting for advice on some sexual difficulties he was having. Sligo's name cropped up and Bethell let himself go.

The counsellor listened until it was nearly time for their appointment to end, then said, "You have a poor opinion of yourself, Mr. Bethell. It shows up in every area. Your friend knows this—subconsciously, of course—and he sees your uncertainty and translates it into a call for help. He wants to look after you."

"But what about when he's wrong and lies about it?" Bethell cried.

"Are you sure he's wrong? If so, perhaps he has his own needs. You never tell people who depend on you that you are fallible. That would seem to be letting them down."

"So what do I do? Avoid him?"

"I don't think so. That would be a defeat. Besides I take it the initiative in this relationship comes from him?"

"Entirely."

"Obviously he loves you. He must be made to respect you as well as love you."

"How? How do I do that?"

"Perhaps by finding some area where *you* are the mentor, the elder, so to speak. And insisting firmly on your role." The counsellor gave a little peek at the clock on the wall.

"I've found a dozen: gardening, fly-fishing, good hotels in Paris—you name it, I've taught *him*."

"And what happens?"

"A month or a year later, he explains them back to me. He never gives me credit for having told him about them in the first place."

Now the counsellor openly consulted his watch. "Mr. Bethell, I have to speak bluntly," he said. "You sound what we would call paranoid."

"I know *that*, for Christ's sake. That's why I'm talking to *you*."

"Well, we've got you to recognize your problem at least. Let's have another go at it next week."

But Bethell never went back. He continued to suffer and dream of an absolute facer that Sligo would not be able to dodge.

When the opportunity finally came, Bethell did not recognize it at first. At the time he was considering simply finding an excuse to pick a quarrel with Sligo (after twenty years!) so that he could cut him off, even though that would be an acknowledged defeat. But when he tried, the result was only a wretched evening and a mystified wife who wondered what had got into him, and made immediate arrangements to get together with the Sligos again (with apologies) to get their relationship back on its old footing. Then one evening Bethell went into a fit of rage on a matter as small as whether one should lock one's doors.

Like most people, Bethell kept his house locked when he was out of it and had even installed a small alarm system to alert the neighbours if anybody broke in. Sligo never locked his house up, or his car, never had, never would. "If they are going to break in," he said, "they come ready. Then not only do they steal your goods, but they break your door down with it. Same with a car. Any good car thief can open a car easy as pie, but if you leave everything unlocked, he might think you are coming back right away."

"How about amateurs?" Bethell asked, getting sucked in again.

"Amateurs won't touch an unlocked house, either," Sligo said, authoritatively. "If you lock it, they just use axes instead of a crowbar. As for cars, amateurs only steal cars with the keys in. They just take them for joy-riding. You always get them back."

Bethell knew this was wrong, and he began to reply, but Sligo had already gone on to something else. "What's the humidity in here?" he was saying when Bethell had got his thoughts together. "You need a gauge. I'll bring over our old one."

Shortly after that Bethell was robbed. The thieves cut the power supply to bypass the alarm, got the door open with a bit of plastic which they left behind, took his television set, his camera, and his trombone, and finding the spare car keys on a hook in the kitchen, drove off in his Rabbit. They were never caught.

"See," Sligo said.

Bethell saw, all right, and began to plan. Sligo was going to have to be robbed, and in such a way that there could be no doubt that the failure to lock his doors was crucial. Bethell set aside, for the moment, the question of whether the robbery would be a joke, to make a point, or whether the robbery would be real. Either way the heist would have to be fairly big and take place in daytime, committed by thieves who evidently acted in the knowledge that they would be able to enter and leave easily. Bethell day-dreamed for a month before the perfect idea fell into his lap. A colleague of his came to the office one morning with the news that his neighbour had been robbed the day before. Thieves using a regular furniture truck had backed up to the man's front door and simply removed the contents of the house in about three hours. No one had questioned them, and when the police went around banging on doors, none of the neighbours could remember what the men looked like—"Kind of guys who move furniture," one neighbour said—or what the name of the company was, or even the colour of the truck.

Now Bethell just had to wait for the next occasion when Sligo was away with his wife, for Sligo left his house unlocked when he went on holiday, too. In the meantime he had to find a furniture-removal truck and four thieves. (He had decided on a real robbery, because he realized that if he made the thing the basis of a practical joke, he would not be making his point; Sligo could afterwards claim that just because Bethell was able to walk in and out of his house in no way invalidated his position. The point was that an outsider would not know it was unlocked.)

The first problem was to get in touch with some thieves. He had heard the phrase "consorting with known criminals" as something thieves on probation must not do, and he reasoned that there must be places where criminals consort—pubs, probably, that they favoured, where they planned the next job. Bethell's scheme to find out about these haunts was to ask for an interview with the public relations department of the police. The inspector was polite, but wary. "A writer, eh, Mr. Bissell," he said. "Not one of those exposé type guys, eh?"

Bethell assured him that the hero of his novel would be a clever policeman, and the inspector listened to his problem. Where did thieves gather in Toronto? He called a sergeant in. "Mr. Bissell here is looking for local colour," he explained. "He wants to know where our clients hang out when they are not working. Are there any particular pubs, like?"

The sergeant considered. "Not that I know of, Mr. Bissell," he said. "We wouldn't allow it. If you find any, let us know, would you?"

The inspector smiled and showed Bethell the door.

Next Bethell asked a number of taxi-drivers to take him to the sleaziest pubs they knew of, where he spent several evenings drinking beer and watching nude ladies jousting in imaginary combat. Nowhere did he find what he was seeking. He considered spending a night in the Don Jail. Surely there he would find what he wanted? But the only offence he could think of that would get him a night in jail but not the possibility of three months was a refusal to pay parking tickets and it would probably take six months or more to build up to that.

Ruminating on the difficulty of getting into bad company, he was presented one day with an alternative solution. There was a knock on his door and a smiling young man introduced himself as a surveyor commissioned to mark out the property next door for Bethell's neighbour who was selling his house. It would be necessary, the youth said, to enter Bethell's garden, and he was introducing himself so that Bethell wouldn't get alarmed and call the police.

Bethell took the surveyor's card and went out to the street and examined the man's car, which had no identifying sign except a CJRT sticker in the window. Bethell switched his plan.

He designed a card, "Royce Dunlop—Surveyor," ordered a hundred from a cheap printer, threw away ninety-eight, and put the remaining two in his wallet. The rest of the plan required the absence of Sligo.

In the three months that Bethell waited for Sligo to go on holiday, the two couples dined together twice and each time afterwards Bethell's wife commented on how well the evening had gone. Sligo chose the restaurant the first time, and the food was horrible. The second time Bethell chose, consulting widely beforehand, even to knowing the name of the restaurant's house wine; they had a splendid meal, and he never felt a thing when Sligo explained why. "This is a Florentine restaurant," Sligo said. "Much better than Milanese."

Then Sligo announced they were going to Bermuda for a week, and Bethell made his move. He chose the Wednesday to avoid any garbage collections on Sligo's street, wanting to eliminate even that much extra activity that might bring the neighbours to their doors. Early in the morning he drove out to a car-rental agency on Eglinton West and picked up the station wagon he had ordered the night before, using his own name. It was the one risk he could not avoid, for he was unable, short of stealing someone's wallet, to think of a way of getting a false driver's licence.

He parked outside Sligo's house at ten o'clock, tucked one of his cards under the windshield wiper, and walked boldly up to the door. Sligo's front door was at the side of the house, obscured from the street, and there was little chance that Bethell would be seen as he opened the door and stepped inside—the first absolutely criminal offence. So far so good. Sweating slightly, he sat down in the kitchen and took off his coat, leaving his gloves on, and ran over his mental list: an antique coffee-pot, a Krieghoff painting, some silver tableware. There was also a gold watch on Sligo's desk. On reflection he decided against the painting and prepared to assemble the loot. As soon as it was piled on the kitchen table he was done for if anyone should walk in. Bethell walked the house like an insomniac, peering out of all the windows at the quiet street, leaping up in the air when the phone rang, then, finally, in a single sweep, he locked the front door, collected the goods together, and looked around for something to carry them in. Here his nerve cracked. A knock at the door had him lying on the floor, then, as he heard faint departing footsteps, peeking through the front window to see the meter-reader from Consumers' Gas leave and move to the next house. He was incapable, he knew now, of walking to the car with a bag full of silver, and he tried to tell himself that perhaps he had gone far enough to make his point. The place had clearly been robbed, and the thief disturbed before he could get away with the loot. Wasn't that enough? But Bethell didn't trust Sligo not to say nothing, to lie silently, and then Bethell would have wasted his time. The solution when it came to him was simple and nearly risk-free. It took him fifteen minutes to set up, and when he was finished he unlocked the front door, drove back to the agency, and returned home in his own car.

His wife said, "Where were you? I phoned the office and they said you'd phoned in sick."

Bethell chuckled. "Caught me, did you? I spent the day in the arms of my mistress, dear."

"No, where *were* you?"

"I took the day off," Bethell said. "I was driving to work and I said to myself, 'I need a mental-health day,' so I kept on driving and took the ferry over to the Island."

"That's not like you," she said. "Male menopause?"

"Could be," he said. "You'd better keep your eye on me."

When Sligo came back he had a tale to tell and he came over to Bethell's house on the first evening to tell it. "They emptied out all the drawers, the closets, all over the floor," he said. "They got Doris's silver, the coffee pot, and my gold watch. Everything worth taking except the Krieghoff. They probably thought that was cut out from a magazine."

"That's terrible," Bethell's wife said. "Losing all that."

"No sweat," Sligo said. "It's all insured. I'll probably make money on it."

"But if the insurance company knows the house wasn't locked, surely they won't pay up?" Bethell said. It was an integral part of his new plan. He intended to let Sligo suffer for a few weeks and then arrange for the loot to reappear.

"I'm not that dumb," Sligo laughed. "Before I called the cops I locked the whole house up and kicked in the back door."

"I see," Bethell said, the room dancing in front of his eyes.

"Oh, sure," Sligo said. "I wasn't born yesterday."

Bethell raged silently. Then a lovely thought occurred to him, the realization that Sligo had delivered himself into his hands. For now, whenever he chose, he could pick up the phone and, anonymously, of course, tell the police and the insurance company that they had been defrauded, that in the basement of Sligo's house they would find a wood-box, and under the layer of scrap wood left over from Sligo's last remodelling, they would find some silver, a coffee pot, and a gold watch. There was no rush. It was only June, and Sligo was unlikely to need kindling before October. At some point during the summer Sligo would become intolerable, and then Bethell would phone.

It was a glorious summer. Bethell's wife remarked on how much more relaxed the two men were with each other. No longer did

Bethell grind his teeth at Sligo's patronage—he seemed not to notice it. Often, when Sligo started to give Bethell advice, Bethell just laughed and told Sligo he was full of it. Sometimes he cut through Sligo's monologues, changing the subject as more important or more interesting subjects occurred to him.

As the summer wore on, Bethell realized that calling the insurance company would accomplish nothing. They *might* assume that Sligo had defrauded them and Sligo might go to prison, which, now that Bethell's sharp need for revenge had faded, was more than he wanted. And, too, they might believe in Sligo's innocence and search for an insider who knew Sligo's domestic habits and where he kept his wood. Bethell knew that if Sligo or the police failed to guess the culprit, his own wife would.

But if he did *not* phone what would happen? Sligo would find the loot, with two possible results. He might keep his mouth shut and try to sell it later, but the coffee pot and the silver were listed with the Fraud Squad, so it would be very risky. He was more likely to announce the find, which would bring the police in asking the same questions and pointing the same finger at him as if Bethell had made his anonymous call. And Bethell had heard that the forensic laboratory could identify him from a single speck of dandruff, never mind fingerprints.

Now October approached with a rush as Bethell grew more and more frightened. In the end he was obliged to improvise, and one dark and rainy night, when his wife was at a movie and he knew that the Sligos were out, he drove over to their house. He tried the door and found it locked, but he had no time to savour his little triumph. He moved round to the back of the house and waited for the noise of a passing car, then kicked the door in. Down in the basement he packed the stuff into a green garbage bag and made a run for it, looking like a cartoon burglar making off with the swag. He drove down to Harbourfront, parked by the yacht basin, dropped the stuff into the harbour, and drove home, beside himself with fear.

When Sligo came home that night, he phoned Bethell after he had finished with the police. "They didn't take anything," he said, "But the police think those guys have got me staked out. Now I'll really have to lock up tight. I was wondering if I could come by tomorrow night and find out about locks and alarms and stuff. You know all about that, don't you?"

"Sure," Bethell said comfortingly. "Sure. I've got information, brochures, on all that kind of thing. Come round and we'll go over what you need."

"Who was that?" Bethell's wife asked as he crept into bed.

"Sligo," Bethell said. "He wants some advice." He kissed his wife and arranged himself for sleep. "I think I can help him," he said.

A Natural Death

SANDRA WOODRUFF

Sandra Woodruff was born in St. Catharines, Ontario, but was raised in Niagara-on-the-Lake. She has a B.A. in English Language and Literature from the University of Toronto. She read her first mystery at age twenty-five and became addicted immediately. For the past four years she has been mystery reviewer for The London Free Press *in London, Ontario, where she lives with her husband and two children.*

EMILY FORBES'S WEEKDAYS unfolded in an unvarying routine. She breakfasted with the newspaper at eight, tidied from nine to eleven, then shopped until her one o'clock lunch. Between lunch and tea she planned the murder of her daughter-in-law. Evenings and weekends were reservea for her many social engagements. She found this routine very steadying. It sustained the illusion, essential at seventy-two, of holding the whip hand over time. She likened it in her own mind to keeping her closets in order, at which she also excelled. She was convinced that if she relaxed her vigilance for even a moment, disorder, with eternity on its heels, would engulf her.

Planning the murder (she would have been shocked to have it described so bluntly) was the highlight of her day. She made a ritual of it, changing from day clothes into a velour lounging robe and tucking herself in bed under a blue mohair blanket which matched her eyes exactly and softened her somewhat beaky features. Thus ensconced she read, thought, and jotted through the afternoon. She was a little afraid of the fascination plotting had for her and was correspondingly scrupulous about confining it within rigid limits: "I mustn't let it take over and poison my life," she said to herself with a small smile.

It would be wrong to think that Emily Forbes disliked her daughter-in-law. Rose had many good qualities and Emily acknowledged them freely. She thought her clever, if a little brittle, and pretty in an overly blonde way. She admired her independence of spirit and the fact, a first for Forbes women, that she had kept her work as freelance copy editor after her marriage. It was simply that, in her mother-in-law's eyes, by marrying Bennett Forbes, Rose had forfeited her right to live. She was a despoiler, plain and simple, and for that she would have to pay.

Bennett was Emily's youngest and favourite child, her only son. They had always understood each other so well (she used to think) and loved each other best. But that was before Rose. Without her it could be so again. Emily cherished the notion, not strictly true, that apart from Bennett she was alone in the world. The late Mr. Forbes was dead if not mourned. "He left us ten years ago," she always said, a little peevishly. He had been charming but a bit of a shirker in life, and she viewed his death as the ultimate shirk, an extravagant way of avoiding responsibility entirely typical of the man. Her twin daughters were negligible. Apart from being twins they had been boringly ordinary as children, not a spark of spirit in either of them. Now as adults they were slotted into respectable lives with respectable husbands and dull children of their own. They lived far enough away that she hardly ever had to see them. A phone call on their shared birthday and a cheque at Christmas satisfied her minimum standards concerning Families Keeping in Touch. When they occasionally visited her she looked forward to their leaving. No, it was entirely on Bennett that her feeling of family, of not being alone, rested. Now that Rose had come between them she felt bereft.

Emily had childishly wished her daughter-in-law dead since before the wedding was suddenly announced a year ago. There had hardly been a courtship. The couple had met, fallen in love (no, she wouldn't believe that), and married within three weeks. The wish had only translated itself into a resolution to kill after they had been married about five months. The idea had taken shape suddenly at the library one morning as she was checking out her weekly selection of books. Among them was a homely looking volume with brown paper covers called *Wild and Wonderful.* She had picked it up thinking it might be the biography of a movie star but kept it as a curiosity when she found her mistake. It had proved to be a cookbook devoted to recipes full of extraordinary and disagreeable-sounding ingredients gathered from woodlots and ditches. To her surprise the librarian had reacted enthusiastically: "You'll have a lot of fun with this one, Mrs. Forbes," she had said. "You probably have some of these plants in your own garden."

Light dawned. From that moment Emily worked steadily at developing and publicizing a knowledge of the edible wild and amassing an unpublicized knowledge of the inedible wild. She was careful not to attract the librarian's attention (really the girl was aggressively solicitous) by taking out books on poisonous plants, but the cookbooks nearly always provided some cautionary information about which plants were dangerous. From this she was able to piece together all she needed to know. As Emily began to work her way systematically through the natural cookery section the librarian congratulated herself on her acumen in starting an old person on a new hobby. "It's so important for them to keep *interested*," she confided to her assistant. After a time Emily, whose social impulses were always correct, brought the librarian a jar of her home-made purslane pickles as a thank you for all her help.

To give herself most scope Emily deliberately chose the crankiest sounding titles for her researches on the theory that the more bizarre her approach the more secure she would be. *Fungus with Flair* inspired less confidence than *From Soup to Nuts*, for example. Everyone, everyone she knew anyway, would be instinctively prejudiced against natural foods, expecting them to be both unpalatable (and privately she thought that every dish she had tried was awful) and treacherous. If she were careful it would be easy to explain away any upsets or poisoning as an unfortunate accident. Because an accident was what she had in mind. "It isn't like real poison," she reassured herself. "Fatal doses and strengths and what not are so variable, almost hit or miss. I'll just experiment a little and if she should die, well it would be a natural death really."

To authenticate her new enthusiasm Emily began speaking airily of nature's bounty and taming the wild. She constantly deplored the terrible additives in everyday foodstuffs and was often heard to say that in her opinion commercially grown vegetables had all the goodness taken right out of them. She served hemerocallis fritters to her bridge club, brought a dish of acorns glacés to a pot-luck supper at church, and offered guests a demitasse of freshly brewed chicory in the evening. When Bennett and Rose came to dinner, which they did every three or four weeks, she always included an interesting seasonal wild dish. And into Rose's portion she sometimes added a little extra something.

Emily Forbes lived only a few blocks from Bennett and Rose in the part of Toronto called Hogg's Hollow, a woodsy pocket off North Yonge Street which has the virtue of seeming secluded while actually being very handy to shops and the subway. All the houses have large gardens; the most luxurious of them are set well back, only just visible from the street through a screen of trees. Emily had owned such a house since the early days of her marriage. She valued privacy highly. But since the death of her husband the thought that burglars might also relish it had caused her to become lavish with locks. The double front doors now sported three: a simple Yale which locked automatically when the doors were pulled shut and two more elaborate ones which had to be locked or unlocked with a key from both inside and out. For further protection she augmented these with a night chain. The locks were the only subject on which Bennett became openly exasperated with his mother. He chafed at standing on the doorstep in all weathers while she fiddled with knobs and keys. "For heaven's sake, Mother, you don't need these things," he would say, knowing it to be useless but unable to swallow his annoyance. Once he had tried to defeat the locks with guile. "If there's a fire, you'll never be able to get out. It worries me," he offered craftily. The reply was unanswerable: "Then no one can get in at me either, dear."

As befitted his junior status Bennett Forbes' house was slightly larger, slightly newer and slightly brasher than his mother's. The breakfast room of his house had been designed by a decorator with tulipomania. Wallpaper and curtains, even the ceiling, were covered with tiny yellow tulips. Both colour and motif had probably been chosen as being conducive to morning cheer, and Bennett did think them fresh and springy. Rose, however, hated them. She was naturally a morning person, but the tulips made her dizzy. They seemed to leave the wall and scintillate past her eyes. Because of them her breakfast conversation was often a little snappish, and she had earned a reputation (most unfairly, she thought) for being untalkable-to until after coffee. Conversation was especially difficult these days, when she awoke feeling ragged from the strain of a marriage which had her husband's mother as its primary point of reference. "What would Mother think? Mother will be so pleased. I must tell Mother." Always Mother, Mother, Mother. Never Rose. "Whatever happened to 'forsaking all others'?" she wondered bitterly.

The morning before her birthday Rose entered the breakfast room to find her husband already drinking coffee and reading the paper. She plunged in abruptly. "I don't want to have dinner at your mother's on my birthday. Couldn't we go out instead?"

"Oh really, Rose," Bennett looked up impatiently from his newspaper. Rose recognized the tone and reacted to it immediately. He always thought her unreasonable if she disagreed with him. Soon he would say so.

She answered, rather shrilly, "She has been trying to poison me for months. You know I always get sick after we've been there."

"Don't exaggerate. You don't *always* get sick. You have occasionally been sick." He enunciated each word precisely. "You know your stomach is a bit peculiar; you just don't like the idea of the food Mother serves us," he continued, one eye still on the business section. "Mother's marvellous, really, taking up a new interest at her age."

"Mother's marvellous, really," she mocked. "You're so bloody eager to take her side. My stomach isn't peculiar. She's the one who's peculiar. No, not peculiar, crazy, batty, dotty, nuts. She hates me. I tell you I won't go."

"You're being unreasonable." (There it was.) "You don't have to eat anything you don't like. Mother just thinks we might like to try new things."

"For the last time, I'm not being unreasonable. Think about it, Bennett. You never get sick. Those beautiful little plates of food she gives us, she arranges them in the kitchen ahead of time, doesn't she? She can easily slip something into mine so it's just me who gets poisoned."

Something in her voice, which had passed from shrill to desperate, penetrated her husband's consciousness. "She really believes it, " he realized, and the realization prompted him to be what he thought of as soothing. He reached out and touched her hand. "You haven't really got to know Mother yet," he began, and hurried on to forestall any protests. "We have to go. Mother's been looking forward to giving you a birthday dinner for weeks. She's really very fond of you. She always asks how you are. But if it will make you feel any better I'll call her today. I'll tell her you're under the weather and can't face anything unusual."

That afternoon, while Emily was finalizing her plans for the birthday dinner, she reviewed past experiments. The shredded iris rhizome in the cucumber and ginger sherbet had produced quite satisfactory distress, she recalled, and the delphinium leaves in the *insalata capricciosa* were effective too. That had been a near thing. The highbush cranberry offered interesting possibilities. She must look at some recipes. That sharp flavour should cover any additions. But for tomorrow night just a few ground lily-of-the-valley berries stirred into her own hot pepper relish. Quite a concentrated source of two cardiac glycosides, she had read, though she tried to avoid technical names. Bennett hated hot things, so it was safe enough. When the phone rang at three o'clock she was first startled, then annoyed. "Who would call me at this hour?" she wondered, composing a frosty put down. She had made it known that her afternoon rest time was sacred. "It's what keeps me going," she had stressed time and again, and it was true. She would not fritter it away in chatter and prepared to say so. She didn't, of course, since it was dear Bennett.

"Hello, Mother. I hope I didn't disturb you," he opened.

"Well, dear, I was just resting, you know. I do every day at this time."

"I won't keep you, but I thought I would just ask you about Rose's birthday party. Her stomach has been acting up again and she can't face anything very fancy. You will keep it simple, won't you? Just a roast or something," he pleaded. "Don't go to any trouble."

"Of course, dear, if that's what you want."

"Yes, yes, I do want. Thank you, Mother."

As she hung up the phone Emily rearranged her features from their nice blend of maternal reproof and accommodation to an expression of simple annoyance and said sharply, "Damn." Not for a moment did she believe there was anything wrong with her daughter-in-law's health. In fact she had grudgingly come to respect her robustness. "Constitution like an ox," she marvelled. "Still, if she's got Bennett to call me she must suspect something." So it was that lily-of-the-valley was out and shrimps were in, or to be more precise, prawns. She had been toying with the idea of prawns for some time. Her fish market, catering to local food snobbery, made a specialty of them. They were unlikely to produce death but could cause considerable discomfort. She had noted and stored away the fact of Rose's bout of illness on her honeymoon in London following a lunch of prawn mayonnaise. Rose and Bennett had dined out on the story for weeks, using it as an example of the perils awaiting the unwary traveller. Silly woman, so quick to blame the mayonnaise when it was much more likely to have been the prawns. Lots of people got sick from seafood. It was certainly worth a try. The menu was revised: prawn cocktail to start, followed by roast pork with potatoes and squash, and birthday cake for dessert. Quite an elegant meal, she decided. If Rose gets sick from it, it will be her own fault: I have nothing to reproach myself for.

Surprisingly the birthday dinner was a great success. Rose was looking worried but vivid with an almost febrile animation. Bennett, anxious to avoid a scene, was protective. Emily herself was in rare form. With the pressures of actual poisoning off her shoulders she was free to exercise her considerable gifts as hostess. She had taken great care with every detail of the meal and was pleased that the table looked perfect. The crystal and silver made the occasion seem formal; the centrepiece of flowers and berries in a basket made it feel intimate. Before dinner, champagne was passed; toasts were drunk; her small gift of fancy soap was presented. Even the meal progressed smoothly. "Bennett love, would you bring in the first course from the fridge please?" Emily asked, smoothly shifting responsibility for the only part of the meal not served from a communal dish. At this request Rose almost visibly relaxed. By the time the roast had been eaten and she was blowing out the birthday candles on her cake, she had almost persuaded herself that her fears were groundless. Mrs. Forbes was doing her best to be thoughtful. Rose became fleetingly sentimental. "How alike they look," she thought as her husband and mother-in-law watched her make a wish with the same politely attentive expression. The cake was delicious; the mood festive. Nothing happened until after coffee. Then Rose abruptly became pale and quivery and rushed to the bathroom, racked with vomiting. Instantly all was concern. "Are you all right? Shall I call the doctor?" from Bennett. "What could it have been? Everything was very fresh," from Emily. Rose heard herself refusing offers of water and rest. "Just get me out of here," she kept saying.

After they left Emily was visited by an unfamiliar and unexpected regret. This was the first time she had seen the results of one of her experiments. Other times the effects had just been reported to her. She had always been careful to choose something that wouldn't begin to act until the middle of the night or even the next morning. She did not doubt her actions; doubt was not a feeling familiar to her. But she felt a passing sorrow at the necessity of suffering. It was the same sort of feeling she had when she caught the eye of a cow being trucked to the slaughterhouse. She shuddered to dismiss the thought, and a spasm of annoyance crossed her face. Why did Bennett marry such an unsuitable woman? Why did he have to marry at all? "She doesn't understand him the way I do; she never will. I *am* doing the right thing," she reassured herself. All the same, she had difficulty sleeping that night.

When the phone rang during her rest the following afternoon Emily made no complaint. It was Bennett, reporting that Rose had been sick all night. She had refused to let him call the doctor until morning, when she was too weak to protest any longer. The doctor had diagnosed a violent allergic reaction, most probably to shrimps. She was in no danger but still feeling very ill. She was to rest and eat lightly for a day or two. And leave shrimps alone. Emily put down the receiver and spoke mechanically, "Not shrimps, dear, prawns."

Two days later Emily Forbes varied her routine. Directly after lunch she went to visit her daughter-in-law, carrying a bouquet of bronze chrysanthemums from her garden. The season had been mild. The late October day was so mellow and golden that she hardly needed her sweater. Rose answered the door herself. She looked pale and remote but showed none of the surprise she felt at being visited unannounced by her mother-in-law alone and, more startlingly, in the afternoon.

"Come in, Mrs. Forbes," she invited. (She could never bring herself to say Emily, or worse, Mother.) "I'm just having tea; will you join me?"

"I will have a cup, thank you," Emily replied, and for once did not discourse on the noxious presence of caffeine and tannin in tea. She proferred the chrysanthemums. "I brought you these."

"They're lovely. I'll just get a vase."

They walked together through the hall to the breakfast room. Neither spoke as Rose arranged the flowers on the table. Emily set down her sweater and purse beside them and twisted the handles nervously.

The silence intensified and lengthened while they crossed the hall to the family sitting room overlooking the garden, where the tea things waited. At last Emily said awkwardly, "Rose, I wanted you to know I'm sorry. The meal was too rich for you. I should have served something else."

It sounded like the conventional apology of a concerned hostess. Only the eagerness of her expression and the beads of sweat on her forehead showed that her remarks meant anything more. But that was enough. Rose thought she had been sure before but now the horrifying certainty that this woman had somehow deliberately poisoned her caused a wave of physical nausea. "Sorry," she thought. "You torment me like this and then decide you're sorry."

"Are you all right, dear?" Emily inquired anxiously. "You look pale."

"No, I mean I'm fine, but I'm still very tired. I want to rest now."

"I'll leave you then," Emily said. "Oh, there's a wasp. It must have come in on the flowers. Dear, I'm so sorry to ask you when you're ill, but I'm terrified of wasps. Would you please take it outside?"

"Where the bee sucks there suck I," Rose quoted irrelevantly with a giggle. "I must keep a hold of myself," she told herself sternly. "If I start to laugh I won't be able to stop." She breathed deeply to steady herself and felt her hysteria fade.

"Certainly, Mrs. Forbes, just wait here while I get a glass and a piece of paper." She returned in a moment, gathered up the wasp, and headed through the breakfast room towards the kitchen door. At that moment she saw Emily's purse and sweater on the table beside the vase of flowers. Without hesitating, without conscious thought, she opened the purse, carefully released the wasp on top of her mother-in-law's house keys, and clicked the clasp shut.

"There, all done, Mrs. Forbes," she said returning to the sitting room.

"Thank you, dear. Don't bother to see me out. I'll just get my things."

The phone call came that evening. Emily Forbes was dead. A neighbour had stopped by and found her collapsed on her front doorstep, her house keys still clutched in her hand. The cause of death was clear; she had been stung on the hand several times by a wasp. The doctor, who had attended the family for years, was sympathetic but matter-of-fact. Yes, such rapid collapse was unusual but by no means unknown, even without a previous history of reactions to stings. Bennett was shattered by the news. Rose tried her best and at last found words which consoled him: "It was a natural death, dear, just as she would have wanted."

The Mandalasian Garotte

JAMES POWELL

James Powell was born in Toronto in 1932. He inherited his sense for justice from his paternal great-great grandfather, High Sheriff of Lanark and Bathurst Counties in Upper Canada, and his great grandfather, Sheriff of Carleton County. He inherited his sense of humour from his maternal grandfather who owned a thirty-room hotel in a southern Ontario town with a population of 706. In addition to his stories about Acting Sergeant Maynard Bullock of the Royal Canadian Mounted Police he has chronicled the adventures of the Ambrose Ganelons, four generations of detectives with the same name who live in a fictitious principality on the Riviera. These and other stories of a mysterious or fabulous cast have appeared in Ellery Queen's Mystery Magazine *and* Playboy. *Still a Canadian citizen, Powell lives in Marietta, Pennsylvania, USA, where he was ambushed by love and marriage.*

THE MINISTER OF Justice admired his own handwriting, the way his plump jade fountain pen tied its clever knots, loops, and hitches. "Legal" was among his favourite words. He liked the way the "l's" went up and the "g" went down. He was writing it when his secretary ushered in Commissioner Baines of the Royal Canadian Mounted Police.

"Kind of you to come, Commissioner," he said, without raising his eyes. "Please sit down. Be with you in a minute." Yes, he liked "legal" and secretly attributed his having been given the portfolio of Justice to the fact that he wrote it with such a flourish.

Commissioner Baines tried unsuccessfully to clear his throat. "May I ask how the Prime Minister is, sir?" he said hoarsely.

"As well as might be expected," replied the Minister of Justice, crossing some "t's" and dotting some "i's." "By the by, what was his name again? Your man who slammed the limousine door on the Prime Minister's hand."

"Bullock, sir," said Baines. "Acting Sergeant Maynard Bullock."

"Well, no matter. That wasn't what I wanted to see you about." The Minister of Justice put the cap on his pen and looked up. "Tell me what you know about Dr. Angus Macpherson."

Baines exhaled and settled back a bit in his chair. "The Johnny Appleseed of Canadian missionary medicine? Let's see. Twenty years of building little hospitals all over Southeast Asia. Finances his work by giving accordion concert tours to standing-room-only audiences. After the last tour he rode a bicycle into the jungle of Mandalasia and hasn't been heard of since."

"Correct," said the Minister of Justice. "Now as you know, the civil war in Mandalasia has stalemated. In spite of considerable American and Communist bloc backing, neither the government forces nor the Communist rebels are getting anywhere. We have reason to believe that each side would like to tip the balance and sway international sentiment in its favour by producing Macpherson's dead body and accusing the other side of having done the dirty deed." He paused. "Speaking of dirty deed, your man—"

"Bullock, sir," said Baines.

"Bullock really did a job on the Prime Minister. I heard the bones go crunch twenty yards away." The Minister of Justice shuddered. "But back to Macpherson. It seems the Americans have an additional reason for wanting Macpherson dead. They've discovered he doesn't charge his patients for his services." Seeing Baines's puzzlement the Minister of Justice explained. "To the Americans that's socialized medicine. And you and I know what Americans think of socialized medicine. The situation is further complicated by Macpherson's steadfast refusal to play at Peking's International Festival of Young Communist Accordion Artists. Chairman Mao, deciding to take this as a personal affront, has recently placed the whole matter in the hands of his crack assassin group, the What-do-you-call-thems."

"Not the Sly Dragons, sir?" asked a horrified Baines.

The Minister of Justice nodded. "But the worst is yet to come," he said. "It seems our friends in the Opposition have gotten wind of the situation. Any day now the Prime Minister can expect a question in the House: What is the government doing to guarantee Macpherson's safety? The thing has the potential of a red-hot election issue.

"Well, late last night the Prime Minister—the pain from his hand kept him up until the wee hours—hit upon another of those wonderful, no-nonsense plans of his: we drop one of your men into the jungle. He finds Macpherson and leads him across the border to safety in Bengalia."

"But, sir," protested Baines, "there's hundreds of square miles of jungle. There's no way my man could find Macpherson."

"Commissioner," explained the Minister of Justice, slowly and patiently, "in a situation like this it isn't necessary that we succeed, only that we try. So the Prime Minister can assure the House that steps are being taken on Macpherson's behalf."

Glancing to the right and to the left, Baines leaned forward and whispered, "Sir, we'd be sending my man to certain death."

"Then I'd advise you to send someone you can spare. I assume you have a man in mind, Commissioner."

"Yes, sir," said Baines weakly.

"Good," beamed the Minister of Justice. "Good. Then tell your man that Canada is counting on him, et cetera, et cetera, et cetera. In fact," he smiled, "as a measure of the importance of this mission the Prime Minister's only regret is that a severe disability in one hand prevents him from packing your man's parachute personally."

Halfway through "A Carnival of Venice" Dr. Angus Macpherson's fingers stalled on the keyboard of his mother-of-pearl accordion. Resting the instrument on the veranda railing he scowled from beneath bushy eyebrows at the ragged mark the jungle made against the sky. For several days now the clearing and the buildings of the modest hospital complex, once a source of quiet satisfaction, had been closing in about him like a noose.

First had come the rumours of armies converging on the spot, and overnight what few old men were left had vanished into the jungle. Then Tang, the little Chinese, had arrived, standing in the bow of the small sampan, wearing an inscrutable smile which had not faltered until the shifting current carried him past the boat landing and around the bend toward the white-water rapids. Macpherson's sigh of relief had proved premature. The next day some down-river villagers had trundled the battered and unconscious Tang back to the hospital.

That same evening a bearded, hawk-nosed man in a torn safari jacket and pith helmet with a leopard-skin sweatband had crashed out of the jungle raving theatrically (until he fell, with a cry of genuine surprise, into the excavation for the new root cellar). He was Michael Patrick Finn, a field engineer for Shamrock Diamond Mines, an Irish company. Or so his papers said.

Macpherson nodded decisively. Yes, it was time to move on. Somewhere out there in the darkness he would start another hospital, another footstep in his flight from civilization.

There was a commotion of voices at the edge of the clearing. Four old women came into the moonlight. They were carrying someone on a litter. When they reached him Macpherson saw the broad-brimmed hat, the trim moustache, and the scarlet tunic beneath the torn jump suit. As he felt the man's pulse, eyelids fluttered. Acting Sergeant Maynard Bullock struggled up on one elbow. His mouth moved.

"Dr. Macpherson, I presume," he said in a weak but triumphant voice, then fell back unconscious.

Oh, lordy, lordy, thought Macpherson, wishing for the thousandth time that week that he had become a lighthouse keeper like his father before him.

Bullock awoke with a roaring ache in his jaw and a monumental stiff neck. During the first tree-top hour hanging upside down in a tangle of parachute his small change and car keys had trickled away into the darkness, followed in short order by his wallet and pistol and the lanyard from around his neck.

But fear—real fear—had not seized him until the survival kit started its inching creep down his body. Without its carefully chosen contents—the sum of his twenty years on the Force—Bullock was just another man against the wilderness. Snapping desperately, he had caught the last strap between his teeth. How long had he remained like that until the old women found him? One day? Two? No matter. Here he was. And there, hanging at the foot of the bed was the survival kit. His luck had seen him through again.

Someone giggled. Bullock's eyes became cautious slits. A small Chinese was sitting up in the bed next to his. His right arm was in a shoulder cast that curved out in front as though he was dancing with an invisible partner. He was reading from a little red book. As Bullock watched he giggled again and underlined a passage with a pencil stub.

"My name is Tang, in case you're wondering, Mountie," he said. Bullock stiffened and squeezed his eyes shut. "Relax," coaxed Tang, "I'm Nationalist Chinese, a loyal lackey of the bourgeois imperialists just like you."

Sensing the jig was up, Bullock opened his eyes. "A bit far from home, aren't you, Mr. Tang?" he asked suspiciously.

"I have the honour of being a troubleshooter for the Taiwan Tract and Gospel Society, a group not unlike your Gideons," Tang explained, holding up his little red book. "Our aim is to place our tracts in every hotel room in Southeast Asia. I mistook the good doctor's hospital for a resort hotel."

Their voices awoke the big-nosed man in the bed on Bullock's other side. He wore a shoulder cast identical to Tang's except that it was on the left arm (his invisible partner seemed to have the lead). "Faith and begorra, Michael Patrick Finn's the name," he insisted, shaking Bullock's hand. "Sure, 'tis out like a light you've been for two whole days, me boyo."

Bullock narrowed his eyes. "I'll bet you're Irish, Mr. Finn," he said.

Finn agreed. "Wasn't it lost in the jungle I was and looking for diamonds and didn't I wander into this clearing by accident now?"

An extraordinarily beautiful woman in a crisp white smock strode briskly into the room. Her jet-black hair framed delicate ivory features. Her eyes suggested the orient. "Begorra!" shouted Finn. "I'll take me shillelagh to any blatherskite that won't admit that Dr. Lotus Lane is the prettiest colleen in the whole wide world. Look, I've made the beauty blush." But Lotus Lane wasn't blushing. She thrust a thermometer into Finn's mouth.

Tang giggled. "Ah, Lotus, is it not written somewhere that when a plum blossom falls into a pond it is the ugly frog that croaks first, not the one that loves the most? I have composed a poem on that theme which—" A second thermometer cut him short.

Lotus Lane took Bullock's wrist and felt his pulse. "Your leg giving you any trouble?" she asked.

Bullock looked down and discovered that one of his legs was in a fat cast below the knee. Immediately it began to itch. "Nothing I can't handle," he said through clenched teeth. "Just tell Dr. Macpherson that Acting Sergeant Maynard Bullock of the Royal Canadian Mounted Police would like to speak to him as one Canadian to another on a matter of national—" Lotus Lane popped the last of her thermometers into his mouth with an exasperated little sigh.

"The doctor's a very busy man," she said flatly. "So would you be with the government forces under General Lo Ding Dok creeping up from the South, with Yem Seng and his Communist rebels slinking down from the North, with Neutralists under deposed Prince Cham Pang sidling in from the West. By tomorrow we should hear the guns. I really doubt if the doctor can spare you any time."

She collected the thermometers and left without reading them. Tang scurried after her, reciting a poem entitled, "Plum Blossoms in the Sunset Far Out on the Frog Pond."

Finn flipped a cigarette in the air and caught it between his teeth. "Don't let that heathen Chinee fool you, me bucko," he warned, striking a match with his thumbnail. "Taiwan Tract and Gospel Society, my Aunt Fanny. Yesterday, scouting around for the Coke machine, I overheard him bragging to Dr. Lane that he was some kind of a Red Chinese agent. He was begging her to run off with him when his job here was done. As if a classy doll like her would spend her life making pig iron in the back yard with a runt like him." Bullock noticed that Finn had lost his brogue. So did Finn. "Begorra," he added half-heartedly.

Dr. Macpherson came into the room, shooing Tang ahead of him. "Yesterday I explained why you must remain in your room, Mr. Tang," the doctor was saying. "I could lock you in, you know."

"Love laughs at locksmiths," insisted Tang, crawling back into bed.

Macpherson scowled at Bullock. "Well, Acting Whatever-it-is Whoever-you-are, what did you want to see me about?"

"I'd prefer to speak to you alone, Doctor," said Bullock.

Macpherson shrugged, filled a hypodermic needle, then deftly put first Tang and then Finn to sleep. He came at Bullock with a thermometer.

"Dr. Lane just took my temperature," protested Bullock.

"Her thermometer's centigrade. Mine's Fahrenheit," muttered Macpherson, slipping home the glass tube. "Hope you're fit to travel," he said after a moment. "When somebody tries to do me in by lacing my string hammock with wet rawhide, it's time for me to move on."

Bullock's noise sounded like "Good Godfrey."

"Yes," insisted Macpherson, obviously pleased by the reaction. "Yesterday I was taking my afternoon nap on the veranda as is my wont. I awoke to find myself immobile, my arms pinned to my sides, gasping for breath, and on the threshold of acute pain. Someone had laced my hammock with wet rawhide. As it dried, the rawhide contracted. I was caught in an ever-tightening cocoon of death.

"Does that shock you? Well, frankly, after twenty years devoted to the service of my fellow man I have no illusions about him at all. The more I see of him with his converging armies and wet rawhide the less I like him." Macpherson's eyes took on a far-away glaze. "Some day I hope to build a hospital so deep in the jungle that no one will ever find it. And shouldn't that be every humanitarian doctor's dream—not to have any patients?"

Bullock tore out the thermometer. "The ever-tightening cocoon of death!" he shouted.

"Ah, yes," said Macpherson. "Well, the rawhide grew tighter and tighter. Without losing my sang froid I started the hammock swinging, timing the swings to intersect with the blades of the small oscillating fan I kept on a nearby table. At first the hammock strings withstood the blades. Then they frayed. Finally they broke and I dropped out the bottom to safety."

"Fantastic," said Bullock. Wait till the barracks started talking about close calls and he hit them with that one!

"Strangely enough," mused Macpherson, "lacing a man's

string hammock with wet rawhide is a traditional way of disposing of tyrants in these parts. The Mandalasian Garotte, they call it."

"Well, from here on in your worries are over, Doctor," said Bullock. "I've orders to get you across the border safe and sound."

"All right," said Macpherson. "I've clearly worn out my welcome in Mandalasia. And I can unload you and those two other pieces of excess baggage, Mr. Tang and Mr. Finn, at the border. Now get some rest. I want you fit to travel in the morning."

"Yours truly has the constitution of an ox," laughed Bullock. "Ask Kingston Billy Wainwright and his gang of counterfeiters about that time they tricked me into handcuffing myself to their backwoods printing press, little thinking I'd drag it sixteen miles to my motel and my spare set of keys." Bullock put his wrists together proudly. "See, the right one is an inch longer than—" Macpherson gave a bored yawn and the briefest of apologetic smiles. Bullock didn't even see the hypodermic coming.

Centuries before, kings and potentates and pilgrims from all over Southeast Asia had taken the Holy Road to the sacred temple city of Batong Wat. Today the jungle has reclaimed the city. And all that remains of the Holy Road is an overgrown path and stretches of heaving cobblestones marked at intervals of roughly a day's march by small temples intended in ages past for the traveller's spiritual refreshment.

Macpherson headed the column, machete in one hand, accordion strapped to his back. Bullock hobbled along behind him on crutches and in full Mountie uniform. He had even browned his cast with polish from his survival kit to match his boot. Next came Tang and then Finn. In a brief cast-butting tussle Tang had won Lotus Lane's make-up kit to carry; Finn, her medical bag. She brought up the rear, looking cool, beautiful, and unattainable.

As Bullock saw his job, he had to protect Macpherson not only from any hostile soldiers they might encounter but also from the mysterious hammock lacer as well. Unless apprehended, would-be murderers invariably tried again. Was Tang the culprit? Was the little Chinese really a Red agent? And what about Finn? Something about the Irishman didn't quite jell. And last but not least there was Lotus Lane.

"Dr. Lane?" said Macpherson. "She's been with me for three years. A most satisfactory assistant. A graduate of the school of hard knocks, her contempt for her fellow man is second only to my own."

Bullock began his investigation by slowing his pace until he was abreast of Tang. "Mr. Tang," he said, using his official voice, "where were you at the time of the murder attempt?"

"This is not Canada, Bullock," said the little man. "Your monkey suit and funny hat mean nothing here. But as a token of good faith I will tell you." He smiled inscrutably. "I was with the beautiful Lotus."

"I can check that, you know," said Bullock, deciding to let the crack about his uniform pass.

"Then why would I lie?" smiled Tang. "That leaves only one unaccounted for, doesn't it? Our Mr. Finn, the phony Irishman. One overhears things. That his name is really Birch Bier and that he's with the C.I.A. He urged Lotus Lane to run away with him after a certain 'hit' had been made. He wants them to grill hamburgers together on some New Jersey patio." Tang quickened his pace and moved ahead.

Bullock remained deep in thought until a voice at his elbow said, "Faith and begorra, me bucko."

"Drop the Irish bit, Mr. Birch Bier of the C.I.A.," said Bullock severely. "Just where were you at the time of the murder attempt?"

Bier was poking at an itch under his cast with a thin stick. He gave Bullock a wink and a nudge. "Kiss and Tell isn't my style, but if it's any of your business I was with Lotus Lane. Ask her if you don't believe me. All right, so I'm here to kill Macpherson. But sneaky stuff like that hammock bit isn't my way. In fact, I'll tell you what I'll do, Maynard," he said, offering his hand;

"you keep out of my hair and I'll make them think his death was an accident so you won't look bad. But just remember the C.I.A. motto: 'We always get our man.' "

Bullock turned purple. "Now you listen here," he said through clenched teeth, " 'We always get our man' is the Mountie motto. Good Godfrey, you people have"—he ticked the items off on his fingers—"expense accounts, fancy electronic gear, fat movie parts. At least let us have our—" Bullock stopped dead and looked skyward. "Listen to the birds," he whispered.

Bier listened. "I don't hear any birds," he said.

"Precisely," said Bullock triumphantly.

Up ahead, Macpherson was signalling them into the bushes. Bullock squatted down behind a particularly unCanadian-looking fern and hoped they hadn't run into the Neutralists. Macpherson had filled him in on them. "The Neutralists are down on anything foreign," he had said. "They rove the countryside smashing transistor radios, making *Time-Life* correspondents eat their ballpoint pens, and burning Marx and Engels in tandem effigy. They've sworn to kill me because I won't make house calls." For a humanitarian, Macpherson sure knew how to make enemies. If it was the Neutralists, their goose was cooked.

There were voices and the sounds of leather and metal on the trail. Seeing Tang and Bier straining to identify the politics of the approaching column, it came to Bullock in a sudden desperate moment that he and Macpherson were just as dead if it was the government forces or the Communist rebels.

Just then from around the bend came heads wearing American-type helmets. Government troops. Bier started to spring but Tang's looping right, cast and all, thudded squarely against his temple. Bier's cry of joy died on his lips and he fell softly to the ground. The Patrol reached them and a moment later passed by.

They rested. Bier sat up, holding his head in his hands. Tang was trying to scratch by rubbing his cast against a tree.

"Mr. Tang," scolded Bullock, "in the West we don't strike a

man when he isn't looking. We warn him. We say, 'Put up your dukes.' "

"Shush!" hissed Macpherson. More voices on the trail. Everyone took cover again. This time the heads that came into sight wore conical wicker hats. The Communist rebels. Bier threw a blind roundhouse swing. The cast caught Tang behind the ear. The rebel column passed by.

"Mr. Bier," said Bullock reproachfully, "doesn't anyone say, 'Put up your dukes' any more?"

Their progress for the rest of the day was slow and bloody. Three more near-encounters with government patrols cost Bier a tooth, a split lip, and a lump on the back of the head. Rebel patrols left their mark on Tang: a puffy eye, a fat ear, and a nose that bled like a faucet. As dusk gathered between the trees they camped for the night at a small temple beside the trail.

Dinner was a hearty meal concocted by Lotus Lane from water and a can of dehydrated food. Only Bullock refused to partake. "Brought my own," he said proudly, producing a grey-brown lump. "Pemmican," he explained. "Equal parts of rendered fat and dried buffalo meat, plus certain herbs and spices I'm not at liberty to reveal, and a healthy handful of Saskatoon berries." Bullock hacked off a leathery strip and chewed at it. But his enthusiasm was forced. It must have been a bad year for Saskatoon berries.

Tang and Bier cleaned their plates quickly and dragged themselves like birds with broken wings to opposite corners where they fell into the sleep of sheer exhaustion. "We should all get some rest," said Macpherson. "Tomorrow we'll reach the Kinkong River valley, a swampy disease-infested no-man's-land that Mandalasia claims is Bengalia's and Bengalia insists belongs to Mandalasia."

Lotus Lane decided to get some fresh air before she turned in. Bullock hobbled out after her. He found her leaning against a tree, deep in thought, her face beautiful in the moonlight. At that moment, as if to add to the scene, from inside the temple Dr. Macpherson's accordion struck up "Nola."

Bullock knew he had a way with women. True, the uniform always worked its magic. But he could turn on the old charm, too, whenever he needed it. Bullock flashed a big smile and wagged his finger. "I should be very, very angry with you, Dr. Lane," he said. "It wasn't very nice not telling me that Tang was a Red Chinese agent and Bier was C.I.A. and that they're both here to kill Dr. Macpherson."

"Men tell beautiful women many things," said Lotus Lane.

"Just the same," said Bullock playfully, "you'd just better come clean and tell me where your own political loyalties lie."

Her eyes flashed in the moonlight. "My father was an American sailor. He abandoned my Mandalasian mother six months before I was born. When her father, a local Communist leader, learned her lover's nationality he drove us from the house at the height of the monsoon season. Dying of pneumonia, my mother left me on the doorstep of an orphanage run by the Neutralists where I was brought up to respect the Mandalasian life of yore when wives could be bought and sold for two goats and a chicken.

"For supper they fed us a thin rice gruel from a large copper kettle. One night I took my little bowl and walked right up and said, 'Please, may I have more?' Punished, I fled to the city where I fell in with a gang of Chinese thieves and pick-pockets. I lived as one of them, sleeping with a loaded pistol under my pillow to protect my honour and my share of the booty until I had money enough to sail away to medical school in Switzerland. And here I am. As for my political loyalties, you tell me."

Bullock was taken aback by her outburst. He cleared his throat. "Let's just put you down as uncommitted. Next question: where were you at the time of the murder attempt?"

"I was alone in my room all afternoon," she said.

Bullock scratched his jaw. "Sure you won't like to reconsider that?" he asked. "You see, if you were with, say, Bier that afternoon, then Tang would be the suspect. And vice versa. On the other hand, if you were alone, then we've got three suspects: Tang, Bier, and you. Take it from me, these cases go a lot smoother if you only have one suspect."

"Sorry," said Lotus Lane. "Neither of those gentlemen has ever set foot in my room."

Bullock chewed on his lip and watched her walk back toward the temple. Obviously Tang and Bier were trying to point the finger of guilt at each other. But what made them think Dr. Lane would go along with their stories? Macpherson struck up "Canadian Sunset."

Homesickness was a lump in Bullock's throat and an ache in his stomach. He wished he was sitting at his own kitchen table across from good old Mavis, his wife. He'd fill up his big teacup and talk things out with her. Yes, a cup of tea and a sandwich or two would go down pretty good right now. Bullock hobbled back to the temple. Before turning in, he'd try the pemmican again.

The morning trail was damp and knee-deep in mist. A weary-eyed Macpherson led the way. "I get these nightmares, Bullock," he admitted. "The population explosion. People cheek to jowl everywhere you turn."

"This may sound strange coming from a Mountie," said Bullock. "But I like people."

They were making good progress. To ensure that it continue, Bullock selected a stout stick. When they met their first patrol he squatted down in the bushes between Tang and Bier and tapped the big stick in his palm. They got the message.

But Bullock's main preoccupation was the murder attempt. As he hobbled along he tried to re-enact the crime in his mind, imagining himself first as the little Chinese slinking out of the narrow shadows and up onto the veranda, eyes darting like evil almonds, rawhide dripping between his teeth—Bullock shook his head.

He tried again, imagining himself to be the big-nosed American. But it still didn't work. He tossed his imaginary tangle of string hammock and rawhide aside in disgust. There was just no way a man could lace a string hammock with wet rawhide using only one hand.

Then was it Lotus Lane? Bullock shook his head again. *Pretty Mary Lacks Vitamins.* That summer Bullock had wangled permission to attend a Mountie seminar: "Murder: Did You Ever Ask Yourself Why?" given by Dr. Montague Dabkin. The celebrated criminologist had insisted that murder motives have remained unchanged since time immemorial: Politics, Money, Love, Vengeance. To help them remember, Dabkin had given a mnemonic sentence: *Pretty Mary Lacks Vitamins.* Well, Politics was out. And you don't go into the medical missionary line if you're interested in Money. Love? Macpherson was hardly God's gift to women. And Dr. Lane had more motive for Vengeance against others than against a harmless Canadian doctor.

Macpherson broke into Bullock's thoughts. He signalled everyone to take cover. They squatted down in the bushes and scanned the trail. Who would it be this time? Bullock had taken his place between Tang and Bier. He wagged his stick menacingly. Then he frowned. The first hat that appeared on the trail was broad-brimmed like his own. Other hats followed. A patrol of Mounties? Bullock grinned. A patrol of Mounties to the rescue!

"Put up your dukes," said Tang and Bier simultaneously. Both sides of Bullock's head burst into pain, then darkness rushed in on him.

Bullock's eyes ached when he cracked them open to the late afternoon sun. He was following Macpherson and the others in a makeshift litter carried by four boys in broad-brimmed hats, plaid neckerchiefs, shorts, and woollen knee socks. A middle-aged Mandalasian, similarly dressed but wearing a whistle, was fanning him with a frond. Boy Scouts. "Good Godfrey," said Bullock dejectedly. The litter hit the ground with bone-shattering force.

The man with the whistle leaned over Bullock. "Ah, sir, you must excuse the boys," he said. "You see, 'good Godfrey' bears a striking phonetical similarity to the Mandalasian for 'Put me down this instant or I shall be displeased with you.' This strange coincidence I have puzzled over more than once."

He offered Bullock his hand. "Bay Den Pol, at your service," he said. "The boys and I are on our way to the Boy Scout Jamboree in Rangoon." In a half whisper he added, "Would you mind returning the boys' salute? They think you are the Scoutmaster General."

Bullock snapped off a quick salute. The boys proudly hoisted the litter and started down the trail again. At the next high point of land Bay Den Pol said, "Look, the Kinkong valley. On the other side is the border."

"Listen," said Bullock, "no offence meant, but I've got some top-level police work to finish up. I'd like to put my thinking cap on, okay?" Bullock folded his arms, furrowed his brow, and settled back in the litter. There would be Embassy people at the border. They'd demand the culprit's name and expect more from a Mountie than a feeble, "Search me." He reviewed his thinking from re-enactment of crime to *Pretty Mary Lacks Vitamins* and found his logic flawless. If that wasn't bad enough, his leg developed a fierce itch.

"I understand you were set upon by the American and the Chinese gentleman simultaneously," said Bay Den Pol when it was obvious that Bullock had doffed his thinking cap. "That reminds me of the old Mandalasian folktale of how Krog the Crow and Lopti the Stork, though Natural Enemies, Joined Forces to Steal the Tail of Chee-Chee the Peacock. Have you heard that one?"

Bullock scowled as though he had more important things on his mind. But he listened. He could never resist a good story.

"Well, it came about this way," said Bay Den Pol. "Each afternoon Chee-Chee the Peacock, resplendent in his magnificent tail and yellow kid gloves, would strut through the forest catching the hearts of the ladies. His amorous successes set the green worm of envy gnawing deep in the vitals of Krog the Crow and Lopti the Stork. From the cornfield Krog would mutter, 'Fancy Dan.' From the frog pond Lopti would sneer, 'Dude.' And each resolved to steal the magnificent tail for himself.

"Now one stormy night as Lopti peered in through the transom of Chee-Chee's fashionable *pied à terre,* who should arrive to peek in at the letter slot but Krog. Now Krog and Lopti were natural enemies. After all, the one was black, the other white. The one squat, the other tall. The one had a short beak, the other a long. Yet together they watched as Chee-Chee banked the fire and bolted the door. Then he locked his tail inside a stout clothes press, placed the key between the mattress and the box springs of his bed, blew out the candle, and retired.

"The stork, thinking how he could not gain entrance through the sooty chimney without pointing the finger of guilt at himself, sighed. The crow, thinking the key was tucked far out of reach, sighed. As one man they looked at each other and sealed the bargain with a wink. In a twinkling the crow flew down the chimney and unbolted the door. Then, thanks to his long beak, the stork plucked the key from its hiding place. The two divided up the elegant plumage and went their separate ways."

They were down on the mud flats now, the litter boys wading knee-deep in soft ooze. Macpherson and the others had crossed a shrunken river channel and reached a ruined temple on a rise of land.

"Noo Noo, my wise old peasant nurse, always delighted in the moral of this story," said Bay Den Pol, struggling along beside the litter. " 'Bay Bay,' she would say, 'politics makes strange bedfellows.' "

"Good Godfrey!" exclaimed Bullock.

It was almost dark. Bullock stood on one leg in a backwater pool and washed the mud from his uniform as best he could. Bay Den Pol and his Boy Scouts had marched on ahead, promising to call the Canadian Embassy from the first telephone booth across the border. Bullock wanted to look presentable for the press photographers when they arrived.

Well, another case was as good as closed. He imagined the Prime Minister's surprise at finding him at his old post, guarding the flowerbeds in front of the Parliament Buildings. ("Back so soon, Bullock?" "Mission accomplished, Mr. Prime Minister." "You're a wonder, Bullock. We've got our eye on you." "Thank you, sir. Here, let me get that car door—") With a smile on his face Bullock hobbled back to the temple, stopping only to cut and strip a pole from a nearby stand of bamboo.

His four companions were having after-dinner coffee around a masked fire—tire-tread sandal prints had suggested that Neutralists were in the vicinity. Bullock noted at once that someone had been into his survival kit. If they'd wanted some pemmican, he thought peevishly, all they had to do was ask.

Well, no matter. He took out a small Canadian flag and tied it to the pole. Then, as the others watched with mild interest, he stuck the pole in the ground, saluted the flag, and announced, "I claim this no-man's-land for the Dominion of Canada." Accepting a cup of coffee from Lotus Lane with a polite nod, Bullock continued, "And now that this is officially Canadian soil, I arrest you, Tang, and you, Birch Bier, alias Michael Patrick Finn, for attempted murder."

Tang and Bier groaned. "Yes," insisted Bullock, "it took two good hands to lace up Dr. Macpherson's hammock. Your right hand, Bier, and your left, Tang. Like Krog the Crow and Lopti the Stork, though natural enemies, you joined forces to steal the tail of Chee-Chee the Peacock."

Bullock really had their attention now. "But why you two? Why not Dr. Lane?

"I'll tell you why," continued Bullock. "If I've learned one thing from my years on the Force it's that your woman murderer never laces her victims up in cocoons of death."

At that moment, Bier, who had been fighting to keep his eyes open, gave up the battle and slumped over, breathing deeply. Tang also lost interest.

"No," yawned Bullock, "when my lady turns to murder you can bet she'll choose a gentler way, something that goes with her natural role as a homemaker. Like poison." Bullock's cup clattered to the floor.

"Eh?" said Macpherson groggily. "What was that? Must have dozed off."

Bullock swayed and tried to work his tongue.

Lotus Lane's laughter was silver. She stood up, her arms crossed over her beautiful bosom. "You men," she laughed, "what pompous Romeos, arrogant fools, and posturing ninnies you are! 'Her natural role as a homemaker,' indeed. For your information, Bullock, I was the one who tried the Mandalasian garotte. I had intended the armies to kill Macpherson. But I was afraid that with your help he might escape them."

Lotus smiled and shook her head. "Tang and Bier weren't trying to give themselves alibis for that afternoon. Each wanted to give me one. Why? Each thought I had tried to murder Macpherson out of love—because I was so impatient to run off with him." She was laughing helplessly.

"But you don't understand," explained Bullock thickly. "You haven't got a motive."

"Motive?" said Lotus Lane. "*Sic semper tyrannis.* I hate all men everywhere because of their suppression of women from the beginning of time."

Suddenly it was all clear. "I really believe you Women's Lib people have got a point," said Bullock. "And I speak for good old Mavis, my wife, when I say that. But why take it out on Dr. Macpherson?"

Lotus Lane uncrossed her arms and revealed the flare gun from Bullock's survival kit. She pointed it skyward, through a gaping hole in the roof. "This will bring the Neutralists on the double. They'll find you here sleeping like babies and kill you all, blaming Macpherson's death on 'foreign interventionists,' their idiotic—but conveniently vague—male catch-phrase of the moment. Tomorrow Denmark, India, Roumania, and the other countries that venerate Macpherson as a great humanitarian will condemn the Americans, the Russians, or the Red Chinese—or all three—for the ghastly act. The day after tomorrow Japan, Chile, Albania, and the other countries that venerate Macpherson for his accordion wizardry will blame his death on ideology, on Capitalism or Communism—or both. A week from now the world will be one immense battlefield. Then, when the smoke of battle clears and there are no more soldiers left to die, it will be an immense no-man's-land."

"Hear, hear," said Macpherson approvingly and pitched forward into a deep sleep.

"Then after a bit the world will fill up with womanly gardenlike things again," continued Lotus Lane. "Grass to overgrow the iron things of war; flowers instead of shot and shell; song birds instead of bugles—"

"But without men you'd all die out," Bullock insisted.

Lotus Lane gave him a pitying smile. "Thanks to science we don't even need you for that any more."

Bullock shuddered like a tree that feels the woodman's axe. He swayed on his crutches.

"Pleasant dreams, Acting Sergeant Maynard Bullock of the Royal Canadian Mounted Police," said Lotus Lane, knowing he would instinctively come to attention and throw his shoulders back. The crutches slipped out of his armpits and clattered to the temple floor. Bullock fell over backward, noting before sleep took him that the moonlit hole through which she was pointing the flare gun was shaped like Lake Huron and Georgian Bay.

Lake Huron and Georgian Bay were dawn-grey. Bullock pulled his crutches to him and struggled erect. A few feet away Macpherson was leaning over Lotus Lane's body while Tang and Bier looked on "She's unconscious," said Macpherson. "A bruise the size of a four-bit piece over her right eye."

"What happened?" asked Tang.

Bullock was examining the flare gun. "These babies happen to be a hobby of mine," he said. "This one's interesting. Watch." When he pulled the trigger nothing happened. "Now what does any normal person do?" he asked.

"He looks down the barrel to see what's stuck," said Bier. Tang nodded agreement.

"Right," said Bullock and did just that. A second later the firing pin clicked. "Heads will roll, believe you me," said Bullock grimly. "This was a personal gift to yours truly from the

Prime Minister. He even had the ordnance boys give it a special tune-up. Wait till he hears they botched the job." Bullock looked at Tang and Bier. "All this means that I can't arrest you guys." He nodded at the flag. "But I can still deport you as undesirable aliens."

"If we go, Macpherson goes," said Tang. "The Hippocratic Oath says he can't abandon a patient."

Macpherson was bathing Lotus Lane's temples. "You're all fit as fiddles," he said. "The casts were just to slow you down a bit. Three against one are stiff odds." Tang and Bier cried out and scrabbled at the plaster with their fingers. Bullock stood stunned. Macpherson shrugged. "Anyone can rent a Mountie suit, Bullock," he said.

Tang and Bier were bashing at their casts with rocks. Though Bullock's leg quivered for attention he took time to advise them. "That's too short range. Mr. Bier, you work on Mr. Tang's cast and vice versa. May this be a lesson in international cooperation for you both." He freed his own leg with a hammer from his survival kit.

A sandy-haired man wearing glasses and a tweed topcoat appeared in the temple doorway. Bay Den Pol and his Boy Scouts were peeking in from behind him. Bullock stopped scratching. "It's Wickett. Hey, Wickett!" he shouted. They had met several years before while Wickett had been cultural and military attaché at the Canadian Embassy in San Marino. Wickett smiled weakly. His lips were blue.

"I see you ran into the Neutralists," said Bullock.

Wickett made a face. "I was gagging on my ballpoint pen when the Boy Scouts sent them scurrying off with some crazy story about a secret Coca-Cola bottling plant in the jungle. I—" Wickett saw the flag. He turned dead-white.

Bullock lowered his eyes modestly. "Welcome to Canada East," he said.

"Bullock," whispered Wickett, "you didn't claim this God-forsaken flood land for Canada?"

Bullock, grinning from ear to ear, nodded.

"But this makes us imperialists," said Wickett, struggling to control his voice. "And we'll have to build a post office and rent a gunboat to protect Canadian interests." He whistled through his teeth. "Boy, wait till Ottawa hears this one!"

Crestfallen, Bullock mumbled, "Couldn't we just unclaim it?" He made the motion of pulling a flagpole out of the ground.

Wickett shook his head. "We're stuck with it. Geography books would be in a heck of a mess if countries could claim land one minute and unclaim it the next. Well," he added, unslinging a camera, "I still need some pictures so the folks back home can see that no harm's come to their beloved doctor."

Macpherson was fussing around Lotus Lane. She was sitting up, her back against a worn statue of the serpent Naga. "This is Dr. Lane, an attempted murderer," said Bullock, by way of an introduction.

"I am?" said Lotus Lane vaguely, touching the bandage above her eye.

"Amnesia," explained Macpherson. "Tragic, isn't it? I had never really appreciated the true depths of her contempt for mankind. And then to have it blotted out in a single blow! But the Scouts have volunteered to carry her to my new hospital. There I will restore her precious memory. After that, who knows? True, she sees man as her natural enemy. But the world of missionary medicine is a lonely place. Together we might steal some happiness from it."

"Like Krog the Crow and Lopti the Stork," smiled Bullock.

Cocking an uneasy eyebrow at the Mountie, Wickett waved his camera. "Some pictures, Doctor. Okay? Let's start with one of you and your accordion." The shutter was soon clicking away.

Those were the next day's front-page pictures around the world. But there is another one sitting in a frame among the mementoes on top of the Bullock television set. Standing there in the over-exposed interior of a Mandalasian temple are, left to right: Tang and his little red book; Bay Den Pol and three saluting Boy Scouts (the fourth was holding the camera); Dr. Macpherson and his accordion; a seated and blank-faced Lotus Lane; Bullock with one foot bare; an uncomfortable Wickett; and Bier with an unlit cigarette between his teeth.

As for all the smiles, Bullock had just called on everyone to say "Cheese"—just as a moment or two before he had shouted, "Listen, everybody! Before we go our separate ways let's have a shot with all of us in it. For old time's sake."

St. Anthony's Man

TIM WYNNE-JONES

Tim Wynne-Jones was born in a house called Ravensheugh on the Spital Road in Bromborough, Cheshire, England. His family emigrated to Canada when he was four. In Canada he expected to find mountains, forests hunted by Indians, Mounties, and bears in the streets. The family moved to Kitimat in northern British Columbia. Canada proved to be all he had hoped for. Somewhere along the way he was urbanized, sang in rock bands, operated a graphic design firm, and received a B.A. and M.F.A. in visual art. His first novel, Odd's End, *was written as a vacation—the only travel he could afford. It won the 1979 Seal Award.* The Knot *followed in 1982. When not writing crime fiction Tim writes children's books and radio plays.*

MUNK HAD THIS idea. He told it to Stretch. "The next person to give me a handout gets double his money back." Stretch said, "Munk, it's too bad your river don't flow all the way to the sea."

Munk scratched his scalp through a hole in his toque. He huddled deeper into his ragged jacket. It was a boy's ski parka. From a tear under his arm he noticed he was losing down. It was cold on Bloor Street; December without a blessed hint of Christmas. Night was setting in with the day hardly out of its shell. The wind tugged at the fringe of Munk's old hair.

"Toronto," muttered Stretch into his collar. "It's like wearing wet diapers on your face." He was thinking about being spilled out of the Mission like dirty water onto Queen Street that morning; how he had let the tide carry him uptown with Munk instead of hanging out on the strip, the home turf. He was thinking what a dumb idea it had been. He looked at Munk. Munk's eyes looked like spit but there was a glint of something there that booze couldn't wash away.

"This is the best part coming up," said Munk, as they stopped at Avenue Road for the lights.

"I shoulda never left Moose Jaw," said Stretch.

The lights changed.

"From here to Varsity Stadium," said Munk, "this is a special place." As they reached the far curb, Stretch surveyed the darkening horizon for a sign of something special. He picked out from the rush-hour crowd a young woman with blonde hair tucked into an angora hat and long legs poured into red jeans. She was wearing a coat the colour of the inside of a plum. Stretch cleared his throat and prepared his spare-change song and dance. Munk beat him to the punch.

"Ma'am," he said. And he handed her a card he pulled from his pocket. The woman took the card without missing a step.

"What was that?" asked Stretch. Munk smiled and his gaze drifted after the woman. He held up his hands while Stretch searched him and then relieved him of a stack of calling cards in a rubber band. Stretch read the printed card out loud: "Walter K. Munkatrink, Uptown Panhandler, Catering to the charitable inclinations of the well-to-do. No appointment necessary."

"That was another idea I had," said Munk repossessing the cards from Stretch's rough yellow fingers. He made a grand gesture with his hand. "This is a classy part of town, Stretch. Folks around here aren't comfortable 'less you can make them feel you're one of them."

Stretch started to cough violently. He spit up mucus the colour of his stained fingers. He wiped his face on his sleeve. "It's too bad your elevator don't go all the way to the top floor," he said.

Munk pointed at the museum. "I go in there a lot," he said. "I like the dinosaurs. The Brontosaurus. He stands around all day eating trees, with his eyes peeled for predators. Like us," he said.

"I think dinosaurs are stupid," said Stretch. "Now let's get going."

"Then there's Philosopher's Walk," said Munk, like a tour guide, unperturbed by the reticence of his clientele. "It's like this green alley down behind the museum and up next to the Conservatory of Music. In the summer I spend time down there listening to the sounds coming out of the Conservatory. Nothing stupid about that."

"It's stupid," said Stretch. "Like your dumb ideas."

"No," said Munk.

"Dumb," said Stretch.

Munk sighed. "You have to keep things happening," he

protested. "Keep bumping the table to keep all the pinballs rolling. It's a game."

"A game!" said Stretch.

"No," said Munk. "It's a challenge. Like what I said before; that I was going to give the next person who shells out double their money back? That's a challenge."

Stretch searched the inside of his coat for a bottle. "You wanna challenge? So run for Prime Minister!" He found the paper bag and sucked on the glass neck protruding from its greasy wrinkled skin.

Munk was thoughtful for a moment. "Things can happen," he said.

"Oh sure," said Stretch, capping his bottle. "Like Lester gettin' rolled last week. Things happen all right. At least Lester lost his money honestly."

Munk clamped his mouth shut. It was no use talking to Stretch about certain things. Easier talking to a Brontosaurus. Friendlier. From his pocket he pulled the change he had made that day: $6.85. Not a lot to lose, he thought.

"The thing is," he said, "beggars *can* be choosers. You choose what happens. You make things happen."

Stretch stopped in his tracks. He wavered a bit. His cheeks puckered, stifling a burp. He looked at the money in Munk's hand. "Tell me one good thing that has ever happened," he said darkly.

Munk looked down at the sidewalk and watched a feather whirl away in the wind: a feather from his torn parka. Then suddenly he smiled brightly. "I'll show you," he said.

"Great," said Stretch, "then double your money back, man!"

"Watch," said Munk. He began to look for a likely target for his latest idea.

"The guys at the Mission are gonna love this," said Stretch.

Harriet Smallpiece fell in line with the crush of uncivil servants filing out of Queen's Park and down into the subway. She felt herself growing smaller and smaller in the press—distilled, like Alice. She clutched her violin case to her breast. She was going to be late. Punctual these twenty years, she was going to be late, today of all days, when nothing must be seen to disturb her orderly ways. She had only one student so late on a Friday afternoon, horrible little Malcolm Brown. He was invariably late himself, and she prayed he might be today.

Harriet found herself flung up against the far door of the subway car. She closed her eyes as the train jolted forward. In the dark she saw the gun. These days she could not close her eyes without seeing either the gun or mother. It was because of the cartridges she was going to be late. Three deadly little packages of powder, primer, and shot, which in her determination to hide effectively, she had completely misplaced. She rediscovered the shells at last in father's tool shed in a bottle filled with orphaned nuts and bolts. Mother never set foot in the tool shed; she hadn't when father was alive, either. It had been six years since he had died. Six years since Harriet, venturing into that refuge, had found his service Enfield wrapped in a blue-green shammy in his kit box. Casually, without the need or stomach for haste, Harriet had discovered that mother knew nothing of the gun's existence. Neither did Major Boothroyd, who had been father's closest friend. The Major had taken the bereaved family under his wing, and to this day they dined with him every other Sunday. Harriet wondered how long she would have to keep that up once mother was gone.

Father's gun—how fitting. He had lived in mother's shadow as completely as Harriet had. They had huddled there together while youth and vitality seeped away like the tint in an old photograph. It was fitting, yes, but the gun's best feature was its anonymity. It had entered the country as an antique; registration had not been mandatory. Officially the gun did not exist. Harriet had learned that much in her usual circumspect fashion. In the same manner she went about acquiring ammunition. It was the good Major who supplied her, without knowing. He collected firearms, belonged to a club. One Sunday, on the pretext of borrowing a book she knew to be there, Harriet slipped into the Major's study. She returned to her sherry in the sitting room with three .38-calibre cartridges of a cut she would never have been able to find in an average gun store had she possessed the temerity to try. She had remembered the book. She even read it, just to be on the safe side. Mother had read it, too. She always liked to keep up with Harriet. It kept her young, she said. The Major never missed the cartridges. But Harriet waited two years, just to be on the safe side. In that time she oiled and cleaned the chambers of the Enfield faithfully. Today, before leaving the house, she had put the stolen ammunition once and for always in its proper place. She had hidden the loaded gun through a tear in the underside of her chair in the living room. She and mother had identical wingback chairs, one on either side of the TV.

The train stopped. More bodies entered than left. The train shuddered back into life, and Harriet closed her eyes again.

Six years. Time had made her cold-blooded. There was not a shred of spontaneity or passion in her plan. Neither would there be remorse when it was carried out. She pressed her eyes more tightly shut as the train whined around the bend leading to the St. George station. There had been no moment of decision. The plan had grown like cancer but without the furious pace. No one would suspect Harriet. Times with mother were good and bad, but always bad again. Harriet's idea gained dimension with each crisis. Her loathing she kept quiet. There were periods of remission, but no cure. No *other* cure. Like cancer, the idea was a part of Harriet now.

The train stopped, mid-tunnel, a victim of the rush-hour back-up. Harriet shifted her weight and found herself face to face with her own reflection in the subway door. The grim expression there disturbed her. I am free of the weight of waiting, she told herself. The shadowy image on the door seemed relieved. There was reason now to act; there was even occasion.

A series of coincidences had galvanized Harriet into the final passage of her drawn-out "cure". Mother's newest and rankling ailment, that was one. Then there was the coincidence of

Leonard's imminent financial embarrassment. Leonard was too much of a gentleman to discuss it with her, but she knew it was a weight on him. She knew he would never come to her for aid, assuming he had the slightest idea of her worth, which he didn't. Harriet couldn't bear the thought of Leonard beset upon in any way. Finally, and most important of all, was the cat burglar who had been terrorizing the neighbourhood. Ironically it was at mother's insistence that Harriet had attended the Neighbourhood Watch meeting at the local school. Mother had been worried about father's money which she kept in the safe in the living-room wall. And well she might. Harriet had learned at the meeting it was the kind of safe a competent burglar could open without difficulty. The sergeant from the Metropolitan Police had supplied a good deal of information regarding the cat burglar's modus operandi. Harriet had taken notes assiduously. Even if this latest crime didn't quite fit the pattern she would be all right. After all, the sergeant had warned them that such a spate of break-ins usually inspired copy-cat attempts.

The subway train lurched into St. George. Using her violin case like the prow of an ice-breaker, Harriet ploughed her way across the car and out onto the platform. She stood for a moment collecting her wits and savouring her freedom. I shall not take subway trains after today, she told herself. I shall not teach. The little brats can learn the accordion. Harriet was certain that was what Leonard would want for her. She let this warming thought carry her up to street level and the cold hard night ahead. She was reminded of the hours of "ordinary" she had yet to face this day before the "extraordinary" crashed into her quiet life and altered it irrevocably. The cold air reminded her of a duty she must discharge, now, despite her lateness for class. She had prayed to St. Anthony to help her find the missing cartridges. Mother had always believed—and had instilled in her the belief—that one must make immediate restitution for an answered prayer. Despite her unholy venture, Harriet was too much a creature of habit to break precedent today. It was mother's idea that one made an act of charity on such occasions; reward a beggar in St. Anthony's name. Mother had never learned that charity began at home, but that was neither here nor there. There was sometimes a man around the Conservatory, a regular. He had given Harriet an absurd little card one day. Standing at the lights at Bedford, she was glad to see him across Bloor Street, leaning on the railing outside the Conservatory. It seemed an auspicious sign. In her elation at being able to so handily dispense with her duty, Harriet momentarily considered giving the man a twenty-dollar bill. She reconsidered. There would be publicity; her picture might appear in the paper. Might a tramp wonder at such a generous donation on the eve of a tragedy? She would stay on the safe side. She would give him a ten. As she crossed the street, she saw her quarry leave the railing and step out onto the sidewalk in her direction. It gave her an eerie feeling as if perhaps he was anticipating her.

"Oh God, let everything work out as I've planned," she mumbled to herself. She would have addressed the appropriate saint but who, after all, *was* the patron saint of matricides?

Munk saw her coming. She was middle-aged and had tidy brown hair held back with two clips like a girl's. She was wearing grey flannel slacks and a black persian lamb coat. One fuzzy-mittened hand clasped a violin case, while the other rummaged in her pocket.

"Here you go," she said. Munk's gaze shifted from the woman's face to her hand and back again. Their eyes engaged a moment before hers skittered away. She had large, slightly protuberant eyes. Mechanically Munk took the crisp ten-dollar bill from her hand but her eyes held him speechless. Her face lightened as if he had removed a thorn from her skin. For a fleeting instance a smile appeared on her full lower lip. Then like a stage-hand unused to the limelight on that fleshy stage, the smile vanished into the safety of the wings.

"You can thank St. Anthony," she said, and then she walked off briskly, her head bowed into the wind. Munk watched her stride up the path to the Conservatory. Then she was gone. He held the bill up to his nose like a love letter. There was no scent.

Stretch tugged the bill from Munk's fingers and examined it. "I liked it better with the snow-capped, purple mountains, and that river coming out at you, but this'll do in a pinch."

"Things happen," said Munk, more to himself than to his sidekick. Stretch snickered. "I'm glad to see you've at least got the sense to let 'em," he said. "That broad coulda wiped you out."

Munk stared at him enquiringly.

"Your big fat idea," said Stretch. "Don't you remember your big fat dumb idea?"

Munk had not remembered. Something quite different had happened. Stretch was cackling now. "Maybe you can give her one of those cards with an IOU on the backside," he suggested. Munk began to nod his head. Stretch stopped laughing. "She's gone, Munk," he said.

"I'll wait," said Munk.

Stretch pointed wildly at the Conservatory. "Maybe she lives in there! Ever think of that?"

Munk shrugged his shoulders.

Stretch started to cough.

"Come on," said Munk. "I'll buy you a coffee."

The north side of Bloor is lined with fast-food eateries crowded with students. Stretch and Munk entered the Donut Queen. Munk bought them each two donuts and a large coffee. Stretch waited at the only available table, the one in front of the door. Munk glanced anxiously over Stretch's shoulder through the window at the bright portal of the Conservatory. Stretch shakily rolled a cigarette, lit it, and spit out loose bits of tobacco on the table. He had wolfed down the donuts. His stomach ached.

"You and me can't afford ideas," he said morosely.

"You watch," said Munk. "I'll show you."

Stretch shook his head and stood up. "I'm in enough pain

already," he said and turned to go. "It's too bad," he said as he leaned against the door.

"What's that?" asked Munk.

"It's too bad your shaft don't go all the way to the ore."

Munk got himself a fresh cup of coffee, glad to be alone with his thoughts. The window steamed up, and he cleared a porthole. She had come this way; if he was lucky she would pass right by the door. There was nowhere he had to be right now, or ever for that matter. His eye never wandered from the clear patch on the window. It was like watching TV but better—there was something to look forward to. Onto the little screen rushed a silver BMW; it stopped in front of the Conservatory and disgorged a small, plump boy. An unseen hand thrust a violin case into the boy's hands and then the car sped off threading its way back into the busy traffic. The boy waited where he was for some moments and then, with a quick backward glance at the Conservatory, he crossed Bloor Street making straight for the Donut Queen. The boy, about ten, plunked his violin case down on the seat across from Munk and joined the line-up at the counter. He returned to the seat with a tray and nudged the violin case onto the floor so that he could sit down. On the tray he had a cup of hot chocolate, a cruller, a dutchie, and a chocolate swirl. Watching him eat, Munk got an idea.

"Better than a fiddle lesson any day," he said.

The boy pretended not to hear. Munk chuckled to himself and sipped at his coffee. He tried again.

"Who you got, anyway?" he said.

The boy frowned. He did not want his time of delicious truancy spoiled.

"I'm one of the supers across the way," said Munk waving in the direction of the Conservatory. "I was just curious who your teacher was, that's all."

The boy examined him warily. "Smallpiece," he muttered.

Munk appeared to check his memory. It was a long shot but why not take a chance? "She the one with the frog eyes?" he ventured at last. The question was met with a minor explosion of half-eaten donut. "And the clips in her hair like she was in kindergarten or something?"

The boy slapped the table and rocked with mirth. "Awright," he said, several times. "That's Smallpiece."

"Awright," parrotted Munk sipping at his coffee.

When the boy was finished Munk said, "Those chocolate things any good?"

The boy looked at the crumbs on his plate and nodded. Munk took a bill from his pocket and handed it to the boy.

"Why don't you go buy us one each," he said.

"Awright," said the boy, clutching at the bill. "Decent!" he exclaimed as he clambered out of his chair. Munk waited a moment until a party of six came through the door, then he made his move. It was easier than he even expected. When the boy returned to the table Munk was gone. So was the violin.

At the pay phone in the subway at Bedford, Munk looked up Smallpiece. His luck was still holding: E and H both at the same address. He dialled the number.

"Harriet's out," came the answer to his enquiry. "Oh, you won't catch that girl tonight. She's got classes and then rehearsal with the quartet until all hours . . ." E rambled on garrulously for some time. Munk liked the way she treated him. Like an acquaintance.

Harriet stared down from the studio window into the bleak emptiness of Philosopher's Walk. There was an old Baldwin near to hand and she tapped tunelessly at the C four octaves from centre. There was a clock on the wall. It was 5:20. She had not yet taken off her coat. Malcolm should have been there at 5:00. Rehearsal wasn't until 7:30. She could warm up for the next forty minutes at Malcolm Brown's expense, and for the first time in their two-year association she blessed the boy. She hummed the Largo from the Shostakovich. She could use the practice. She must be good at rehearsal tonight, but not too good. She must play competently. What else was expected from a second violin? Above all, she must resist the urge to show off. She must not play too close to the bone. The others might not notice, but Leonard would.

The quartet met every Friday at Leonard's place. Harriet was in love with Leonard. Until she had met him, love had frightened her. She had imagined it nothing more than a pretty but fragile mask behind which Duty hid her ugly face. Time had revealed no such duplicity in Leonard.

It had all started so innocently. She had arrived early for rehearsal and joined Leonard for dessert and coffee. She now arrived early on a regular basis by invitation. Their relationship had blossomed quietly under the midwifery of companionable chatter, without the need for dates, gifts, or vulgar display, all of which were, to Harriet's way of thinking, too frivolous, not to mention frightening, for mature consideration. Once or twice Harriet had felt the need to stifle what showed every indication of becoming an emotional outburst on Leonard's part. She could not risk getting into a pother herself and perhaps letting slip the horror which was life with mother. In all her planning the one thing she feared most was to imagine, let alone perceive, the slightest suspicion in Leonard's eyes afterwards. She took every opportunity to stress to him her devotion to mother. There had been no scenes lately, which was just as well.

Mother knew nothing of Harriet's fondness for Leonard. Harriet retailed bland accounts of the quartet's progress over tea when she arrived home from rehearsal. It was the same every week. There would be the light on above the side door and the lamp on dimly in the dining nook. Harriet would put on the kettle and while it boiled, watch TV. The TV would be on at a barely audible volume but just as Harriet was settling down with her cup of tea, mother would appear from the darkened hallway blinking furiously, doing up her dressing gown, and wondering what all the commotion was about.

"Just me," Harriet always said, hidden behind the wings of her chair. "Go back to sleep, dear."

To which mother would reply, "I'm up now, aren't I?" She would then turn up the TV to a scream and plunk herself in her chair. Harriet would set a cup on the tray "just in case", and then they would talk above the TV's blare. Mother liked to hear what the quartet was up to. It kept her young, she said. Tonight, thought Harriet, she will hear quite a different report!

Suddenly Harriet leaned heavily on the edge of the piano. She felt weak. The clock had scarcely moved. There were still hours of "ordinary" left in the day, and she could feel the timid creature of habit she was, slipping from her grasp. She couldn't bear the studio another moment. Buttoning up her coat and grabbing her violin, she left. She passed no one in the hallways. No one at the front desk saw her leave. Again the cold air snapped her from her reveries. It was beginning to snow. She wanted a coffee or a drink. She let herself consider going to Leonard's that very minute but the gravity of such a rash move cancelled the desire. Squinting into the snow she tried to imagine in which of the dives across the way she could nurse a coffee for an hour or more. The harsh lighting was somehow disconcerting: the arrival suddenly of two police cars outside the Donut Queen positively repellent. She set off in the general direction of Leonard's house. If she walked slowly enough she would not be too intolerably early.

Munk got fifty dollars for the violin from a pawn shop on Church Street. He bought himself a mickey of good Scotch and a two-pound box of chocolates and set out on foot for the shared dwelling of E and H Smallpiece. They lived off the Danforth at the end of a little street in a bungalow with a hipped roof. It was a plain house. Through a crack in the curtains of the front room Munk caught a glimpse of a fat woman in a flowered housecoat. The TV was on so loud he could hear it out on the snowy street. It was cheery. About a hundred feet from the house on the other side of the street there was a muffler shop. It was closed for the night. Munk made himself comfortable in a nest of cardboard boxes which had overflowed from the dumper out back. The wind had dropped off with the coming of the snow. Munk was warm enough. He made a little raised shrine for the box of chocolates. Munk felt good. All the pinballs were moving now. He tried to remember the last time he had been in love.

The Scotch was almost gone when he saw Harriet coming up the street. He had already decided not to approach her until she was safe inside. No use scaring her. The lights in the house had gone out some time earlier although E had distinctly mentioned having tea with Harriet once she got home. It was tea Munk was aiming for. He smoothed down his hair under his toque and popped a couple of mints into his mouth. He watched Harriet safe inside, watched the lights of her progress—kitchen, front room. He began to unwind himself from his cardboard lair, and that's when he heard the shot.

For a moment Harriet stood transfixed by the noise and sucked into the silence which followed it. She stared at mother lying half in the living room and half in the shadowy front hall. There was no need to check—the woman was dead. All Harriet could think of was how remarkably the scene resembled the mental image she had lived with these last few months. She had known it would be like this; mother's death was no more than a fact delayed. There was nothing to fear, Harriet told herself. Yet she could not move. Gradually, however, the low murmur of the TV roused her from her shock and it was that same low murmur that brought on the second wave of shock and nausea. *She had forgotten to turn the TV up loud.* Panic set in. She had already jumbled her carefully constructed schedule. She forced herself into action. She must unlock the front door—*he* escaped through the front door, she reminded herself. Harriet crossed the room, stepped over mother, and unlocked the front door. Now the gag and the bonds—No, that was later. The safe, she had to open the safe. She recrossed the room and was about to lift down the painting covering the safe when she realized she was still carrying the gun. *She was still carrying the blasted murder weapon.* Harriet began to whimper. She braced herself against the wall.

"It's a concert, Harriet," she said out loud. "No matter how nervous you think you are you must will yourself towards the coda. One bar at a time."

Harriet wrapped the revolver in its blue-green shammy and returned to the front door. Bending down, she removed the loose heat vent and pushed the gun as far along the duct as she could. She stood up a little dizzy but with renewed hope; the first movement was underway. She opened the safe and took out father's money. Each denomination was wrapped with a rubber band and a chit of paper recording the amount. From the cache in her chair she removed a pillowcase and deposited the money in it. From the pocket of her cardigan she took a length of string and wrapped the parcel tightly. No use having stray hundred-dollar bills floating into the room when the furnace went on. She set about placing the parcel in the duct but was interrupted by a knock at the front door. Some instinct told her it was too tentative to be the authorities. One of the neighbours? She cursed herself for not having turned up the TV.

"Hello?" called a voice from the porch. It wasn't Mrs. Scargall from next door. Still Harriet could not move. She prayed for the voice to go away. There was a more frantic knock. As if in a trance Harriet forced herself forward. Stepping over mother she bent to place the parcel in the heat vent. Her knees cracked noisily. The front door opened. Harriet rose as slowly as a vapour. In the doorway stood a man backlit by street light. They stared at one another. Light from the living room picked the pattern of his face out of the shadows. Harriet did not recognize him.

"Miss Smallpiece?" His voice sounded like water running through rusty pipes. He cleared his throat. If he was vaguely familiar in appearance, Harriet did not know his voice. It might have come from another planet.

"Are you all right?" the voice asked, clearer now. "Oh Jeez!" He had seen mother. To Harriet's surprise, the stranger quickly closed the door behind him. He looked from Harriet to the corpse and back again. He pulled the toque off his head and held it respectfully to his scrawny chest.

"We've been robbed," whispered Harriet.

She watched the movement of the stranger's eyes: the pillowcase, the open duct, mother. No words could have implied so unfavourable a verdict.

"Was she awful?" the man said with great feeling. Harriet could not believe her ears.

"Was she awful?" the man reiterated.

"Yes," said Harriet, grasping it fully. "Yes, yes, yes!"

The man nodded his shaggy head and regarded Harriet with compassion. "These things happen," he said matter-of-factly.

Harriet wondered if she had died and gone to some second-rate heaven. If she had, Peter was smiling at her affectionately. It was then that she finally recognized him. He saw the comprehension in her eyes.

"St. Anthony, remember?"

Harriet heard police sirens.

"Here!" she said, thrusting the pillowcase at him. "Take it, go away. Run!"

The stranger looked at the bundle uncomprehendingly.

"It's twenty thousand dollars!" said Harriet. The man shrugged uncomfortably and took the bundle. Then he pulled a large box from inside his ski parka. He handed it to her. It was a shiny red box of chocolates and shoved under the ribbon were two crisp ten-dollar bills. Harriet stared at the gift with blank horror. The sirens grew nearer.

"It was a bet," said the man. "But actually, I mostly wanted to see you again."

The sirens Dopplered, speeding west on Danforth. The sound of a TV commercial filtered into Harriet's unfocused attention.

"Don't need to worry about any of this," the man said gesturing vaguely at the floor. "It'll be our secret."

It was no longer a concert. It was as if the others were playing Handel while Harriet wrestled with the Largo from the Shostakovich.

"My name is Walt Munkatrink, but people usually call me Munk." He said this with all the polite nervousness of a gentleman caller.

"I can't see anyone now," said Harriet.

Munk nodded. "I can understand," he said. "Maybe next week? I mean when all of this has blown over."

Harriet smiled. Gently she tugged the pillowcase parcel from Munk's grasp. There was only a slight resistance.

"All right . . . Munk," she said steadily, her thoughts racing. "Yes, next week." After all, she thought, I still have the Enfield. "Come at . . . Come in the evening," she said.

"Thank you," murmured Munk. There was a brief wrangle about the chocolates, but Munk insisted she keep them. He glanced wistfully at the pillowcase parcel as he opened the door, but he smiled at Harriet. She summoned up what she hoped was an expression of sociable inclination. Then at last he was gone.

Harriet leaned her cheek on the cold hard surface of the door. After six years of waiting what was another week? She noticed a feather in the vestibule floor. She stooped to pick it up, stopping herself in the nick of time. It was a clue. Perhaps, she dared to think, this uninvited visitor would prove more useful than she could have ever dreamed.

With renewed enthusiasm she hid the money and replaced the heat vent. She opened the box of chocolates, flushed some down the toilet, and placed the box beside mother's bed. She pocketed the twenty dollars. She felt in complete control now. When she had surveyed the living room and assured herself that everything was as it should be, she peeked cautiously through the front window. She was half afraid Munk would still be there watching the house. She was half afraid he had never existed at all. He was part of her plan now; the Lord in his mysterious ways had provided her with a burglar. He had even left footprints behind on the front path. She gathered up the extension cord from the dining nook; she shoved her hankie in her mouth. One more week, she thought as she tied herself into her chair. She had practised this before and felt certain she could make a convincing job of it. She pulled the cord abrasively across her wrists, enjoying the sting.

Mother's friend, Theresa Baxter, would phone first thing in the morning as usual. She would be over like a shot when no one answered the phone, but still, thought Harriet, it would be nice not to have to wait so long. With great difficulty she spat the hanky from her mouth.

"Help!" she called. "Help, help!"

Her shout grew louder and louder until it was a scream. Screaming thrilled Harriet. She had never known she could scream.

Munk showed Stretch Harriet's picture in the *Sun*. Stretch remembered her.

"And she likes you?" he said. Munk nodded sublimely.

Stretch re-examined the picture. "An old lady'd be nice to have around," he admitted. "But personally, I'd have taken the twenty thou."

Munk clucked benignly. "You'll never understand," he said. "You gotta make things happen."

Stretch nodded agreeably. "I'm beginning to see your point."

Munk got an idea. "Why don't you come with me next week to meet her. Then you'd really understand. Next week, okay? After all of this has cleared up."

The Capitalist

MARION CROOK

Marion Crook is the author of five mystery novels, The British Columbia Mysteries *series, set in different parts of British Columbia. The latest, set on Mayne Island, is* The Gulf Island Connection. *She is a contributor to several magazines including* Canadian Aviation *and balances her crime writing with factual feature stories. She was born in British Columbia, graduated with a Bachelor of Science from Seattle University and returned to work as a Public Health Nurse for several years. She now writes full time and lives with her husband and three children in Williams Lake, B.C.*

LIGHT SNOW WAS just beginning to fall in the early evening darkness. From the warmth of the office Ryan could see the sparkling flakes reflect the neon lights from the Esso sign and drift in against the gas pumps. Snow might change to rain. It was only November and winter didn't come in deep snowfalls and persistent arctic temperatures for a month yet.

He rubbed his cold ears and then shoved his hands into his pockets.

"Christ! I hope we don't get cars in tonight. I sure as hell don't want to go out there."

"It's a little cold out there all right," the older man said, shaking his newspaper and folding it, "but I'd just as soon keep busy."

"No one should have to work in this cold." Ryan's blue eyes flashed an angry reaction to injustice. "Work's all wrong anyway. I should get cat work or a good loggin' job and work a couple of months a year. This piddly-assed job is for old men."

"It pays."

"It pays? Minimum wage! How can a man live on minimum wage? And only a day's work a week!" Anxiety sharpened his voice. "Do you think we're in line for more work?"

"Only if there is some kind of evening activity in Ashton. Tonight there is a wrestling match. The more people who come to town to see it, the more cars, and the more business at the station."

"So we only get work if there is something going on in town?"

"That's right. Otherwise, the boss just closes the station at six."

The bright glass office seemed to be the only thing warm or alive in this dark section of town. The cash register, counter, two chairs, the cans of oil on the shelves, and the various gadgets hung on the wall were warmed by the one gas heater that laboured to keep the cold on the other side of the twin seal. The snow on the ground reflected the overhead lights that trimmed the roof above the pumps. The gas pumps themselves were brightly lit from within, advertising availability to passing motorists. Beyond the steamed glass wall of the office, the bright, almost glaring, empty gas station defied the dark night around it.

Ryan rubbed his hands together again. "If I was in charge of the country I'd see that everyone got a couple of weeks' work and then got unemployment for a couple of months. They keep saying that there isn't enough work in the country. Well, why don't they spread it around to everyone and let us live on unemployment between jobs? And we'd get it automatically. We wouldn't have to go to the Welfare and *ask* for money."

Gordon eyed his nephew thoughtfully and decided against trying to teach basic economics to such an angry malcontent.

"One day, Gord, I'm going to have so much money I'll buy myself a ticket to Hawaii in November and a return in May."

"You're cold?"

Ryan nodded.

"Don't you own a hat?" He eyed Ryan's shaggy, sandy hair and the red tips of his ears.

"No. I had one at the last job at the Pinewood Mill. They supply you with all the stuff you need to keep warm there but they make sure they take it away from you when you quit."

"Did you quit there?"

"Yeah. Christ! Have you ever stacked lumber?" He didn't wait for an answer. "All shifts, every hour, reach and stack, reach and stack. It breaks your back and puts your mind to sleep. I wasn't staying there to end up an old man creaking and groaning while the company made money. I quit."

"No unemployment benefits that way though."

"Yeah. Well, that's why I'm here tonight. I can't get unemployment and, you know, I went to the Welfare and this snotty broad told me I couldn't get welfare either. What am I supposed to do, starve?"

"What did she say?" Gordon carefully folded the paper at the Lotto Canada results and put it beside him on the counter.

"She said that eating was *my* problem. She sat there, you know, in her wool sweater that probably cost more than six meals and told me that she could care less."

"I think you have to wait six weeks for welfare if you quit your job."

Ryan looked over at his uncle. The end of Gordon's nose was pocked with tiny broken blood vessels; his eyes, while clear today, had the habitual droop and strained look of a man used to alcohol. Gordon had drifted into Ashton a couple of months ago and introduced himself to his nephew and niece. They had heard of him—an itinerant labourer, sometimes working on the fish boats out of Bella Coola, sometimes working in the mining towns up north. Ryan was fascinated by the older man's stories of the places he'd been. Gordon knew the country. He knew all the relatives too, and the details of family events. In some cases Gordon had been close to the event and could tell Ryan and his sister all about it. He'd been picking fruit in the Okanagan when Aunt Olive and Uncle John had died in a house fire. He had helped fight that fire and told Ryan how hard the fire brigade had worked and how hopeless it had all been. Gordon's stories made the family seem closer and gave Ryan a feeling of being part of an exclusive club with right of membership by birth. Ryan envied Gordon his trips and his freedom to roam the country. Ryan had no money to move anywhere. Some days, the younger man's envy was transposed into irritation and a sarcastic condescension.

"I guess you'd know all about unemployment."

Gordon nodded. "You have to be laid off to get either unemployment or welfare. Couldn't you manage to get fired?"

"Hell." Ryan was impatient with the planning and manipulations that had kept Gordon fed and clothed for thirty years. "I couldn't wait for that kind of crap. I wanted out of that mill right then. I wasn't going to put one more board on that pile."

"I see. And now you are broke. Have you worked any place else?"

"A few places. They never seem to pan out though. I had a few jobs when I was in high school, and times were good when I dropped out of grade ten and worked in construction. You know, then I could work a little while, quit and pick up another job, and work a while and quit. The pay was always good."

Gordon nodded slowly. "Things are different now. You have to plan carefully how to acquire money and how to spend it."

Ryan shrugged. "Things'll change. I'll make out. How many nights have we done this now? Once a week for three weeks?"

Gordon took a small notebook from his inside pocket and consulted it. "No, just two."

"Do you keep everything written down?"

"Just my finances. I want to make sure I can eat next week, too, so I plan ahead."

"What happens when you go on a drunk?"

Gordon looked at Ryan steadily for a moment. "I am not an alcoholic. I do not *have* to drink. I can plan to enjoy my liquor at times when I can afford it."

"Oh? Well, you must be able to afford it pretty often then. I seen you downtown lots of days sloshed to the eyeballs."

Gordon either hid his resentment or had none. He continued to sit comfortably and quietly.

"How can you afford it?"

"I buy tickets on the Western Lottery. I've made enough from my winnings to keep buying tickets and have a little over. I get a hundred and seventy-five dollars from welfare for support and that helps."

Ryan was impatient. "Yeah. I can get that in another four weeks but I can't see living very good on that. I'd like to see that bitch of a welfare worker live on that. And you've got to have more money than a hundred and seventy-five. Look at that coat you're wearing. That's got a warm lining. How can you afford that? And I seen you eating in the Texaco café by the Blue Mountain turn-off. You had a full meal there and that costs money. Does Welfare know you've got money?"

"Of course not. I'm careful to keep it from them. And I don't have a lot. Just a small insurance policy that I had on my mother. It pays me a little every month now that she's gone."

"I remember her. She died in that car accident a couple of years ago, didn't she? She must have been old."

"Eighty-five."

"Oh." Ryan lost interest. There was no get-rich scheme for him there.

"I got to get some money and I got to do it without stackin' lumber."

"Think it over carefully and plan well—"

"Ah, shut up, Gordon. You're not much better off than I am."

Gordon looked at Ryan speculatively. The only evidence of any emotion from him was a small muscle that twitched at the side of his mouth. He made a short, neat entry in his notebook then put it back inside his jacket pocket.

The next week the weather had warmed slightly, but there was more snow. In the evening the temperature dropped below freezing. Ryan swung his arms and walked back and forth in the small office.

"Last week was bad enough. This week my sister won't even let me eat at her house. She says I don't pay her anything when I do have money, and she's not feeding me when I don't. I went back to the welfare office and that s.o.b. wouldn't even *see* me. Christ, I can't live on the peanuts I make here."

"You could eat on this." Gordon sat with his chair close to the heater, his gloves warming on top of it.

"Maybe. But I can never buy a beer or go anywhere. I got no car, no money for anything."

"It will be another two weeks before you can get welfare. The worker wouldn't give you an advance?"

"She wouldn't even see me. You couldn't lend me some, could you?"

"No, I'm sorry. I don't get any more money myself until the end of the month."

"Yeah. Family or no family, you probably wouldn't give it to me anyway. Every man for himself in this lousy system."

He peered out the window. "Why are we working tonight? What's on?"

"There's some kind of concert across the street."

Ryan moved closer to the glass wall, rubbed a circle of condensation away and read "Ashton Community Theatre presents 'The Importance of Being Earnest'—Dinner and show." "Should be some customers coming soon."

Three cars drove in for gas. The snowfall was light tonight but this early in the winter many of the cars still had summer tires and slipped on the wet pavement.

Gordon buttoned his wool coat. Ryan zipped his thin leather jacket and both men pumped gas and took credit cards and money for the next hour. Just before eight o'clock and the beginning of the concert a small blue Chev pulled up to the pumps. It was Ryan's turn. He was very cold; his ears, not yet bitter white were bright red in the freezing air. His bare fingers grew numb holding the cold metal gas pump. He thought longingly of the pictures he'd seen of Hawaii and the warm sand and sun there.

He brought a twenty-dollar bill into the glass office. His hands were shaking, and Gordon could see the red surge up his neck marking his erupting anger.

"You know who's out there? That broad from the welfare office! She's going to the show. And she said "hello" to me. She smiled at me and talked to me because she knows that she's met me but she doesn't remember where. Get that! She doesn't remember that she told me to starve to death. She sees so many people. Big deal! She sees so many people, and I'm just one of them. I'm a nothing! She's driving a nice warm car, spending money on a bloody show, and I'm working my ass off in the cold because *she* doesn't think I should get any money."

"She probably grew up in a monied family, went to university, always had enough to eat, and really doesn't understand poverty."

"So?"

"So perhaps you should make allowances for her ignorance."

"Allowances!" Ryan was almost screaming his frustration. "I'd like to teach her about hard luck. I'd like to show her what it's like to have nothin'."

"One day you might get a chance to do that. She would be a better worker if someone taught her to understand deprivation."

His calm voice did not pacify Ryan.

He took the money from Ryan's hand. "Do you want me to take her the change?"

"Yeah. Do that. I might shove it down her throat."

Gordon buttoned his coat, put on his hat and his gloves, warm from the heater, and took the change from the till. He approached the Chev, handed the money to the woman, smiled and talked for a moment, then touched his hat.

Ryan stamped around the office.

"Did you have to be so polite?"

"She gives me a hundred and seventy-five dollars a month. I'm allowed to make fifty dollars on the side. It pays to be polite."

"That makes me sick. Where's she going?"

"As you said. To the show. She's parking her car across the street here near the station so that we can keep an eye on it."

Ryan looked sharply at Gordon.

"I'll keep an eye on it all right. The minute she's in there I'll give her nice new paint job a scratch."

"I suppose you could scratch it. That might annoy her, but it would hardly teach her what it's like to do without."

Ryan flung himself down in a chair and clenched his fists.

They sat in the cocoon of the office watching the cars pass by on the street blurred by the condensation on the glass. Few customers came after eight.

Ryan jerked irritably, jumped to his feet, and paced back and forth in the small office. He cleared a spot on the glass and peered across the street.

"She parked that car right in front of us. Shit! I'd like to smash it for her. Serve her right. That would teach her. Why should she drive when I got no car? What does she ever do for anyone but pass the money around like God Almighty?" There was silence for a moment. Then Ryan turned back to Gordon. "What time do we close here?"

"In about half an hour."

"I'm going to take her car."

Gordon said nothing.

"I'm going to take those two cans of gas out from the back of the station and load them into her car, drive it away, dump it, and torch it."

Still Gordon said nothing.

Ryan was excited now. "I won't even have to hot-wire it. I bet one of these keys will fit." He opened the drawer below the till and grabbed a handful of keys. "What time is the show over?"

Gordon got to his feet and looked through the cleared spot on the window to the marquee across the street.

"It says 9:30."

"Good. We close at 8:30. It won't take me fifteen minutes to get in and get away.

"Look, Gordon. You're my uncle. Do me a favour. Take that station truck there"—he pointed to the small Toyota with the Esso decal on the door—"and follow me up the Blue Mountain road. I'll need a ride back. I'll dump her car over the edge at the top, put it in gear, and let it go over. It'll burn at the bottom, and she'll never get it out. You can give me a ride back, and we can leave the truck back here. No one will even know we took it. I'll say you were with me here, and you can say I was with you."

There was silence in the office. The heater hissed as Gordon's jacket brushed against it.

Ryan stepped closer. "It's safe! Foolproof! I never asked nothin' of you before. You said it yourself—that dame needs teachin'. What d'ya say?"

Finally, Gordon nodded.

"All right. But there's no money in it."

"I don't care!" Ryan was almost yelling. "I want to *get* that bitch!"

"All right." Gordon's voice was thoughtful. "But be sure to

get enough speed going up that hill. She still has her summer tires on, and if you slip and have to stop on the mountain you won't get going again."

"I know. I know." Ryan was impatient. "I can drive. I'll get it up there."

"You'll give it lots of speed?"

"Yeah. Yeah."

Ryan ran out to the back of the station with his leather coat unbuttoned, ignoring the bite of the cold air.

One of the keys from the drawer fitted easily into the door lock. In less than ten minutes Ryan drove away in the Chev.

Gordon methodically closed the station, turned out the neon lights, picked up the key to the Toyota truck, and followed Ryan.

The highway was slippery even under the winter tires of the Toyota. Gordon thought of the winding mountain road and of the light fall of snow that had melted during the day and was now frozen.

"Lots of speed," he murmured to himself.

At the intersection of the Blue Mountain road and the highway he put the Toyota in four-wheel drive and gave it gas. The truck responded steadily with a sure grip of the studded tires. Ahead of him he could see Ryan fish-tailing a little on the curves of the road. Ryan had lots of speed. About a third of the way up the road Ryan spun on a corner. The back end of the Chev swung dangerously close to the drop-off.

He can't do that farther up, Gordon thought. There's no shoulder on the road on the outside curve near the top. But if he stays off the brakes he might make it.

But Ryan didn't know the road or the car well. He followed Gordon's advice and gave the car speed. Three-quarters of the way up Ryan hit a patch of ice. The sun had shone on the south slope of the mountain all day. The snow on the road had melted to water that now, in the cold of the evening, had turned to ice. Gordon saw the tail lights swing in towards the hillside, then the bright red brake lights flash. The back end of the car swung wildly towards the precipice as Ryan over-corrected and skidded the tires on the ice. There was no one else on the hill—no other traffic—just the dark, deep black of the night and the quietly drifting flakes of snow. There was no one but Gordon to see the twin beams of headlights reach out into the black at the edge of the cliff and the blurred red splash of the tail lights arc out over space and disappear.

Gordon stopped his truck in the centre of the road, well short of the icy patch. He didn't want to leave tire marks on the side of the road.

He did not get out of the truck. He rolled down the window on the passenger side and listened. He heard a muffled bang and then saw a ball of fire billow past him about thirty feet out. He heard the sudden roar of flames but couldn't see anything but a glow of light off to his right.

He backed the truck down the hill, turned at the first opportunity, and drove back to the station.

The theatre-goers had not yet emerged. He parked the truck and replaced the keys. While he was in the office he took his small notebook from his pocket and turned to the page headed "Insurance".

"Ryan Maclean," he wrote, "$72,000, short-term insurance. To be received in quarterly instalments."

He turned to the back page of the notebook and meticulously drew a pencil line through Ryan's name, fourth on the list.

Then he turned out the lights and left.

Strange Archaeology

JOSEF SKVORECKY

Translated, from the Czech, by Paul Wilson

Josef Skvorecky is Professor of English at Erindale College, University of Toronto. He emigrated to Canada after the Soviet invasion of Czechoslovakia in 1968, and he and his wife, the novelist Zdena Salivarova, continue to keep Czech literature alive through their Czech-language publishing house, 68 Publishers. Skvorecky's novels include The Mournful Demeanour of Lieutenant Boruvka, Miss Silver's Past, The Cowards, The Bass Saxophone, *and* The Engineer of Human Souls.

Paul Wilson lived in Czechoslovakia for ten years, working as a translator and English teacher and playing with an underground rock band. He was expelled in 1977. In addition to many novels and short stories by Josef Skvorecky, he has translated works by several Czech authors. He now lives in Toronto.

IT HAD BEEN Boruvka's first case. Back then he wasn't allowed to deal with homicides, only missing persons, and someone called Kvetuse Rerichova had disappeared. She was a clerk with the State Savings Bank on Wenceslas Square.

He looked around the little room she shared with her mother. Against one wall stood two narrow couches made of old packing crates. They were painted red and doubled as beds at night. The room itself was narrow with a window at one end that looked out on a litter-strewn courtyard with open-air walkways running around its perimeter. Swinging in the breeze on clotheslines strung across the yard were brassieres, long underwear, and delicate blouses with flower and polka-dot patterns. The room also contained a modest bookshelf constructed from orange crates. It held volumes of poetry, and a cheap bakelite record-player rested on top of it. There was a man's shaving mirror on a small table between the couches. Since the girl's mother slept on the second couch, and her ten-year-old brother, whose bed was in the kitchen, was the only male in the household, the mirror obviously served as a vanity table. It made you seem bigger when you looked into it.

"They moved us in here when Dad and Ota fled the country, Commissioner," said the old lady tearfully. She was wearing a threadbare housecoat and her hair looked like what Boruvka's former boss, Lt. Soukup, called "piss-soaked straw". "We used to have a three-room flat for the six of us. Now there's only four of us and all we got is this room and the kitchen, but there's no window in the kitchen."

"Four?" asked Boruvka, who was still a constable at the time. "How's that? There's you, your daughter, your son—?"

"Ruda—well, he tried to escape with Dad and Ota, but they caught him. He's still doing time."

"Oh, I see," said Boruvka. His eyes wandered to the wall where among magazine reproductions of Van Gogh's golden yellow sunflowers hung a photograph of two men, one younger, one older, leaning nonchalantly against a large American car. The sign on a store in the background read BEN'S BURGER BURG. Constable Boruvka had no idea what that meant, but he could guess where the picture had been taken. The woman saw what he was looking at.

"Well, that's where they are—New York," said the woman. "Dad—my husband—writes that he's the manager of some company that rents apartment buildings. Only in America, he says, he's called a 'superintendent'. But he doesn't manage to send us much money. If it weren't for Kvetuse, I don't know what we'd. . . . I can't get work anywhere because of my husband. Libuse's moved out and lives on her own, but Kvetuse's a good girl. She hands over all her wages to me except for a little spending money she keeps back for herself." The woman with the straw-coloured hair began to cry.

"That's all right, ma'am," said Boruvka. "We'll have the matter cleared up in no time. Now, tell me what happened. I understand your daughter told you she was just going away for the day with her boyfriend on Sunday. Is that what she said?"

"That's right, Commissioner. She packed a suitcase—and I—"

"You what."

"Officer! After she went, I looked, and she'd taken everything she owned with her!"

"What do you mean, everything?"

"Well, she took the business suit I altered for her when Libuse left, both her dresses, all her underthings, two rings and a necklace she got from her grandmother, and both pairs of shoes. And she said she was only going away for the day—"

Constable Boruvka frowned. Once again, he looked at the photograph of the two smiling men beside the shiny big car. The case began to appear very straightforward.

"What did she leave behind?"

"Nothing but this record player and a couple of books. She even took her favourite books with her." The woman looked at the constable in alarm. "Maybe I shouldn't even have reported it."

An inexplicable sadness came over Boruvka, but he managed to put on a severe expression. "It was your responsibility and you did the right thing. But"—he hesitated—"I don't think you have anything to worry about." He looked at his assistant, the old chief constable Sintak, whom they allowed to remain on the force only because he had agreed to leave the Church, although Boruvka was aware that each Sunday he drove all the way to Kremosin, where no one knew him, to attend Mass. From Sintak's expression, Boruvka could see that what he was about to say would remain confidential among those present. He smiled at the weeping woman. "To tell you the truth, ma'am, it probably won't be long before you'll be hanging a picture of your daughter beside the other two, in front of that"—he leaned closer to the photograph—"BEN'S BURGER BURG, whatever that is."

"I pray to God you're right, sir."

"I'm afraid I am, " said the lieutenant. Then he resumed his official composure. "Of course the fact remains that your daughter has done something that is not only very foolish, it's also against the law." The old lady began to sob so plaintively that the constable, after another glance at Sintak, added: "Anyway, let's hope the border guards"—and he stopped.

Sintak broke into a wide grin. "No way, Mr.—I mean comrade constable. They'd have nabbed her long before this. She's been gone a week already. Your daughter must be a pretty sharp kid, ma'am."

Constable Boruvka soon had reason to agree that Kvetuse Rerichova was indeed a pretty sharp kid.

"Twenty thousand?" he asked her department head at the State Savings Bank. His voice was incredulous.

"That's right. She withdrew the lot a day before she disappeared."

She gives all her wages to me, except for a little spending money for herself. Hmm, thought the constable. This is going to be more complicated than I thought.

"I'm afraid I may have had a hand in it myself," said the department head. He was a youthful, dark-haired man with a Young Communist League button in his lapel. "At the league meeting last week, I proposed that she be fired."

"Why?"

"Loss of confidence. She was a good teller. But as a citizen?" And he began to count on his fingers: "Father a small businessman, arrested for provocative behaviour towards a government inspector right after the Revolution in 1948. As soon as he gets out of prison, he escapes to the West with his elder son. Her second brother is caught attempting to cross the border. Her mother is unemployed and has had run-ins with the Security Forces for making inappropriate political statements. And the money we handle here belongs to our working people. We can't afford to employ comrades who don't enjoy our full confidence."

"Where did the twenty thousand come from?" asked Boruvka.

"I don't know. I had no idea myself she had so much money. She had a password account."

Constable Boruvka frowned. Her account was empty, her suitcases packed with all her worldly possessions, her father in America. Everything pointed to the same simple, unmysterious conclusion. All that was left to explain was where the twenty thousand crowns had come from.

That didn't remain a mystery for long, either. Looking through the files, Boruvka discovered that the friend with whom Kvetuse was to have gone on the trip had a criminal record: three years for attempting to cross the border and for poor behaviour in prison. So the girl had been surrounded by criminals and the circumstances of her disappearance were becoming clearer all the time. Except the money.

"She won it in the lottery," explained the friend, Miroslav Jun. "She bet half her spending money each week, and this February she hit the jackpot."

Jun had nervous eyes, but he was a handsome young man. Despite his criminal record, the constable felt he could trust him. The waste-paper depot where the lieutenant was questioning him was a dark room with a large weigh-scale in the middle and stacks of old newspapers piled up along the walls. A long line of aged women stretched out of the door; each woman carried a bundle of old newspapers in a shopping bag, obviously gathered from garbage cans and tied with bits of knotted string. An elderly man in a pair of ragged overalls stood by the scales. He weighed the bundles, then handed each old lady some coins.

"So you didn't go out with her on Saturday?"

"No."

"Where were you?"

"At home. I'm learning . . . English. I studied all weekend."

"Can anyone vouch for you?"

The young man said nothing and shook his head. "No. My landlady went to see her son in Benesov."

"Do you know why I'm asking you these questions?"

The lieutenant's eyes met the young man's. They were guarded but bold. "No," replied the young man rebelliously.

"She's missing, her money's gone from her bank account, her suitcase—"

"So how come I'm still here?" His voice was now arrogant, with a trace of sarcasm in it.

"Maybe you figured it wasn't worth risking it a second time."

"That's God's own truth," said the young man with feeling. "But what's Kvetuse's taking off got to do with me?"

"We don't know if she actually has —taken off, as you put it."

"So what do you want of me?"

For a moment, Constable Boruvka merely looked into the young man's nervous eyes. Then, thoughtfully, he replied: "In an abandoned quarry near Karlovy Vary we found the bodies of seven girls. It was always the same story: bank accounts cleared out, suitcases packed. The first one disappeared two years ago. The last one nine months ago."

The young man grinned. "I was still behind bars, in case you'd forgotten."

"I hadn't forgotten. And we've got the scoundrel. He promised to take those poor girls across the border. They all ended up in the quarry."

"I don't see what that's got to do with"—the young man began, then stopped. "Oh, you think—"

The lieutenant nodded. Then he said, "Those girls in the quarry aren't the only case like that, just the ugliest."

The young man's insolence suddenly vanished. In a trembling voice, he said, "But I was fond of Kvetuse. I'd never have—for a lousy twenty thousand. And anyway, I tried to per—" He stopped suddenly.

"What did you try to persuade her?" Boruvka said encouragingly.

Jun saw at once that he had said something he couldn't take back. He looked at the lieutenant, and then at Sintak. The lieutenant's round face was not like the faces he'd been used to seeing in the past three years. Even Chief Constable Sintak seemed more human than the goons in prison. In his irrepressibly good-natured way, Sintak said, "Come on, out with it. Don't be afraid, we're not going to"—and he glanced at the lieutenant, who pretended he hadn't heard.

The young man was intelligent and his instincts were sound. "Kvetuse did want to skip the country," he said, "that's a fact. And I didn't report her to the police, that's also a fact."

"But you tried to persuade her not to go," said Sintak. "In my book that's an ex—an ex—what is it the lawyers say? Anyway, it lets you off the hook."

"It's an extenuating circumstance, that's true," interrupted the lieutenant. "Tell us what happened."

"I told her not to be crazy, but she wouldn't listen. You know, her dad and her brother are already living in the United States; she told me her brother was doing well selling cars, and she was fed up to the teeth with that hole she was living in. She had nothing to wear, either. Once we were out on a date"—and he stopped. "But that has nothing to do with this case."

"Go ahead, tell us," coaxed the lieutenant.

"Well—it was last January. Before she won the lottery. It was freezing cold but a nice, sunny day. She showed up in a purple corduroy jacket and we went for a walk on Petrin Hill. She wasn't saying much that day, and I was blabbing on—you know, about books, because she loved reading and talking about them—and suddenly, it seemed strange how quiet she was, like a wooden statue, so I look and she's all blue, shaking like a leaf. The thing was, not only did she not have a winter coat, she didn't even have a sweater on underneath. She had no money. So I took her into a pub and poured at least five mulled wines into her before she got her voice back. Then I bought her a sweater. I'm only telling you that, sir," the young man went on, "so you'll know how hard up they were, so you'd understand that she had good reason—even though it doesn't excuse her, naturally."

"Well—" Sintak began but the lieutenant quickly interrupted him.

"You tried to dissuade her, but she—"

"She wanted me to put her in touch with someone who would take her across, but I didn't know anybody. If I had, I wouldn't be working in this scrap-paper depot today. And then she"—Once more he fell silent.

"She what?"

"Well—she still wanted to clear out. She was obsessed with the idea."

The lieutenant sighed. "Look, Mr. Jun. You didn't report an intent to commit a crime, and now you're holding something back from us again. As for not reporting her—well, there *are* extenuating circumstances, I agree. But they'll only be extenuating if you tell us *everything* you know, not just *something*."

One of the old ladies in the line began to cough uncontrollably. The man in the overalls took the bag out of her hand and removed a pile of newspapers. They were of pre-war vintage and the paper was brittle and yellowed. The woman had obviously found them stashed away in someone's attic.

"Where did you get these, ma'am?"

The old lady tried to reply but she was still coughing too violently to speak.

"Sit down here, ma'am," said the man in the coveralls, indicating the scales. He began leafing through the old papers with great interest. "I'll buy these from you myself. There's a lot of good reading here, ma'am." He looked at the scales. "That's thirty-eight kilos, which makes"—and he pulled a wallet out of his back pocket. It was well worn, but made of snakeskin, and he extracted two banknotes from it.

Boruvka was fascinated by the scene. This man can't have spent all his life weighing scrap paper, he thought. For a moment, he forgot the investigation, but the young man himself brought the lieutenant back to the subject.

"All right, I'll tell you," he said dejectedly. "She was at my place the day before she disappeared. She came to say goodbye. And she said she'd found a way herself. I thought it was better not to ask for any details. I tried to persuade her not to go again, but her mind was made up."

"Hmm," said the detective, looking the young man in the eye. For the first time, he saw a flash of contempt that would, later in his career, become a familiar sight. For the first time too, he felt defensive about his job. The young man's expression made him feel ashamed and sad. The story of the shivering young girl had moved him. Ever since his youth, Boruvka had been more than ordinarily sentimental. "Hmm," he said. For the young man's sake, he came up with a ridiculous conclusion. "You thought she was just paying you back for your unwillingness to help her. You didn't really believe her but you let her think you did because you were fond of her. Isn't that how it was?"

The contempt disappeared from the young man's eyes and

was replaced by something else. Boruvka was glad the young man had been able to exclude him from a certain category.

"Yes, lieutenant. I knew all along she was just kidding."

And thus the case of Kvetuse Rerichova, a teller in the State Savings Bank, was closed. An illegal crossing of the border, successfully completed. It was a common occurrence at the time. Boruvka was praised for his quick work, and very shortly afterwards he was assigned to his first murder case, which he solved with equal swiftness. For a while, he gave serious thought to requesting a transfer to petty theft. The case had involved a perverted driver's mate who had murdered his wife, packed her in ice, and kept her in the basement for two months while having sexual intercourse repeatedly with the corpse. For a month afterwards, the lieutenant had nightmares and would wake up soaked in his own sweat, wondering whether it was all worth it. At last, thinking the worst was now behind him, he decided to remain with the Homicide department.

Eleven years had gone by since the disappearance of Kvetuse Rerichova. By this time, the lieutenant—now a true lieutenant (he was never promoted beyond that because he remained reluctant to join the Communist party on the grounds that his consciousness had not yet been sufficiently raised)—had a reputation which, in criminological circles, extended beyond the borders of the state. He had even been invited to give a paper to an international criminological congress in Warsaw. The paper was reprinted, after having been stylistically overhauled by a certain policewoman, in the *Criminological Gazetteer*, along with an abstract in three languages.

One day, the lieutenant was summoned to a new housing development in Krc on the outskirts of Prague. Some workers digging the foundations for a co-operative apartment block on a piece of land where a small woodlot had once stood had unearthed a human skull.

The skull, cleaned and beautifully white, stood on Dr. Seifert's laboratory table, gleaming like alabaster in the afternoon sunshine. Dr. Seifert turned it over, revealing an ugly hole in the elegantly elongated cranium.

"A blow from a pointed object," said Dr. Seifert, who enjoyed speaking technically whenever he made professional statements. "That's what killed her." He turned the skull over again and pointed: "A fractured supra-orbital margin, broken nasal bone, both maxillae have sustained blows from a blunt object, the right maxilla has collapsed and bone fragments lodged in the nasal cavity, teeth quite sound, but three have been knocked out. Left temple punctured—"

"A maniac?" asked the lieutenant.

Dr. Seifert slowly shook his head. "I doubt it. It might look that way, but there's one circumstance that gives me pause—"

"You mean the fact that he separated the head from the body and buried it separately?"

"No, not that. A body without a head is difficult to identify. It's something else."

The doctor placed a finger on the bare, chalk-white crown. "It hasn't been in the ground for more than ten, fifteen years. It's a female cranium. Looking at the teeth, I'd say a girl of about twenty-five. And there's no sign of her hair."

"Maybe it rotted."

"No, no," said Dr. Siefert. "There would still be something left after ten years. The murderer scalped her."

"But, why?"

"Perhaps he'd read some true crime stories," said Dr. Seifert, shifting from his technical style to the language he usually used when dealing with the detective. "Something about Dr. Crippen, perhaps. They nailed Crippen on the basis of an appendix scar on a piece of skin from the stomach of his wife. Our killer simply scalped his victim so we couldn't identify her by the colour of her hair." He was silent for a moment, then added: "And I would say he did something even more gruesome. First he tried to deform the face, and then, just to make sure, he boiled the head"—Dr. Seifert stopped and looked at the lieutenant, who had become almost as pale as the skull—"and he disposed of the fleshy parts. Otherwise there's no explanation for why the bone is so clean and white."

The old detective swallowed and stared at the skull. It was narrow and well shaped. The girl must have had a narrow, noble face. It reminded him of something. Something he had read recently and put down in disgust. He couldn't remember what.

"He must have cut the rest of the body into pieces, like Crippen," said Dr. Seifert. "I wouldn't be surprised if we heard from other building sites. There's a lot of construction going on these days."

"They found a hand not long ago," said lieutenant in an unsteady voice. "It was impossible to identify. No fractures, no tattoos, no forgotten ring—"

"Well," said the doctor, "I guess the scoundrels are learning too."

The lieutenant overcame his squeamishness, took the skull carefully into his hands, and examined it. Its teeth were in excellent shape; unspoiled, small girl's teeth. It even seemed to the detective that they still retained a slight, pearly sheen. Three were missing: two canine teeth on the left and one molar on the right.

He examined the jawbone more closely. "Doctor," he said, "look. That molar is only broken off."

Dr. Seifert almost snatched the skull out of Boruvka's hand and looked into the mouth. "Good Lord, Joseph!" he said in astonishment. "A good thing you noticed that. Those teeth weren't knocked out, they were *pulled* out. That stump!" And he pointed to the missing molar. "That's exactly how it looks when you try to pull out a tooth and it breaks off in the pliers. Look!"

The lieutenant looked, but the shattered remains of the tooth told him nothing.

"He tried to pry it out. Didn't know what he was doing, and it broke on him. Then he gave up." Dr. Seifert examined the holes where the canine teeth had been. "Just as I thought. These weren't knocked out either," he said. "He pulled them out very neatly. It worked with the canine teeth, but not with the molars."

The lieutenant frowned. "Well, it was a mistake. Those blows to the face and the scalping won't do him a bit of good now. There's only one reason he tried to pull those teeth out."

Dr. Seifert nodded. "Exactly. But Joseph, that was fifteen years ago. How are you going to track it down now? In fifteen years, they've probably accumulated hundreds of thousands of dental records in the clinics. And back then they still had private dentists. God knows if they even keep their records. Even though they should."

It still reminded the detective of something. He sat in his easy chair and tried to read a novel about the founding of a co-operative farm. It was homework in a compulsory course in politics, and besides, the author had taught him German in the Kostelec grammar school. The novel was an exercise in socialist realism and told of how the efforts to build the co-op had been sabotaged by a gang of Catholic criminals led by an American agent from Washington who had been sent to the village of Zalesi by the CIA. But the lieutenant's mind wandered back to that unidentified person who, ten or fifteen years ago, had played the dentist on a delicate female skull. Once again, it reminded him of something.

He got up, put the novel down, and walked over to the bookshelf. Beneath *The Collected Works of Alois Jirasek* (he had inherited them from his father) was a short row of books belonging to his thirteen-year-old daughter, Zuzanka. *Sylva's First Film, Irene Leads the Class, Zdena's Teacher.* Those works had been inherited too, from Zuzanka's mother, who of course was still very energetically alive. The books were dog-eared and well-read, whereas the books that the lieutenant had given his daughter on various occasions still looked brand new. *Wuthering Heights, War and Peace, The Gold Bug and Other Stories, Madame Bovary, Gulliver's Travels.* The lieutenant didn't know what had drawn him to the bookshelf. He stood there a while longer, then returned to his chair and the American saboteur in Zalesi. He fell asleep just as the American had managed to destroy the co-op's rabbit hutch, leaving behind him at the scene of the crime a vial of poison with the legend "Made in U.S.A." on it.

The next day at the office, however, he continued to be haunted by the very unprofessional sensation that he had read something relevant somewhere. He was going through a list of people who had gone missing between 1948 and 1953, eliminating the men and putting the young women to one side, when once more he came across the name of Kvetuse Rerichova.

He read through the eleven-year-old report—written by himself—and the more he studied the document, the deeper his frown became. It had been a very, very superficial job. The lieutenant flushed with shame. How could he have been so careless? Of course, he'd been young at the time. But youth is no excuse for negligence. It was true that not much attention was paid to cases like that, except perhaps by the *other* police, to which he did not belong. To make matters worse, he'd been praised for his work. Cold sweat drove away the flush of shame. At the bottom of the report, in red pencil and his own handwriting, were the words: *Case closed; illegal exit to West.*

God! At the time he hadn't even questioned Libuse Rerichova, Kvetuse's sister. And no one had rapped his knuckles. Nor had he provided a detailed description of the jewellery which the mother said the missing woman had taken with her. All his report said was : "Two rings (gold) and a necklace (silver)". In the bank, he hadn't checked the manager's story. He hadn't bothered to find out if the woman had gone to a dentist, either. How could he have been so sloppy? If his partner, Malek, had done slipshod work like that for him, he would have given him an official reprimand. And he, Boruvka, had been praised for it!

He sighed. That was how it had been in those days. Disappearances were daily occurrences. Most of the missing persons surfaced some time afterwards in camps in Germany; some didn't, and some showed up ten years later in places like Australia or Argentina. And murders? At the time, they were treated as a lesser crime. They didn't even hang people for it much. It was not that he had anything against this reluctance to use "hard but just" punishments. It did bother him, however, that people went to the gallows for less.

He realized that his shirt was sticking to his back and his face was burning, as if from a fever. With a sensation of self-reproach, he put the report bearing Kvetuse Rerichova's name back into the file and began to read furiously through the remaining seventy-four entries. So great was his embarrassment that he read the male ones as well.

And still he felt that premonition, or whatever it was.

Suddenly, he stuffed everything back into the filing cabinet and quickly left the office.

Old Mrs. Rerichova was already dead, and her dark kitchen was now occupied by her son Peter and his eighteen-year-old wife. In the narrow room, where the small bookshelf had once stood between two red couches, there was now a crib.

And Peter couldn't remember. He had been ten years old at the time. Kvetuse must have gone to a dentist, but he didn't know which one. Perhaps Liba, the sister, would know. Yes, Liba was married. Her husband was an engineer. They lived in Jamaica Street in Letna.

There were three nameplates on the door of the flat: Arpad Hruska, LLD; Arnost Hruska, Prof. Eng.; Rudolf Cerveny, PhD. A family of intellectuals, thought the lieutenant. But the sounds emerging from the other side of the door sounded more like what one might expect to hear in the slums. Two women were shouting at each other: "I've had enough, I tell you, and from now on, I forbid you to—" "You can't stop me! It's my own son." "And he's my husband!" A male voice intervened: "Girls, please, I beg you—" and a second male voice: "For Christ's sake, I've had it—" Overlapping this cocktail of hysteria, or so the lieutenant guessed, was the screaming of at least two infants, and then the reproachful voice of a third woman: "You've woken up little Jindriska again!"

He rang the doorbell. The voices fell silent. The door was opened by a young woman in a turquoise dressing gown. She had beautiful chestnut-brown hair and a desperate look in her eyes. Several strands of hair had come loose, and she was gathering them away from her face and trying to fix them back in place with a hairpin.

"Yes?"

"Mrs. Hruskova?"

"No, I'm Cervena. Do you want to talk to my mother-in-law or my sister-in-law?"

"Your sister-in-law," said the lieutenant. He was embarrassed. "That is, if I'm not interrupting anything."

"Not even the cops could make things worse than they already are," said the pretty but desperate-looking woman, and the lieutenant blushed.

Soon he was sitting alone with another woman in one of the rooms. This woman was older, at least thirty-five. Once, perhaps, she had been pretty too, but now her hair was prematurely grey, and she was overweight and terribly high strung. They were sitting alone only because the lieutenant finally had to show his badge to get the red-haired Mr. Hruska, the engineer, a seven-year-old girl in a dirty dress, and a nine-year-old boy with a bloody nose out of the room.

On the wall were pictures of people in folk costumes and there was a bookshelf there as well, dominated by a row of Jirasek's *Collected Works* in leather binding. The shelves also contained *Wuthering Heights, War and Peace, Gulliver's Travels,* a row of crime novels, and several other volumes that seemed somehow familiar to the detective. The woman's irritable voice interrupted his reverie on the literary taste of so many multi-generation households.

"So what is it you want to know? What is it I'm supposed to remember? It's been so long."

"Some new evidence has turned up," said the lieutenant, still embarrassed, "indicating that in this case, there may not have been an illegal exit from the republic, but—"

"It certainly took you long enough to figure that out, didn't it?" said Mrs. Hruskova, with a sarcastic grin. "Eleven years it's been, and we never heard a word from Kvetuse. Do you think she wouldn't even bother telling her own mother where she was? Or that she wouldn't have gone to join her brother? He's got three car-repair shops of his own now, and a house in Florida," she added with undisguised pride. "And poor Mama, when she was still alive, reported it to you several times—"

"I—" The lieutenant tried to interrupt.

"—but you had other problems to worry about, didn't you, and no time to help look for an old woman's poor daughter that some bastard probably did in."

For the second time in this case, the lieutenant had been unjustly identified with a department of the police force he did not belong to, and he felt ashamed.

"Just after your sister disappeared I was transferred to another branch. A colleague took over missing persons."

"Then he should have realized that something rotten was going on."

"You're quite right. But now some new evidence has come up, and that's why I've come—"

"So get to the point. What do you want to know? The sooner you leave the better. As you may have noticed, things are in a bit of a state around here. Six grown-ups and three children in two rooms—it's enough to drive you crazy."

"Couldn't you join a co-op?" said the lieutenant, and then he bit his lip because he remembered where they had found the skull.

"A co-op? We did—five years ago. They say we're going to get a flat the year after next, but I'll believe it when I see it. That is, if I don't end up in the bug house before then."

"I only need to know one thing. Do you recall who your sister's dentist was?"

"I do. We've always gone to Dr. Heiser. Now he's working at a clinic in Prague 7. But Kvetuse always had good teeth. Our parents were poor when we were kids. No cakes, no candies. And later we weren't the proper kind of working-class kids either, not like Madam La-di-da, the respectable comrade who looks after these barracks. . . ."

From the next room came the sound of muffled but angry voices. The lieutenant stood up and made an apologetic farewell. He hurried out of the tenement house into the street and took a deep breath of the spring air.

Dr. Heiser, he discovered, was allowed to have private office hours twice a week. He tended to his patients in a family villa, which was now occupied by the families of two of his sons and a daughter who had remarried. The daughter's first husband slept in the doctor's office. In the attic, under a pile of old rugs, the doctor had a carefully preserved card index of all the patients he had treated since beginning his practice.

The lieutenant found Kvetuse Rerichova's card with its schematic picture of the teeth. The dentist had marked three teeth on it: the two canine teeth on the left and a molar on the right. In faded ink, he had recorded payment for the filling of three simple cavities.

That evening a very chastened lieutenant took Kvetuse Rerichova's folder out of the missing persons' file and transferred it to the Unsolved Homicide file. He blackened out his original conclusion with ink and wrote above it in red pencil: *Murdered in May 1952. Murderer as yet unapprehended.*

Nine months went by. Kvetuse Rerichova's killer remained at large.

At eleven o'clock one morning the telephone rang. The detective lifted the receiver. "Lieutenant Boruvka," he said.

"We've got a murder here, Lieutenant. Can you come right away?"

"Give me the address," said the detective automatically. "And don't touch anything.'

"It's at Klarov Number One," said the voice. To the detective's ear, it sounded rather jovial. He hoped this wasn't just someone playing a practical joke on him. Such things had happened. But he had a duty to investigate.

"Who's calling?"

"Professor Gebert. There's no particular hurry."

The man hung up. Lieutenant Boruvka had a growing suspicion that this was some kind of silly joke, but even so he woke the drowsing Malek, went into the laboratory and interrupted Dr. Seifert, who was eating lunch over the remains of an exhumed leg, picked up the coquettish fingerprint expert Babincakova from the next office, and they all got into the Volga squad car and drove off.

Klarov Number One was a gap where the old building had been torn down and foundations were being laid for a new one. A man with a full grey beard stood by the wooden construction fence surrounding the site, along with a girl in jeans wearing her hair in a pony-tail, and a young man in blue coveralls and thick glasses. They didn't look like masons.

"I'm Professor Gebert," said the robust, elderly man. "This is Miss Vostra, and this is Jise. They're my colleagues. Miss Vostra discovered the body."

"I hope you left everything just as it was?"

"Yes, of course," said the girl, and opened a door in the wooden fence.

An unexpected sight greeted the lieutenant's eyes. Instead of the usual gang of workers with shovels and bulldozers, there were about ten young men and women working in the excavation. Some of them were digging in the ground with spoons—or at least they looked like spoons to the lieutenant—others were carefully scraping away at a stone wall that emerged from the clay. At the edge of one pit a young man with a moustache sat dunking a piece of cotton wool in a bowl and delicately wiping off a mud-covered bottle made of green glass and chips of stoneware. Another man was carefully cleaning an object that looked like a court jester's boot. The lieutenant stared at it, amazed.

"Isn't that something?" said Professor Gebert, who was standing behind him. "A perfectly Gothic slipper, complete with bells on its toes. There's nothing like it anywhere in the world. Now we're looking for the mate."

The detective came to his senses and asked, "Where's the body?"

"Right this way."

The professor climbed down a ladder into the pit, followed by the lieutenant and the fingerprint expert Babincakova, who immediately began to curse violently. She had come to the police force directly from the army and had just recently finished a course in fingerprinting. Her high-heeled shoes had become stuck in the clay.

The professor led the little group across an exposed section of stone flooring that had obviously been cleared during the excavation to the corner of the stone wall. He stopped and pointed dramatically to a hole broken in the wall, which was made of unfinished stone.

For just an instant, the lieutenant's breath was taken away. A human skull stared at him out of the hole. It wasn't pure white, but brown. On the other hand, it was undamaged.

He looked at the professor, who grinned toothily. "It's murder, Lieutenant. It happened some time ago, of course—about five hundred years ago, to be as precise as we can. But it's murder all the same."

"Comrade!" said Malek darkly. "Do you realize that summoning the police on false pretences is a punishable offence?"

"God—or someone—preserve us!" cried the professor. "I didn't call you here on false pretences. Our ancestors were not in the habit of burying their dead standing up, nor did they wall them up in their basements. This is a bona fide murder you're looking at. Of course," and he paused, "the murderer really comes under the jurisdiction of the Royal Court of His Majesty Charles the Fourth, Emperor and King by the Grace of God. But since his majesty has been in the bosom of the Lord these five hundred years, the investigation is now a matter for the People's Court of the Capital City of Prague."

"Don't make fun of us, Comrade, okay? The statute of limitations on murder is twenty years, and that was four hundred and eighty years ago, which lays you open to a charge of malicious interference in the work of the Public Security Forces."

"Hang on a minute, Pavel," said the lieutenant. The sight had awakened all his investigative instincts and something else besides.

"There's no need for me here," said Babincakova. "I don't suppose there'll be any fingerprints," and she looked at the archaeology students who were busily scraping away in the dirt with their spoons.

"I don't suppose there will," said the professor.

"Then I'll just take a gander round the site," she said, and in her narrow skirt and high heels, she tottered unsteadily towards the young man who was cleaning the bottle.

"Please don't take this amiss," said the professor in a conciliatory tone. "I only thought that as professionals, you'd be interested. It's not every day you find a five-hundred-year-old corpse."

"Certainly, Professor. This is really quite interesting indeed. Pavel," said the lieutenant, turning to Malek, "I believe that in legal terms, this does concern us, even though it's well beyond the statute of limitations." The lieutenant frowned. "Are you absolutely sure that this was a murder?" he asked, addressing the professor again.

"Look," said the professor, inscribing a wide arc in the air with his finger, "there used to be an ordinary nineteenth-century tenement house here. It was declared unfit for habitation and they tore it down. When they began to dig out the foundations, they found a few medieval coins and other bric-a-brac. So they called us in. We discovered that part of the foundations go back to the fourteenth century. Beside them we found the pile of glass and stoneware bottles you see over there," and he pointed towards Babincakova, who was already flirting with the moustachioed archaeologist. "It wasn't difficult to deduce how they got there. Before it was regulated, the Vltava River meandered through Prague and it also had several "dead arms" or inlets. The original building here must have stood beside one of those inlets and the people who walked out of it must have thrown their empty bottles into the water. We found several hundred of them. Why so many bottles? Well, because the building was a tavern. Perhaps one of the ones where King Charles the Fourth, disguised as a commoner, came to get sauced up."

The lieutenant looked around. The Vltava was some way off now. He could see the green roof of the Rudolfinum concert hall, and he could hear the screeching of a streetcar braking at the Klarov stop. Dank air was rising off the site, and the skull leered straight at him from the broken hole in the wall. Once again, he felt the tingle of intimation at the back of his neck, a nagging thought, a memory, but he did not know of what.

"And wherever you have taverns, you have brawls. When we uncovered the foundations, I thought it odd that while three of the corners were right angles, that corner over there was rounded. So I authorized my assistants to dismantle it, and Miss Vostra here uncovered this beauty."

The girl with the pony-tail smiled happily.

"Can you dig out the whole skeleton?" asked the lieutenant.

"Of course," replied Professor Gebert. "In fact I would say we're obliged to, since you're here. Even though it's beyond the statute of limitations."

The girl with the pony-tail, the young man in the blue coveralls, and the professor very carefully removed the stones from the rounded corner of the wall. The lieutenant's premonition, which seemed to be tugging him in the direction of literature—though he had no idea why—strengthened. Gradually, they uncovered the skeleton, and when it was exposed as far as the top of the pelvis, the professor gave a whoop of delight.

"And here we have the *corpus delicti*," he cried, pointing to a rusty object eaten away by the centuries and protruding ragged-edged from the left side of the skeleton's rib cage. "A dagger! He was stabbed in the heart."

Feverishly they kept up their work until they had completely uncovered the skeleton. It was wearing the remains of a belt with a large metal buckle and a leather pouch. Scarcely legible on the buckle was a date, MCCCXLVII, and what was left of a coat of arms. Breathlessly, the professor leaned closer and then turned to the lieutenant. "And we even have a motive. This is the insignia of a royal messenger. Obviously the poor fellow was carrying a lot of money," and he touched the pouch delicately. "He must have stopped by the tavern for a drink and some thieves did him in. They buried the corpse in the cellar, but now, after centuries, as they say—or rather, as they write—the cellar has yielded up its secrets."

About a week later, the archaeologist invited the lieutenant and his wife for supper. The detective didn't lead much of a social life, and Mrs. Boruvka was worried about what to wear. She was an elegant woman in her thirties, the mother of thirteen-year-old Zuzanka and nine-year-old Josef, and she was on the plump side, with a pretty face, grey eyes, black hair, and a beautiful olive complexion inherited from her Italian ancestors. At last she chose a black dress and a large cross of pure gold, although the lieutenant was somewhat reluctant to see his pretty wife decked out in such an ostentatious symbol of Christianity.

He needn't have worried. Professor Gebert's attention was immediately attracted by the cross—and to tell the truth, Mrs. Boruvka as well—and he identified it as a work of Italian provenance from the sixteenth century, stylistically related to the famous Cross of Assisi. Mrs. Boruvka was flattered and she reciprocated by admiring the necklace worn by the professor's wife, who was in turn admired—in spirit, not aloud—by the always potentially unfaithful lieutenant. She was a young woman, scarcely twenty-eight and as it turned out, she had been a student of the professor, far from his best, although almost certainly his favourite. Her necklace had come from the Chod region of the country, fashioned from Josefine coins by folk artisans, as the professor once again informed the company, for the wives of well-to-do farmers in the late eighteenth and early nineteenth centuries.

After dinner, as they sat around in armchairs sipping Cointreau and smoking, the professor said: "I wanted to tell you, Lieutenant, because I assume it will interest you, despite the statute of limitations, that I've solved the murder of that messenger at the Swan and Star Tavern."

"Seems like you've missed your calling," the lieutenant laughed.

"Wrong," said the professor. "The methods of archaeology and crime detection are remarkably similar. But as it turned out, I needn't have bothered. The murderer was, as they say, or rather as they write, given a hard but just punishment. He was drawn and quartered alive, and all four pieces of him were put on display by the Bridge Tower. The only thing is that this hard but just drawing and quartering was for another murder. On the other hand, of course, you can only execute someone once, so whatever it was for, he got his just desserts."

The lieutenant looked at his host uncertainly, wondering if perhaps the artful scientist wasn't just making the whole thing up as an allegory for a recent report in which a judicial commission stated that the leader of a particular renegade political faction group was not, in fact, guilty as charged but that he was otherwise evil and therefore there had been no real miscarriage of justice, except for the fact that the formally innocent person in question had already been executed. Mrs. Boruvka, thinking it would be suitable, tried to turn white (it was the lieutenant, rather, who turned pale) and declared, "That's simply awful! Drawn and quartered, you say?"

"Yes. In those days, justice was cruel. But it was just. Times have changed." And the professor winked at the lieutenant.

"How did you come to that conclusion?" said the lieutenant noncommittally and then realized at once that what he said sounded ambiguous.

The professor grimaced—perhaps it was only a habit—and said, "It was easy, and logical. The messenger had the year 1347 on his belt. From the old land registries we learned that the name of the tavern was probably the Swan and Star. It's mentioned several times in contemporary sources. Then I looked up the old black books, as they're called—that means the trial records—and I discovered that a certain Matej Ctyrkusy—which, by the way, is a wonderful *nomen omen* is it not? Makes your blood run cold. Anyway, this Four-piece Matej was the inn-keeper of the Swan and Star. He had bought the place in the Year of Our Lord 1335 and was later put to the torture and convicted of the murder of his neighbour Cenek Liska, a money-lender from the old town, and sentenced to death, and as I've already said, the chief executioner, called Hynek Urvany—they all had such wonderful names—and his acolytes cut him in pieces with a saw, first vertically, then horizontally."

"Ludvik, please, couldn't you leave out the details?" said his naturally blonde wife, Mrs. Gebertova, and then she smiled, but only with her eyes, at Lieutenant Boruvka. Professor Gebert, however, ignored her suggestion.

"I'm a little bothered by this notion of being 'put to the torture'," the professor continued with a grimace, and the lieutenant's suspicion that he was talking in parables increased. Was it possible, the detective wondered—even with the archaeologist's undoubtedly superior education—that so much could be known about the fourteenth century? And did our ancestors really have such names? But the professor continued in an entirely authoritative tone: "First they had to put Matej Ctyrkusy in Spanish boots, then they stretched him on the rack and applied hot coals to his loins before he would confess. Then he withdrew his confession, so they put him on the rack and applied fire to his loins again, and this time he didn't withdraw his confession. I don't know how it would have turned out if the age of Charles the Fourth had enjoyed our rehabilitational techniques," and he winked at the lieutenant again, so that Boruvka had no choice but to smile back.

"But the circumstantial evidence would suggest," Boruvka replied, "that Matej Ctyrkusy didn't exactly have clean hands. Anyone could have killed that messenger in his tavern. But is it likely that just anyone could have walled him up in the cellar without his knowledge?"

"He was a professional. Anyone can see that," said the professor. "Matej tried to withstand the torture because he knew that something even worse would follow confession. And he wasn't wrong in that. It is true that the head executioner gave him a bottle of spirits before carrying out the punishment—I don't think even the hangman could have enjoyed carrying out an execution like that—and it worked somewhat like an anaesthetic. Even so, before the saw reached his vital organs, Matej Ctyrkusy, according to the Black Book, lamented in a mighty voice."

"Ludvik," said the blonde professor's wife, "how would you like to change the subject? It's turning my stomach."

The lieutenant had not noticed that part of her body. On the other hand, he did notice that nestled in the deep décolletage of her dress and framed by the silver necklace, were beautiful snow-white breasts that went wonderfully well with her naturally blonde hair.

The night was full of spectres and foreboding, and Boruvka couldn't help feeling that there was something on the tip of his tongue, something that was stuck just beneath the threshold of full consciousness. He woke up covered in sweat, tossed down his breakfast, and rushed to the office. There, he pulled out the file marked MISSING: KVETUSE RERICHOVA. The word "MISSING" had been crossed out and replaced with the word "MURDERED."

Feverishly, he read through the file. He found what he was looking for. "Two rings (gold) and a necklace (silver)." He jumped up, sat down again, and looked out the window at St. Sidonia. There was not the slightest reason why the two things should have anything to do with one another. The beautiful necklace, made by folk artisans, adorning Mrs. Gebertova's beautiful breasts. But in a walled-in corner of a medieval cellar, the professor had discovered first a skull and then the whole skeleton of a man murdered five hundred years ago. Perhaps, thought the lieutenant, there did after all, exist mystical correspondences between things. Once again, he experienced that unpleasant, involuntary sensation that there was something literary about the case. He too had discovered a skull during another excavation, although it was only twelve years old. And criminology is *not* archaeology. Or is it? The professor's deduction, this necklace, the other necklace—experience had taught the lieutenant that correspondences between people, murder, and providence never happened according to the rules laid down in detective stories. Sometimes they followed logic, but neither coincidence nor intuition could ever be ruled out. Not even mystical, undefinable things like literary sensations.

Half an hour later he was sitting once more in the flat in Letna, looking at the bookshelves with those familiar volumes, listening to the middle-aged woman who was saying bitterly: "Of course I remember. At the time I was angry with Kvetuse about it, may she rest in peace, but that necklace belonged to me, too. And she disappeared with it. Grandmother gave it to both of us. But what of it? I wish it were the only thing in life I'd ever lost," she said sentimentally. The lieutenant thought she seemed calmer today.

"Can you describe it to me?"

"It was silver, " said Libuse Hruskova. "Obviously made by some village craftsman. It was supposed to have been from the eighteenth century. It was made of Theresian coins. There must have been at least thirty of them in it, joined with silver wire. A beautiful pattern. Whenever I wore it, people would just stare at it. And at me, too. I didn't always look the way I do now. But eleven years of marriage in the same flat with a mother- and father-in-law and a sister-in-law and three kids doesn't do anything for a person's looks."

"You'd never know it to look at you," said the lieutenant, and blushed, for there were some lies he could never manage to get successfully past his lips. "And perhaps the co-op flat will improve things."

"Maybe. At least they're saying now it'll be ready by the fall."

"Was there something about the necklace by which you could positively identify it from others like it?"

"Yes, there was," said the grey-haired woman. "All the coins had Maria Theresa on one side, and only one had Josef the Second. Right here in the middle," and she pointed to the centre of her chest, where the professor's wife had those beautiful, pristine snowy slopes.

"Oh, my, Lieutenant," said the woman's voice gaily into the telephone when the detective had dialled the professor's number and asked to be excused for disturbing them. "You're not disturbing me in the least, Lieutenant."

"I'm glad. You know, I was just thinking—my wife is having a birthday soon, and when we were at your place, she was very much taken with your necklace. Do you think I could buy one like it somewhere?"

For a moment, the woman at the other end was silent.

"Perhaps. I don't know, though. It's a piece of folk art, and most of the ones like it are probably in the ethnographic museum."

"Where did you get yours?"

"It was—that is, I bought it in an antique shop."

"Which one? I'd like to ask about it."

"Which one? You know, I don't really—I think it may have been the one on National Street, but I couldn't say for certain any more."

"And when did you buy it? Perhaps they'll still have some like it."

"When. . . ? It must have been about a year ago, or so. They only had the one at the time."

"That doesn't matter," said the lieutenant. "I'll ask anyway. Thank you for your help. And I hope," he added, and he didn't even have to make an effort to have his voice sound sincere, "I hope I'll see you again some day."

"So do I. . . Lieutenant."

The detective felt she didn't say this as warmly as she had greeted him.

The next day after lunch he rang the bell at a door with a nameplate on it that read: "Professor Dr. Ludvik Gebert, Member of the Czechoslovak Academy of Sciences." She opened the door, her blonde hair like a halo of sin, a tight-fitting dark blue dress and the necklace around her neck. The lieutenant noticed that the coin lying right at the foot of those snowy mountains had the image of the Austrian Eagle stamped on it.

"Oh, my, Lieutenant!" she said again, joyfully. "How did you make out?"

"I didn't," he said mournfully. She invited him to come in.

They sat opposite each other, and the professor's wife poured him a glass of liqueur. Her hair had been given a fresh wave and a smell of perfume that reminded the lieutenant of something drifted towards him across the coffee table.

The professor's wife looked over at a big grandfather clock. "I still have half an hour's time. Then I have an appointment at the doctor's. Tell me about it."

A smile played around the grey eyes, but they contained a thought, a question.

"They didn't have one," said the lieutenant. "I'm very eager to get one because my wife was so fond of yours. They called around to all the other stores, but it's obviously a very rare thing. They told me they hadn't had anything like it for at least five years."

"Is that a fact? I do know it's relatively rare." White fingers with pink nails played with the beautiful necklace, and the coins jingled.

"Perhaps you made a mistake."

"That's possible. I have a very bad memory. And then—my husband is always buying me things. You know—he has a vain wife," and she laughed, but her eyes remained strange.

"Well, I suppose there's nothing to be done," said the lieutenant. "In my profession I don't have much time to comb the stores."

"At least your work isn't boring," said the beautiful young woman, taking the bait which the lieutenant had subtly offered her. "In fact, it must really be very interesting."

"Not as interesting as your husband's work, I'm afraid. Even though—believe it or not—I'm working on a case now that is very much like the one your husband solved. I mean the murder that took place in Charles the Fourth's time."

"You don't say!"

"A skull was unearthed at a construction site on the outskirts of the city. It wasn't as old, of course, only about twelve years. It was a female skull, not a male. And I've managed to identify it. Her name was Kvetuse Rerichova. She disappeared twelve years ago. Someone murdered her."

"That's astounding!"

"Not really. My main concern now is to find her killer because this crime is well within the statute of limitations and the murderer could well be still alive and at large. And if he's murdered somebody once. . . . But I only have a single clue, and that's led me nowhere."

"Oh, but you'll solve it, I'm sure. Would you like another drink?"

The professor's wife leaned over to reach the bottle, and her necklace swung like a pendulum.

"That's interesting," said the lieutenant.

"What's interesting?"

The young woman followed the direction of the detective's glance and interpreted it inaccurately. She laughed.

"Have you noticed," said the lieutenant, "that all the coins on your necklace have portraits of Maria Theresa, and only one has the two-headed eagle?"

"D'you mean this one?" said the young woman, and with her white fingers she picked up the coin that was resting on the spot where the white hills vanished beneath the dark blue neckline.

"Yes," sighed the lieutenant.

"Look on the other side!"

She leaned forward towards the lieutenant so that he could see properly. The scent of sandalwood wafted around him but even so, he resisted the temptation to look at her breasts. He examined the coin closely.

Suddenly he straightened up. The young woman stared at

him in surprise. "Where did you get it?" he asked unhappily.

"But I've already told you."

"I *know* what you told me. What I want to know now is *who* gave it to you."

She was silent.

"Your husband? I certainly hope it wasn't!" cried the lieutenant almost desperately.

The blonde woman took a drink, then looked searchingly into the lieutenant's eyes. The lieutenant, who was usually shy, returned her stare.

"You're investigating a murder, aren't you?" she said quietly. The lieutenant had meanwhile managed to relax. No. The necklace had not been a gift from the sympathetic professor. He had, of course, showered his young wife with jewellery, but young wives with older husbands certainly remember the origin of their jewellery much better than anything else.

"Yes," he said, "I am investigating a murder. But don't worry. I won't tell your husband."

Once again there was a long pause while her eyes made searching enquiries. This time she glanced away. She may not have been the professor's best student, but she was clearly the prettiest and she was certainly very intelligent as well. Or perhaps she was merely clever. When she spoke, her voice trembled slightly. "Why are you interested in where I got my necklace from? I mean, if it's a murder you're investigating."

"I don't think I need to go into detail. I think you can work that out for yourself."

The young woman shuddered. Once again, she took the beautiful silver object in her white fingers. "This clue of yours. . . ." The lieutenant nodded.

The professor's wife let go of the necklace as though it had suddenly become red hot. She turned pale.

"I feel ill," she said, and took a sip of her drink. Then, more hopefully, she went on, "But perhaps it's a mistake. The murderer could have sold it—after all, it was twelve years ago and — he"—she hesitated, and the whiteness that reminded the lieutenant, in his dreams, of the beautiful skull gave way to a blush—"he could have bought it in the antique shop."

She shook her head. The hope was extinguished; the flush died.

"I feel as though I've just reached out and touched something horrible in the dark," she said and tears began streaming down her face. But they were tears of horror more than anguish. "And he looks—and behaves completely—and I —"

"It happens all the time," said the lieutenant. "Particularly with murderers who kill for money, like him. Of course," and he thought for a moment as he remembered something the blonde woman's husband had said, "in his case there was a clear pathological aspect to it. I mean more obviously than usual in a murderer, because every murderer in fact is sick."

"But he really does behave—just like you'd expect—expect a bank manager to behave."

The lieutenant, however, was not listening. He was absorbed in his own thoughts.

"The fact that he cut her up into pieces and even boiled the head and scraped away all the fleshy parts . . . What did you say your—friend—did for a living?"

He looked at the blonde woman.

Her complexion was green and she was just rising from the couch. Then she rushed out somewhere into the hall and for a long time the lieutenant sat in the room alone, his shame and sadness mitigated only by a very tiny sense of satisfaction. That the girl who twelve years ago had been fed up with everything would now finally be—what, really?

And it was a case full of strange correspondences. When the lieutenant went to see Libuse, to tell her that her sister's murderer had been arrested, she was no longer living in the flat on Jamaica Street. She had moved, the concierge told him, to a new co-operative flat.

"Where?" asked the lieutenant, a sense of foreboding tingling at the back of his neck.

"Krc," said the concierge.

So the detective told Libuse nothing about where they had found the beautiful skull and said only that he had based all his deductions on the coin bearing the likeness of Josef the Second. But Libuse was not really interested in his deductions.

"A nice flat? You call this a nice flat?" she said bitterly when the lieutenant praised their new one-bedroom suite. "Just take a look!" And she led the lieutenant into the bathroom, where she demonstrated some of the features of the apartment. The bathroom was too small for both a bathtub and a sink, so the inventive architect had designed a washbasin that could be attached to the edge of the tub when no one was having a bath. When the washbasin was in place, it was impossible to get into the bathtub, which otherwise was long enough to lie down in, as long as you could put your knees up around your ears.

"At least you have the whole flat to yourselves."

"Look, lieutenant or whatever you are," said Libuse, "when I got married, I was twenty-five. Now, when I'm thirty-seven I finally have an apartment of my own and an eleven-year-old daughter. She's *already* mad about boys, and by the time she's seventeen at the latest she'll be in trouble and then we'll have three generations crowded around that detachable washbasin all over again."

The old detective said nothing. He thought about the manager of the savings bank who, because of numerous extenuating circumstances (the time elapsed since the crime, no other criminal offences, a wonderful political record, a long history of dedicated party activity, and an immediate and full confession) would get, he guessed (accurately, as it turned out) no more than fifteen years, so that in relative security (he would certainly continue to co-operate with the prison authorities) he would await his forty-eighth year, or more likely the nearest amnesty. Whereas the driver's mate who had committed an act, invented by a perverse Mother Nature, upon his dead wife's body, had, lacking party connections, swung at the end of a rope.

"So I'll have this flat to myself for six, seven years at the most. And then I'll be forty-four," Libuse said bitterly.

The lieutenant could think of nothing to say. He looked around, and on the walls saw the same figures in their folk costumes, and Jirasek in his leather bindings was in the bookshelf, a gift edition of Nemcova, detective novels, *Wuthering Heights, The Gold Bug and Other Tales, Jane Eyre, War and Peace.*

"And then my boy will get married, naturally with some stupid girl who has nowhere to live. . . ."

The lieutenant rose to his feet guiltily.

"Why am I telling you all this?" said the grey-haired thirty-seven-year-old woman, rising as well. "It's not your fault. And it was nice of you to take the trouble to avenge our Kvetuse's death. I hope they hang the creep. He deserves to be drawn and quartered, the bastard."

But the lieutenant knew that punishment in the people's democratic states was no longer cruel, only hard and just. And if a person co-operates with the party and doesn't commit anything worse than murder. . . .

He shuddered. At what Libuse had wanted to happen to the murderer. At those correspondences.

That night he couldn't sleep.

Next day, towards evening, he sat in his room and, through the open door, watched while his eleven-year-old daughter Zuzanka struggled over her Russian homework. He marvelled at how they had come by this little love nest, through circumstances that were almost mystical: the landlady, although she was only forty-seven, had suddenly died, so that when Zuzanka was born, they had not just a back room, but a whole flat to live in. What luck that had been! And how lucky he had been, all his life in fact. Perhaps the world wasn't such an evil place after all, even though many evil things take place in it. On the other hand, there are so many wonderful things to compensate. He looked at the girl over her homework, at the bookshelf behind her and at the rows of volumes. There it was again, that strange sensation at the back of his neck. He stood up, walked into the next room and pulled a book off the shelf. Yes. He had seen it in the new flat in Krc. *The Gold Bug and Other Tales*. He opened it up and read:

> I asked myself—"Of all melancholy topics, what, according to the *universal* understanding of mankind, is the *most* melancholy?" Death—was the obvious reply. "And when," I said, "is this most melancholy of topics most poetical?" . . . "When it most closely allies itself to *Beauty*: the death, then, of a beautiful woman is, unquestionably, the most poetical topic in the world. . . .

The lieutenant didn't understand that. He remembered a photograph of Kvetuse, a pretty blonde girl with a beautiful, long face that had been transformed into a beautiful, long cranium. He leafed through a few pages and read again, shuddering:

> With a shriek I bounded to the table, and grasped the box that lay upon it. But I could not force it open; and, in my tremor, it slipped from my hands, and fell heavily, and burst into pieces; and from it, with a rattling sound, there rolled out some instruments of dental surgery, intermingled with thirty-two small, white, and ivory-looking substances that were scattered to and fro about the floor.

His whole body trembled. The beautiful white skull stared at him through the open window. I'll not encounter anything more terrifying than that, he thought, not after this. He turned a few more pages and read again: ". . .the strange anomaly of life. . . feelings, with me, *had never been* of the heart, and my passions *always were* of the mind"—but he didn't understand that either. Still, it horrified him. How could passion—and emotion — from reason. . . .

He didn't understand it for a long time. Not, in fact, until he saw those two dead girls in the long, green grass.

Common or Garden Murder

ELLEN GODFREY

Ellen Godfrey was born in 1942, in Chicago. She graduated from Stanford University in 1963 with a B.A. in History. She has lived in West Africa, Provence, Ontario, and now makes her home in Victoria, British Columbia.

Ellen Godfrey has worked in advertising, promotion, editing, and publishing, and is now the president of Press Porcépic, a literary publishing company, and Softwords, a computer-software firm.

Ms Godfrey has published three books: two mysteries, and a true-crime book, By Reason of Doubt, *which won the Mystery Writers of America, Edgar Allan Poe Special Award in 1982.*

The story in this collection is her only published short story.

NEIGHBOURS. THEY'RE GREAT when you need them, but it's better not to get too involved with them. Especially when you've got kids, and they don't; sooner or later there'll be trouble, and there's no escape from a neighbour. They're always there; and you can end up sneaking out of your own house, hoping not to be seen by a neighbour you're in trouble with.

Of course it's ridiculous to be a prisoner in your own house, but it's the kind of thing that happens to me. My curiosity tricks me into going too far, and then I'm not clever enough to get out of trouble. Trying only makes things worse; I ought to know better by now. At forty, quite the worse for wear, I'd like to think I've learned some common sense for my sins, but the signs all point in the opposite direction.

When I moved into my new house by the sea the first thing I decided not to do was get too involved with my next-door neighbour. I was going to keep my curiosity under control. Even now I'm not sure how it happened, how I got mixed up with my neighbour, Tory Barton. I look back to try to understand how it all happened and to see where I went wrong. I really want to know.

It was his garden that interested me, not him. It was too beautiful for me to resist. And who would ever dream that a beautiful garden could draw in a person too far, draw in a person until she was involved in murder?

There really was something very special about the effect that garden had on me. It seemed almost to be promising me something, something that I wanted, something that was very important to me.

In that first autumn after I moved in, I would walk over the rocky bit of ground that separated his property from mine, just to look at it. Standing there and looking down, I would think that the sunshine was more mellow in Barton's garden than anywhere else. Apple and pear trees, their branches so heavy with fruit that they leaned upon their stakes, cast soft restful shadows on the smooth green lawn. The leaves of the trees were full and heavy with sunshine, holding and reflecting the light. Beyond the fruit trees, the runner beans climbed vigorously on the white-painted trellis. Hedges of colourful dahlias separated the rows of dark green cabbages; there were prickly red currant bushes under their netting, and squash, cucumber and tomatoes, each without a blemish, without a mite, the soil turned and worked and weedless around every plant, vine, and stake.

Barton's crowning glory grew on the slope on the seaward side of the garden. There, sheltered from the sea breeze, warmed by the sunlight reflected off the rocks, and thick on their vines, grew the dark luscious fredonia grapes which Barton was so proud of. Still, who could argue when Barton boasted, "Have you ever seen a vine like it? Does anyone else on this coast have grapes like this?" You had to agree. I had read in the gardening column of our newspaper that the climate was too harsh for grapes . . . and yet, there was Barton's vine, a masterwork.

I had quickly learned that I had to be careful not to be caught looking at the garden. But it was hard to resist, especially when I was having a rough day with the kids, and the damned dog, and the house getting to be just a bit too much, and most likely the van on the fritz again. Even though I knew that the last thing I needed on days like that was to have Barton making a pass at me. And that's all it seemed to take—just seeing me looking at his garden was enough to give him the idea that I was longing for a little fun and games.

Women in my position are vulnerable, and we are supposed

to be careful. I know it, and I knew right from the start I might have trouble when I rented a house next to a divorced single man. In fact, when I heard about him I even wondered if I ought to go ahead and take the house. But the old, two-storey tudor-style place, with its big windows and funny nooks and crannies, was too perfect to pass up. The house was just run down enough for me to afford, yet it was big enough and had a sea view. Down behind, there were lots of neat places for the kids to wander. I thought the funny old house might help make up to the kids for what they had lost by me making a hash of my marriage and losing them their father in the process. I know I'm not supposed to put it that way—everyone says it takes two to break up a marriage—but I tried my hardest and still my husband left me for someone else. Whose fault could that be, if not mine?

Anyway, a lecherous neighbour is no reason for the kids not to live in the kind of house they had always wanted. I told myself he'd probably take one look at me driving by in the big yellow van with my hair every which way and the tailpipe (which I've been meaning to get fixed and *still* haven't) tied on with rope, and not even bother to try anything.

Of course I was very lonely and pretty unhappy. I was trying not to think about my husband, Marcus, and his new posting in Paris, and his pretty new girlfriend. I don't know, it might even be that, without realizing it, I was hoping to like Tory Barton. Maybe that is why I accepted so easily his invitation to come in and have a glass of wine, the first time he caught sight of me, on the rocky spit of land that divided our properties, feasting my eyes on his wonderful garden.

"Well, I'm not sure," I said, thinking of my dusty, ratty jeans and feeling not really up to his smoothness. I knew right away, as soon as I saw him, that he was one of the "perfect" people. He was wearing sharply creased khakis, and a blue cotton crew-neck sweater that matched his pale blue eyes.

I'm sure my looks will be enough to put any flirtatious thoughts out of his mind, I told myself as we walked along his spotless marble foyer (how *do* other people keep the entryway carpets of their houses from going all grungy?) and along a thickly carpeted hall into a perfect kitchen, like an illustration in *Western Living* magazine. It was easy to see that appearances meant a lot to him, and in that department a woman like me, surely, would not be a very worthwhile conquest. Turning forty, ten pounds overweight, too many sad lines in her face and the general falling of everything that can fall after four children—I didn't belong in that shiny, spotless kitchen.

But Tory Barton did not seem to notice how uncomfortable I felt, sitting awkwardly on the spindly barstool at his gleaming kitchen counter, while he poured wine into large, long-stemmed glasses.

"I have, quite literally, the best view in this city, don't you think?" Tory had asked, turning to look out of his kitchen window and to show me his perfect profile, his thick, silvery grey hair, blow-dried in the latest style, sweeping away elegantly from his temples.

"Yes, yes it certainly is," I said, for the view over the straits was magnificent. The architect had set the house and placed the windows along the seaward side, to show a wonderful sweep of coast that made the viewer feel he was a lord, high up in his castle, surveying an isolated, uninhabited, perfect realm.

"Naturally I had to pay plenty for it," said Tory. "But it was well worth it. What else is money for? To buy beauty. That's what I always say."

Again I agreed. With four children to feed on a fixed monthly alimony it was an idea I really didn't have to worry about one way or the other.

"And you, Sylvia," he said, pausing over my name almost like a dog positioning a bone between its paws, "how do you find that old house you rented? Pretty creaky I bet. Not much spent on maintenance over there, as far as I can tell." He didn't wait for me to answer. "It's nice for me, having a single woman living next door; I hope we can get to know one another better. Not that I'm lonely, of course—I'm never lonely—but you . . . tied down with all those boys . . . I'm sure you could use. . . ."

His voice tailed off into a knowing smile. "You must find it . . . very. . . ."

"Not at all," I said hurriedly, wondering what was wrong with me, that I would let the conversation start to go wrong when I had only been in his kitchen for a few minutes. I knew already that I didn't like Tory Barton very much, although I felt, for some reason, a little sorry for him, maybe because he did seem kind of lonely. Still, I wished I was almost anywhere but alone with him, drinking his wine, and not knowing how to get out of what I could see was coming.

"One of my wives was a movie star," he told me with pride in his voice. "Sara Blixen."

I said, without thinking, that I had never heard of her.

"You're kidding." He mentioned some movies I had never heard of. "And she's on 'Hollywood Squares' a lot."

I wasn't sure about 'Hollywood Squares' either. Was it a TV show or a kind of filmstar-world drug? I could see it would be better not to admit my ignorance and seem even more a fool.

"I used to rub her back when she was under pressure," he told me, "but she turned out to be as heartless as the other three, no matter what I did for her."

I knew it wasn't a good idea to let a man tell you about his bad luck with women, so I tried to change the subject, but Tory had the conversation under his control and I didn't have a chance. I found myself listening to him going on about how he had done "everything" for his wives, but how he found out they were only interested in one thing, money. He said sadly that nothing would satisfy them.

When he wasn't talking about his past he was prying into mine. He wanted to know how much my husband had earned a year, and what stocks and property he had, and how much alimony I got. When I told him—I couldn't figure out how not to —he told me firmly that I had been badly treated.

"Royally screwed, in my opinion. I could have got you more, if you had known me then; I would have helped you. I've helped a lot of my friends whose marriages broke up. And what is really good about it is, both of them—the husband and the wife—thanked me afterwards. Now *that's* unusual, but, to tell you the truth, I could have been a professional negotiator. It's a knack I have. . . . "

I interrupted. "But I didn't want more." Somehow it seemed important to me not to be lumped in with the actress on 'Hollywood Squares'. "Marcus worked really hard for his money and *he* earned it. I have to admit it, I was just not very good at helping him. And I didn't want to either, so why should he owe me anything? The kids, yes, and he's doing that; but me, I don't see it. I wanted to stay out of that life at External, all the entertaining and that kind of thing. I just wanted to have babies and take care of them. As it turns out, now I'm unemployable, but, after all, whose fault is that?"

He smiled at me, and I could see he thought I was trying to prove to him that I wasn't one of those women who were only after a man for his money. And although he knew that that was all women wanted, he liked me for lying to him about it. He expected it and felt good to have things work out the way he expected. His smile suddenly revolted me.

"Look," I said, trying to explain, "wives in External are supposed to be elegant, and charming, and good at running a house, and they're supposed to entertain beautifully. It's part of the job. Marcus's new girlfriend is French; she's perfect at that stuff. But I just never did it the way Marcus wanted. I wasn't a help; I was a hindrance." I didn't say, although I thought about it as I spoke, how Marcus complained that the kids got in the way of his "professional obligations" and how he wanted to send them away to boarding school. I didn't see things the way Marcus did; how could anybody send little boys of five and seven and nine away? Even the oldest, at twelve . . . you only had them such a short time, surely it wasn't right? Marcus said that if I wanted to keep the kids around I should be able to manage the way other External wives did.

"I just gave up trying," I told Tory Barton. "I just didn't want to try any more. Nothing I did was done the way he wanted. So what does he owe me for?"

"You handled it very badly, in my opinion. But it isn't your fault. Women like you need good lawyers and friends who rally round in time of trouble." He gave me that awful smile again.

"I have to be going now," I said gulping down my wine. "The children will be coming home from school any minute and. . . ."

"But I wanted to show you around my house," he said, his smile fading.

"Maybe some other time," I said weakly, cursing myself as soon as the words were out of my mouth.

He brightened a little. "You're such an attractive woman, a desirable woman. . . . I feel that somehow, you and I. . . ."

It had turned into a farce. I got myself away as quickly as I could. I decided after that afternoon that Tory Barton was a phoney (expecting me to take him seriously when he said he found me 'attractive', 'desirable'; it was really pretty insulting) and the only thing he had going for him was his garden. I know it was an over-reaction, but I think I was still quite easily hurt then, and it did hurt that I had seemed to him so easy, so vulnerable, and so dumb that I would believe such a feeble line.

After Tory Barton got over being annoyed about the rude way I had "run out of the house in the middle of a friendly drink", he used to talk to me about whatever was obsessing him at the time, if he could catch me when I was walking the dog, or when he came over to borrow something. So it wasn't long after his trouble with Kieran began that I got all the details from him first hand.

And then, after Kieran was killed and I had made up my mind to forget all about his death because it really had nothing to do with me, I still kept thinking about Tory Barton, and his garden, and his grapevine, and the perfection of his house and his life . . . compared to the slap-dash, screwed-up life the kids and I led in the big old house, looking over his garden. And I kept seeing the image of old Kieran lying dead between the two houses, like a symbol of unfinished business.

The municipal trucks were the first sign of trouble. I heard the thrum thrum of their motors early one morning as I hustled around the kitchen making breakfast. The noise distracted me from my usual morning hassles: reminding the kids not to forget their homework, checking on who had soccer practice and who needed a dental excuse and doing all the other last-minute stuff other mothers probably have made careful lists of the night before. When all four of them were off, and I had made sure that no one had forgotten his knapsack, I sat down with that most blessed cup of coffee and cigarette of the day. Then I heard the sound of earth rolling down the rock slopes and workmen calling to one another. I stuck my bare feet into a pair of wellingtons, buttoned a heavy sweater over my bathrobe, and ventured out.

Carefully skirting the eucalyptus hedge that shielded our front yard from the lane, I peered around without letting myself be seen. Two bright yellow municipal trucks were dumping fill on the rock outcropping between our house and Barton's. This was peculiar because that narrow rocky spit was the property of the municipality. I had been told that when I moved in. It was dedicated as a "sea access" and no one could put a house on it. My landlord's assurances of this had surprised me, because the lot was a funny triangle. The point at the road was no more than fifteen feet wide, widening out towards the sea to a sharply sloping rocky coast of about a hundred and fifty feet. No one could or would want to build on this triangular piece of rock, high on my side, but sloping sharply downwards towards Barton's. Now, as I watched, peering out from behind the eucalyptus, the contours of the rock were disappearing under torrents of earth.

Forgetting my unmade-up face and my bathrobe hanging out below my sweater I approached one of the workmen.

"Hey, what's up? What're you guys doing?"

"Dumping fill."

"But why?"

"How should I know?" the workman said, looking around

for his mate. "Hey, Rick, the lady wants to know why we're dumping fill," he called out, his voice just audible above the sound of the engine and the fill falling out of the dump truck onto the rocks.

The second workman approached. "No idea, lady, nothing to do with us. Call the municipality if you wanna know anything."

Just then I saw Kieran coming towards us along the lane. The old man was a figure of fun to my kids. He walked down to the end of our road every day, slightly stooped over, wearing a dirty tweed cap and an old worn plaid jacket with several layers of shirts under it, each of a different colour. The kids had told me that old Kieran had once owned half of the land in the neighbourhood. They were probably right; he must have become a millionaire many times over as he sold it off, parcel by parcel, over the years. The main road was called Kieran Road. I had heard stories of his peculiar tastes in houses and had sometimes seen him on a tractor, or a bulldozer, working a piece of wasteland, which soon after was subdivided, given a cute name, and then built up with fancy, ugly houses.

Now he shuffled towards me and gestured towards his cap. "Morning," he said in a surprisingly strong, young voice. As he got closer, I could see that he was really very old and frail-looking, despite the voice; well into his eighties, I thought, with bits of white whiskers poking out of the crevices round his sunken mouth, and his small eyes vague and bleared over.

"Good morning," I said. "You're Mr. Kieran?"

"That's right, and you're the lady that rented the Morris place last September, around there, eh?"

I nodded. "What's going on here, Mr. Kieran?"

"It's to be a fine house for my sainted sister, God rest her soul. In her memory. I'll rent it out, just by the month, you know. Because I might decide to live in it myself. Haven't quite made up my mind."

"But I thought this land belonged to the city. That's what they told me when I rented my house."

He laughed, showing a row of perfect, white teeth. "Bound

to say that, but it doesn't mean a thing. This land is mine. Has been for fifty years. So was the land your house is on, and Mr. Barton's there. All of it my land once. Mine and my sister Mary's. This is last piece left along here, and I'm going to build some house here, you'll see."

"But the lot's so small, and all rocky."

"For the moment. Just for the moment. A course we got to pass the percolation test, so the municipality's dumping the fill here for me. It'll all be just fine. Architect's got it all worked out—you'll see. No problem. Amazing what you can do these days to make land fit your plans."

"But look, the dirt is sliding over into Mr. Barton's garden onto his grapevine."

"We'll clean it up later," Kieran said without much interest. "Building things is always messy. Right now we got this work to do. Clean up's the last step."

He turned away from me and began shuffling back towards the workmen. Remembering my bathrobe and my morning coffee, and the chance that Barton might look out his window and see me, I took off for home.

It was an unusually warm day, and by noon it was hot enough to leave the front door open, so I could hear the kids coming towards the house, fighting and arguing in the distance. Timmy was threatening to tell Mommy on Jackie if Jackie didn't let Timmy ride his ten speed. The screen door banged, and they came rushing in, leaving muddy footprints on the carpet, each anxious to be the first to get his side of the story across. There was no point in listening, really. As they talked, Jackie's cheeks flushed with indignation, and Timmy hopped from foot to foot in his excitement, dropping clods of mud on the kitchen floor with each hop.

It was perfectly obvious what had happened. Jackie's breath smelled unmistakeably of peanut butter and chocolate; he must have stopped on the way home, contrary to standing orders, and bought a candy bar. It was clear from Timmy's manner that he hadn't gotten any, and the oval smudge of fresh mud on his pants' leg was where Jackie had kicked him when he argued for his share of the booty. When the candy was gone, Timmy had tried blackmail, seeing if at least he could barter his knowledge of Jackie's forbidden behaviour for a ride on the coveted ten speed. The oldest, Mark, was smirking in the background. At thirteen he felt himself beyond such arguments, unless he had started them. The littlest, Robert, was waiting breathlessly to see what I would do.

Knowing what had happened ought to have helped me to know what to do, but it didn't. I usually *did* know what had happened behind my back. That was one thing Marcus had eventually hated about me, even though he had loved it at first. He called me a witch and said that I could see right through him. When that stopped feeling like love to him, it started being very unpleasant indeed.

I can understand that. Knowing what people want to keep secret doesn't give you a clue what to do about it. Should I let Jackie know I knew he had disobeyed my rule about candy between meals? I couldn't enforce it, obviously. Yet telling him I knew would only prove to him that I wasn't serious when I forbade something.

Then, knock on wood, when he was tempted towards something serious like drugs, he'd already have the habit of sneaking, of going against my will. Or did he have it already. . . .

"Oh be quiet all of you, you're giving me a headache! And look, mud all over the rug and kitchen floor. Haven't I told you and told you to take off your shoes before you come screaming in here? Now just sit down and eat your lunch and don't say a word."

"But he hit me. . . ." "No he started it. . . ." "No, he's a tattleface. . . ." "Well he said. . . ."

"SHUT UP!"

Luckily lunch was clam chowder, and for a few minutes there was no sound but the clinking of spoons, and the crunching of crackers, and the spilling of milk—as it did at least once each meal-time.

When I had mopped up, I asked the boys if they knew what was going on next door. They knew of course. Where curiosity was concerned they took after their mother.

"Old Kieran's going to build a humungous house next door," Mark told me.

"It seems impossible, there's just rock there. The city won't allow it."

"Yes, but I heard at school that Kieran can do whatever he wants, Mommy. They say the city is afraid of him because he's so rich and he has so many houses and so much land—all that stuff. So if anybody doesn't like it, they all say it's just too bad on them. Is that true, Mommy? Is it?" Mark was worried. "I don't think it's fair."

"*I* think it sucks," said Robert, not wanting to be left out.

"A new house on that little bit of rock? Totally awesome," said Timmy, who was always hoping for a friend to move in nearby, a friend to help him gang up on Jackie.

I said, "Well what does Mr. Barton think? If they build up the land next to him, his garden will be in a hole."

"The old creep was out there screaming at the workmen when we came home for lunch today," Mark said. He had always hated Tory Barton.

"The old fart," said Robert.

We had a brief discussion about language, and the kids rushed off, back to school. In the echoing silence left behind I could hear the municipal trucks and the sound of fill pouring onto the rock, and the new "lot" being created between my house and Tory's. When I thought of Tory, who always had everything under control, and Kieran, who seemed always to get his way, I felt a chill, and I wondered how it would all come out.

This was my kind of mess, but this time it was happening to one of the "perfect" people.

There was never any doubt about who killed Kieran. But then, *that* wasn't the point. Tory admitted it, and I myself was a witness.

There had been a party at the house of Dr. Mills, an orthodontist whom I knew rather too well (two of the boys were already under his very expensive care). Most of us in the neighbourhood were invited. I put on my dress-up outfit and went over. I didn't intend to stay too long, since Mark was "babysitting" as usual and I wanted to limit the damage. I went to the party for the same reason I always go to parties: I was hoping I would meet a rich and tender man who could hardly wait to sweep into my life, hire me a housekeeper, and take me away to Hawaii for a long holiday. This fantasy always made me look forward to going out. After half an hour or so, when I realized that once again the dream man hadn't shown up, I tended to drink too much and go home early.

The first person I saw when I got there was Tory Barton, looking a bit pissed, leaning warmly over the cigarette of a young woman I had never seen before. I avoided him and found myself talking to another stranger, a man who turned out to be a very nice person. Maybe I wouldn't have liked him so much if we'd met in other circumstances, but in the din of the party, and after the first two drinks (which I tend to drink very quickly when I arrive in a crowd of people alone), we seemed to get along as if we'd known each other for a long time. Nothing particularly exciting, and he certainly wasn't going to sweep me off my feet and rush me off to Hawaii, but still. . . .

He looked to be in his late forties, with a wrinkled face, as if life had dealt rather harshly with him and he had accepted that. He laughed easily and had a sweet smile which made me smile back no matter what the point and feel happy inside. His name was Rob MacNally and he practised law in town. It sounded boring to me, mostly real estate and business law, but he said he liked it. He saw how people acted when money was at stake. He said they were worse than he thought people would be when he was young, but as he got older he expected a hell of a lot less, so he was more and more often pleasantly surprised when they acted better than he had expected. I liked that. We laughed a lot, and when I apologized for talking too much he looked at me and said he hadn't enjoyed himself this much at a party in a long time.

I didn't believe him. But I liked him for saying so, and more for the way he said it: sort of gentle and relaxed, his eyes looking out of that worn face as if to say that I too had delivered more than he had expected, and that was good enough. He was just easy with himself, and I felt more comfortable with him than I had with anyone—and that includes myself—for a long time.

But it was a party and I knew I had to circulate. So I spent quite a long time talking to Mrs. Mills. We compared the "woes" of a rich orthodontist's wife to the "joys" of being a single parent. She had a lot more problems than I had, or at least so she said, and I found the idea comforting.

I didn't notice until later than I should have that, as usual, I had drunk too much and that it was getting towards the time the porno movies started on TV, and I had to get home, to be sure the kids weren't watching them.

Tory saw me leaving. "Hey Sylvia, going so soon? Worried you'll turn into a pumpkin at eleven? Ha, ha."

It was obvious that he was even more pissed than I, and I edged away from him.

"I noticed, you always leave before the fun. . . . What are you afraid of ?"

"I'm walking, I really have to be going, and I left the boys without a babysitter."

"No problem, no problem, I'll just zip you home in my MG—you've never ridden in it anyway, and now's your chance. Chance of a lifetime." He smiled at the young woman next to him, and she smiled back.

But I had no intention of going with Tory Barton, particularly when he was so pissed, and I made excuses and hurried out the door before he could catch me and insist. I wondered if everyone in the world thought I left parties early because I was afraid of something, and I didn't like the idea. Still there wasn't much I could do about it. When you marry young and stay with one man for twenty years and think of no one else, you often find yourself acting like a prude. The problem is, the choice usually seems to be between being a prude or letting yourself go completely.

It was a very dark night. The wind was high, off the sea, and the trees shook and groaned and leaned over me as I walked through the blackness. I didn't mind. It wasn't cold, and the fresh air felt good and clean after the fug of the party. There were no sidewalks most of the way, and the streetlights shed barely any light in their unequal struggle with the moist dark night air. Around each was a soft misty halo of light, and I could hear some of them humming like noisy insects hidden in the night air.

Always cautious, I walked against the traffic, and when I saw a car approaching (there weren't many at that time of night, it was past eleven), its headlights dim blurs until it was almost upon me, I walked far onto the shoulder until the car had passed. My sweater and hat were dark, and I knew that I must be practically invisible.

As I turned into our lane, I heard a car coming from behind me, very fast. As it approached, the headlights wavered. Thinking that someone might have had too much, and possibly be tight enough to drive over the middle, I stepped off onto the shoulder and looked back and "saw" the whole thing. The headlights of the car wavered again, there was a thud, and a screeching of brakes. The car door opened, and by its light I saw that it was Tory Barton's snazzy little MG. We both ran towards the dark patch on the road, he unsteadily, I, fully alert, sobered by my half-mile walk in the wind and by the shock of what had just happened.

"I didn't see him. Nobody could have seen him. He was invisible, just invisible," Tory was saying in a high, frightened voice. We both came upon the figure at the same time and saw him, lying thrown onto the soft muddy shoulder. It was Kieran, and he was dead.

So that was all there was to it, it appeared. I testified at the inquest; Tory was given a scolding by the coroner, and the city came and took away the fill on the land next door, at Tory's expense.

Yet, even after I got over the shock of what had happened, I found I couldn't stop thinking about it, going round and round, worrying over it. Sometimes I was craven enough to think that if, just for once, I had remembered to get the van looked after, I would have *driven* and been home half an hour earlier and missed the whole thing. Then, at least, I would not have been a witness to death.

But the van was parked at the end of the lane, in front of Tory's, useless that night, and I *had* walked, and I *had* seen it all. If I had had less to drink, would I have seen Kieran as I came walking towards him and told him to walk on the shoulder? If I had taken the ride with Tory, would he have left earlier and so not been at the wrong place at the wrong time?

Pointless thoughts; at the time, the best thing seemed to be to try not to think about it at all. I told myself, over and over—as I had testified at the inquest—that it was no one's fault. Even if Tory hadn't been drinking, he very well might not have seen Kieran. *I* hadn't seen him. I knew the best thing would be to try to forget about it as soon as possible.

The morning after the accident, when I was walking the dog, I saw the rubber marks on the road, and the fine sparkling crumbs of broken glass. Saw, but did not look at; I did not want to look at the bloodstains on the edge of the road and the depression on the soft shoulder where the body had come to rest. I didn't want those images to go into that place in my mind where all the other sad things collect, the ones that I can't help or do anything about. Things like Marcus not wanting me and the kids, and how my life seems always to be more than I can handle.

After all, whose fault is it if an unloved, unlovable, frail old man, a neighbourhood laughingstock, and a developer of eyesores, gets run down accidentally late at night? And what was he doing there, anyway, after 11:00, on a Saturday night?

The morning after the inquest was a beautiful one, warm and sunny. I knew I ought to get out and do some gardening, so I put on a pair of gardening jeans, looked for my gardening gloves with no success, then collected what tools I could find and went out into the yard.

But I didn't get much done. Instead, I found myself, drawn by the soft warm air and the sunshine, out of my weed-filled yard and over towards Tory Barton's. I moved cautiously around the hedge and lurked behind a tree, checking to be sure he too wasn't out, directing his gardeners, or working himself. But no, the garden was peaceful and silent in the morning light. I approached over the rocks between, now stripped of the loads of fill but still muddy and slippery, and looked down into Tory Barton's little Eden.

The spring blossoms had fallen from the apples and pears and been replaced by clouds of tiny pearly green leaves, the grass was already very lush, and shoots of vegetables showed up in their rows, rising out of the neatly tilled soil. But Tory Barton's garden did not look beautiful to me that morning. It looked rigid, lifeless, and sinister. I was astonished. It was as if you had unexpectedly come too close to a painted backdrop. Scenery once full of splendour was revealed to be coarsely painted smears of colour, meaningless and flat. I backed away and hurried home.

At lunch, the children seemed to sense my mood. They were subdued as they ate. All except Robert, who said suddenly, as he reached for the last of the Sara Lee brownies (I had meant to bake that morning, but somehow had not gotten around to it), "Mom, why did Mr. Barton kill Kieran?"

The question hung in the air, and I shrank back from it, hating it, wishing it unsaid, and feeling, at the same time, the awakening of that stupid curiosity of mine that makes me find out what I would be oh so much better off not knowing.

"It was an accident, Robert," I said. "Wipe the crumbs off your mouth please. Not with the tablecloth, for God's sake."

"What's the difference, Mommy?"

"Oh, be serious," Timmy said. "Even babies know what an accident is. Even teeny tiny tots."

"So then tell him yourself, smartass," said Jackie.

We had the usual talk about language, and then when the

kids went back to school I sat for a long time at the table, finishing off the brownies, looking out the window, and smoking, thinking about everything. My thoughts went around and around and I felt worse and worse, until I knew I couldn't stand to let things stay the way they were.

Then the doorbell rang, and it was Rob MacNally. He had been at the inquest the day before, sitting among the spectators, in the back row, watching everything. It had surprised me to see him there, surprised me even more that seeing him made me feel happy, and made the whole experience more bearable for me.

He had come up to me afterwards and we had talked a bit, but I had been in a hurry to get back before the kids came home for lunch and hadn't been able to stay. Although we didn't talk long, I had felt his sympathy, felt that he knew how hard I found the whole thing. So that, when he said he might come by to talk about it with me when I wasn't so rushed, I hadn't made the kind of excuses I usually do. I'd just looked at him and said, "Yes, thank you, I'd like that." Then he'd smiled without replying, and I thought, oh dear, I probably fouled it up again by being too pushy when he was just being polite. But now, here he was, and I would have been more glad to see him if I hadn't been still in my grimy gardening jeans, with soil under my fingernails, and no brownies left to offer him.

But we had a cup of tea together, before the kids got back, and we talked about the inquest, and about old Kieran.

"He had everything the way he wanted in this city, you know," MacNally said. "It's a pretty corrupt place; most of the aldermen are in real estate or are lawyers heavily dependent upon it. They won't cross a man like Kieran."

"I know. It doesn't seem right, but somehow I can't believe God knocked him off because he contributed to the corruption around here."

MacNally smiled. "I know what you mean. His death does seem just a tad too neat."

I felt very comfortable with MacNally. Maybe that's why I could tell him about what was worrying me without feeling foolish. "That's just it. It's all so neat . . . too neat. I can't stop worrying about it. I knew Kieran was wrecking Tory Barton's garden. It's awful of me, but I think, maybe Tory . . . but I know that can't be right. I was there that night, and it was so dark you couldn't see your hand in front of your face. There was no way in God's green earth that Tory Barton could have known that Kieran would walk down the street at that time, and there was no way, even in the last minute before the accident, that Barton could have seen that he was about to hit him."

"That makes sense."

"So why do I keep worrying about it? It's not my fault, what happened. It's not my responsibility."

"Well, what do you think?"

"I wish I knew. Something about it is really bothering me. More than just the sad death of an old man, I mean." I found myself boasting a little. "I've always been good at figuring things out, putting the pieces together, you know? And somehow these pieces don't fit."

MacNally looked thoughtful. "Maybe you don't have all the pieces, maybe that's the problem."

"My husband always said that about me," I said, feeling my face go hot as I wondered if MacNally was laughing at me. "He used to say, 'You can't manage what's on your own plate; you shouldn't keep wanting to explain what's on other people's'."

"He sounds like kind of a jerk to me," MacNally said mildly.

"No, not at all," I said. "He is actually a very fine man. Very highly respected in External. Everyone says so. It's amazing how fast he's moved up. I just wasn't the right wife for him."

"Or he wasn't the right husband for you." MacNally looked around, noticing the shabbiness of the house, and the fact that there really wasn't quite enough furniture. "For a guy in External he doesn't seem to have looked after you as well as he might."

"That's what Tory Barton said. Do you think so too?" For some reason I felt I had to defend Marcus. It made it all worse somehow, if he too was at fault. "Why should he, if he doesn't want to? It's up to him, isn't it?"

"It's not just a measure of love," MacNally said. "It's also a measure of responsibility. But anyway, this isn't my business. I'm sorry if I seem to be pushing in." He smiled. "Just the lawyer's habit I guess, seeing everything in an adversarial light, with winners and losers. Please excuse me."

"Oh no, that's all right. But maybe you're right about Kieran. Maybe I don't have all the pieces."

"I'm pretty sure you don't," MacNally said. He was looking out the window as he spoke, not at me.

"Maybe I'll try to find a few more."

"I think you should. I think that would be a good idea. And will you let me know what you find out?"

"Do you want me to? You really don't think it's silly?"

"Not at all. I think it's eminently sensible."

"I'll do my best then."

He looked right at me this time not smiling. "Yes, please do. Let's keep in touch."

"Sorry you're so upset." Tory's face was all concern. He grasped my arm and drew me solicitously into the top level of his living room. There were big soft chairs and a sofa full of cushions positioned around the window. There was also a low glass table with a gold cigarette case, a big crystal bowl of cashews, and a silver wine bucket, sweating, with a bottle of French wine in it. Syrupy music with a heavy beat was playing, coming out of very large speakers.

"I'm upset too; I think it would do us both good to talk it over," he said.

I nodded, and tried to suppress my nervousness. How could I have been so stupid, I thought. Of course he would think my request to "talk over what had happened" meant I wanted him to make love to me. I ought to be used to awkward situations like this, but I'm not.

I sat down in a chair and ate some cashews. Luckily there wasn't any problem making conversation with Tory Barton.

He lounged back into the sofa. "I wake up in the night and feel the thud and see it all pass before my eyes," he said. "Poor old man. I bet he didn't even know what hit him."

"What I can't understand is," I said, through the cashews, while he gracefully poured me a glass of wine, "what the old fellow was doing out at that time of night."

"I can't understand it either," said Tory. "It's a total mystery to me. I just never would have expected it, not in a million years. A person would think that if he wanted to go down there to see how his building site was coming he would go in the daytime. Or drive his car, or at least be walking around with a flashlight, for God's sake!" His voice rose.

The very words "building site" seemed to cause his face to redden. "Did you see it? Did you see what he was doing?"

"Yes, I—"

"What he was doing was, it was inexcusable! The fill was falling over onto my grapevine and wrecking it! And cutting off the view of my garden!"

"I can't understand how the city— "

"I called our alderwoman. I said to her, 'I'm a taxpayer and something has to be done. Has to. This is a travesty! Doesn't a man have the right to enjoy his property in peace? Isn't your home still your castle, even in this day and age? But there's more to it than that,' I said to her. 'Do you know that I paid over twenty thousand dollars extra for the view rights? Do you know that? I'll fight this,' I told her, 'and I can afford to. I'll get an injunction. But that the city should be a party to it! It's unconscionable. Why do you do his bidding? The city—at his beck and call! Make no mistake about it'—I told her quite, quite clearly, believe me—'make no mistake about it. I'll sue the pants off him, and I'll sue the pants off the city.' "

"And what did she say?"

"Oh, she was upset. Mind you, aldermen don't have as much say as they used to; it's all planners nowadays. But she said she'd get right on it. Yes, I have to give her credit for that, at least. She called the municipality and this Mr. MacDonald came around and talked to me personally. But the long and the short of it was that they were going to go on loading up the fill until the damn site passed the percolation tests."

"And so, what did you do?"

He had forgotten me, forgotten to offer me another drink, a cigarette, forgotten to look meaningfully into my eyes.

"I have my contacts, you know. I got a look at the plans for the house. And I couldn't believe my eyes."

"What do you mean?"

Tory stood up and began walking around the room. "A monstrosity!" he cried out, waving his arm, indicating a large, shapeless something or other. "The house was an unbelievable abortion. A concrete bunker, a huge block of a thing which would shut out my view, shut out the sun from the entire east side of my garden. You know they had already just about killed my grapevine. I honestly thought that was the worst thing I had to face. But when I saw those plans I couldn't believe it. I called MacNally, my lawyer, as soon as I got home."

"What did he say?"

"What's that got to do with it? You don't ask your lawyer what to do. You *tell* him what to do, and if he won't do it, you get another one. I've had lots of lawyers and I know how to deal with them. That's what I was trying to explain to you when you told me about your divorce. You have to remember that lawyers are just hired help. I simply gave MacNally the outline of the case myself, and told him we had to get on to it at once."

At the sound of MacNally's name my heart made a sudden and surprising bang inside my chest. If he were involved why hadn't he said anything? If he were Tory Barton's lawyer it would explain why he was at the inquest. What else did it explain? I didn't have time to work it out, Tory Barton was in full flight.

"Of course, I had to warn him about running up costs. Lawyers think nothing of charging you every time they sneeze; you have to keep control. So naturally, I warned him I had no intention of paying for his ignorance. If he didn't know the law on this kind of thing I'd find someone who did, I told him straight out."

I felt suddenly that I was fed to the teeth with Tory Barton's obsession with money. Everything seemed to come down to that in the end. I guess my expression showed my disgust, because he became a bit defensive.

"Well, these lawyers, they'll charge you for their own research if you're not careful. After all, what other profession makes *you* pay when they have to look up information they should have learned in school or kept up on? Anyway, I told him, if he didn't know the law on this I'd find someone else who did. But, not to worry, he knows me and there was no problem. After all, we're old friends, MacNally and me. He knows how I think. Why a couple of times he's told me I ought to have been a lawyer myself. I've got the legal mind, you see. But then. . . ."

His voice sank, the pride went out of it, he sounded almost disappointed as he went on, ". . . for once, luck was on my side. Oh, I don't mean that the way it sounds. God knows, I wouldn't wish what happened on anybody. But there's no point in being a hypocrite . . . and I have to admit, that, at least . . . about the garden. . . ."

In the awkward pause that followed, I tried to lead the conversation back to the night of the accident. I tried to get a clear description of what happened. But Tory wandered off, first talking about his garden, obsessively, then trying again to see if I would confess that I was lonely and wanted his comforting embrace.

"Oh no, not lonely, not at all," I said with as much conviction as I could. "What with the kids . . . and the housework. . . ."

I thought "housework" would be a good word. I never knew a man who didn't find the very word off-putting. It's guaranteed to break up the kind of steamy atmosphere he was trying to create by talking about our loneliness, our need for comfort, and by pouring on the wine. I recognized the spacey feeling I get when I have drunk a little too much, and I noticed Tory's words were moving by in a kind of smooth rhythm, making a lot more sense than they should have, without really meaning anything. He was talking now about his loneliness, his need for someone understanding, about how two people. . . .

I got up and began looking for my purse.

"But why are you leaving? It's so nice, talking to you like this, I thought maybe we could. . . ." He came up to me and took my hand between his and stroked it gently. He was standing very close to me, looking into my eyes. The smell of his aftershave was overpowering.

I was angry and frightened. I pulled my hand out from his, stepped backward, and stumbled against the coffee table. He grabbed me and pulled me close, and I tensed at his touch. He didn't notice and I had to wrench free. His passionate expression changed to anger.

"What are you playing at anyway? *I* didn't ask you to come here, you know. God, how I hate women who tease."

"But . . . I just . . . a talk between friends . . . awfully upset about Kieran. . . ." I hurried towards the door with Tory right at my heels, talking angrily, his face red.

"I suppose you won't be happy unless you have the whole game: expensive restaurants, presents, flowers. . . . I thought we were both too old and too sensible for those silly games. And frankly," he went on, his voice spiteful, "you're lucky to get the chance. God, why do all women have to dance around beforehand. Jesus, it really pisses me off. We both know. . . ."

By then I was at the door, and I opened it gratefully. "No, I'm sorry, Tory, really. I'm sorry I gave you the wrong impression." Hating myself for apologizing to him, I hurried away, leaving him standing angrily in the doorway.

I turned back to look at him, and to wave apologetically, despite myself. He did not wave back. His face was dark red and his expression was spiteful and vindictive.

The kids were late coming home from school that day, and I was glad. I still wasn't over what had happened at Tory's house. Had I really led him on? Was it "asking for it" even to suggest to a neighbour that you were worried over the death of someone and needed to talk about it? It had seemed like a harmless way to get more of the "pieces" Rob MacNally and I had discussed.

But I had been kidding myself and I should have known better.

The stupid scene was all my fault. Probably it could have been handled properly—but it was too late for that now.

Only the two youngest, Timmy and Robert, were due back that afternoon. The other two had soccer practice. When they came in, Timmy was bleeding from a long cut on his shinbone. I bandaged it, worrying about whether I ought to take him to Emergency and get it stitched up. I never know for sure which cuts need stitches and which don't. But the thought of waiting in Emergency for an hour or two while the other two kids came back to an empty house decided me to take the chance this one would be okay.

"What happened?" I asked, when the tears were dry, the comforting done, and the bandage securely in place. There was a long silence. Robert looked stricken. "I won't scold you, Robert," I said. "I'm sure it was an accident."

"Oh it was, Mommy, it was," he said eagerly, running up to me and butting his little head in my lap, where I knelt, gathering up Band-aid wrappers from the bathroom floor. "I didn't mean to do it; it was an accident. Truly. Cross my heart and hope to die, stick a needle in my eye."

I shuddered at the image. "Don't say that." I took him in my arms and his tears soaked into my shirt.

"I didn't mean to knock him off his bike and he fell in front of a car and almost got killed like Mr. Kieran and it *really* was an accident. You said, Mommy. Like that. But I don't get it. How come, if Timmy got out of the way and got his bike out of the way, how come Mr. Kieran didn't?"

I sat down in the wicker chair in the bathroom, feeling very weak, suddenly, and seeing, in that instant, the headlights of Tory's car wavering the instant before the impact, as if the car had turned towards the road edge. I held Robert tightly in my lap with one arm and reached out and drew Timmy close with the other. With the boys held close, I listened to all the details of the boys' near accident.

"Let's forget all these horrible things." I hugged the boys. "But what *I* don't understand," I said, half to myself, "is what Mr. Kieran was *doing* that night."

"Oh, Mommy. I'm surprised at you," crowed Timmy, mimicking my favourite phrase of reproach. "You're supposed to know everything and be a witch like Daddy said."

"Yes Mommy, I'm surprised at you too," Robert said happily. "'Cause *we* know all about it."

"I give up," I said.

"Mr. Kieran went every night, exactly at eleven, to the place where they were putting the dirt, Mommy," Robert told me.

"Yes, and he stayed for half an hour *precisely,*" Timmy added, using Jack Webster's voice.

"How do you guys know that?" I wanted to know. "You're supposed to be asleep at 11:00." But it was obvious. They must be sneaking out of their room at night to watch the smelt fishermen. I had noticed wet running shoes the last few mornings and sand on the kitchen floor when I swept up after breakfast.

The boys gave each other meaningful looks. Robert said, "It was Mark's idea. But once we saw that old Kieran out in the middle of the night, we kind of spied on him. It was neat; Mark said you could set a watch by the old bugger."

Ignoring Robert's language I said, "But why? What did he do there?"

"He just sat on the big rock, there, you know, and sort of talked to himself," Timmy said.

"You didn't happen to hear what he said?"

But I had already realized what Kieran was doing there. I understood why he came, in the night, to sit alone and look at his new building site that meant so much to him. He was dreaming of the fitting tribute he would build for his sister, Mary.

I had heard people talking about his devotion to her, or maybe his obsession would be a better way of putting it. He came to sit there and commune with Mary, and to discuss the house with her. Promising that nothing and no one would stop the project which would store up glory in heaven for her, and give him honour in her eyes.

I had a talk with the boys about their sneaking out at night, and later, I knew, I would have to ground Mark who, it appeared, was the ringleader. Probably have to ground all of them. They knew they were forbidden to go out at night, and most especially forbidden to go near the water. How do you get kids to obey? I wish I knew.

Finally I asked the question whose answer I feared. I asked it of Mark that night, just before the goodnight kiss. "Mark," I said hesitantly, "do you think Mr. Barton knew about Kieran coming down here every night?"

I waited for the answer. Mark took after me. He had the habit of making leaps from small details to the explanation of what had happened, and he, too, usually turned out to be right. It was a quality which his father had never liked in him; Marcus would shout at him and call him a know-it-all. That was one of the reasons I didn't miss Marcus as much as I might have.

"Yes, Mommy," said Mark. He was drowsy. The long scolding, the tears, a hot bath, and now the goodnight kiss, warm and relaxing. He was half asleep. "I've been worrying about it anyway, after the accident. Mr. Barton used to stand in his kitchen window and watch Mr. Kieran sitting there. I saw it, Mommy. Just before eleven, just before old Kieran came along, Mr. Barton would turn off his kitchen lights. But you could still see him, if you knew he was there, sort of a faint shadow. And he'd stand there, in the dark, and look, and watch old Kieran. And old Kieran would sit on that big rock, and smoke that stinky pipe, and talk to himself out loud. Sometimes he'd look up at the house where Barton was standing but I don't think he could see him. *I* wouldn't have known Mr. Barton was there if I hadn't seen him turn off his lights so he could look out into the dark. Anyway, Kieran sat under the streetlight at the end of the road; it kind of shines on that rock, you know? He was easy to see. They were in a fight, it seemed like, sort of looking at each other and figuring out their plans. Something like a game. But not knowing the other knew he was there, you know what I mean?"

His voice was getting fainter. "The whole thing made me

feel yucky. They were both real losers, Mommy. I wish somebody else besides Mr. Barton had that awesome garden. . . ."

So Tory had lied. He knew Kieran came down to his plot of land at the end of the lane every night. He knew then. And if he watched as Mark described he must know everything about it. Where on the road Kieran walked, what time he arrived, what time he left—everything.

Was Tory Barton clever enough, and mean enough . . . or was the word, evil? Was Tory Barton clever enough and evil enough to plan to kill a helpless old man and then to carry through the plan in such risky circumstances?

And if it were true, what I feared, what was my part in it? Was I partly at fault? I realized I had been frightened all along that somehow I was part of the bad thing that had happened.

I struggled with the idea of Tory doing this thing; and I found I couldn't believe it. He was one of the "perfect" people, one of those people who are always in control, with his neat, orderly elegant house, and his neat, orderly elegant garden. How could such a man take such a risk: trusting in his position in the community to escape blame, and using a neighbour as a witness, to run down a frail old man?

I didn't want to think about my part in this little play.

Had Tory Barton been sizing me up all along? Casting me for a part in his terrible drama? I remembered his remark at the party about my "turning into a pumpkin at eleven". Because he knew that, he might have been able to time the accident. If I had agreed to accept a ride with him, he could have delayed our departure until the time was right. But he hadn't worried. He had known that because I always left before the 11:00 porno movies, he could count on my being on that long stretch of the road at the right time one way or the other. And, remembering his surprised and angry face when I ran from his house that last time it was easy to believe he had thought I was completely foolish and controllable until that moment.

The plan itself—that was easier to deal with. It was hard to escape the idea that there was no simpler way to kill someone in Canada right now and get away with it. Pretend to be a bit drunk, pretend it was an accident. Even if you were tried and sentenced—and that hadn't happened to Tory; the police hadn't pressed charges—if you were rich and had good lawyers you could keep appealing and eventually get off with a fine. But the most likely outcome was what had happened to Tory—nothing. He had only to pick a night of a neighbourhood party and find a fool for a witness. He had succeeded in doing both.

But then, I told myself, I was making something from nothing, blowing it all up out of proportion. After all, Tory himself had told me that he could stop Kieran's building legally; and that he had been going to do it.

But he had lied when he said he didn't know what Kieran was doing, walking down the lane that night. Lied that he didn't expect to see him. Maybe there was another lie in the story about his conversation with his lawyer.

I remembered, suddenly, the way MacNally had looked when we had discussed the accident. I knew now that he had known more than he had been able to say. Why had he come to see me the day after the inquest and encouraged me to find the "missing pieces"? He surely hadn't been drawn by my beauty.

No, even in my misery I knew that wasn't fair. MacNally liked me, and had been concerned about me. It was a surprise to me to realize that I was sure of that; sure that the friendship we felt for each other didn't have something nasty lurking behind it too. But even so, even with that understood, I realized for the first time that MacNally had some other purpose as well. Lawyers had their professional ethics; there were things about their clients they couldn't say. But something must have happened to make him suspicious. What if MacNally thought Tory had a motive, but knew he couldn't talk about it unless he was sure enough of the other things—that Tory *knew* Kieran would be down there, and when he would be down there?

I felt sick inside. My head ached, and I wanted to escape into some fresh air, but the pressure was inside me. It looked as if I would have to bear up under it until I knew the whole story. I reached for the phone to call MacNally and tell him I had got hold of some pieces, the picture was taking shape, and he had better come over and see if, now, any of *his* pieces looked like they belonged in the puzzle.

"I came to the inquest because I had reason to be worried about that accident," Rob MacNally told me.

We were sitting at the kitchen table the next morning. The kids were gone, the house was quiet and peaceful, with the sounds of the waves on the rocks coming in quietly through the open window. I felt sickish and dragged out. I had not slept the night before, even when Rob said he would come over first thing next morning. Hearing what I had learned he had promised to tell me everything he knew, explaining that he had not wanted to talk about it before because of lawyer-client privilege. Now, he said, things had gone beyond that. We agreed we had to thrash the whole thing out right away. The more I talked to Rob MacNally, the more I liked him; and it ought to have been comforting to have him on my side. But when I remembered how I stood there and watched as the car struck the old man I felt so bad that it seemed as if nothing could help.

Still, in the morning, after several cups of coffee, I had my wits about me a little more than I had the night before, and I was starting to get used to what then had seemed unthinkable. "And the inquest put your mind at rest, did it?" I asked Rob.

"Yes, at first. Just as you said yourself, there seemed no way that Tory could be criminally involved. My problem was that knowing him, as I do, and knowing how he felt about that old man and his house, I couldn't stop worrying about it."

I understood that. "He consulted you about the house, I know. But he told me he was going to sue, so I thought that side of things was all under control. He said there was no problem."

I noticed the rims of Rob's ears go pink as I spoke. "Well, he lied. I told him as I would tell you, or anybody that asked me, that it was impossible in this city to succeed in stopping a man like Kieran from building a house on his own property—"right to enjoyment of the view'' clauses or easements notwithstanding. That's a reality around here, and a man as experienced as Tory Barton would know that as well as you or I would.''

''But if he still wanted to fight, why would you object?''

''You don't take on a case when you haven't a chance of winning. It's against legal ethics. Sometimes we lawyers try to talk a client out of something because we know the chances of success are slight, and we want to be sure the client is really keen enough to go on to the finish. I've had conversations like that with Tory and with plenty of other clients. I make it a principle never to let a client sue on principle. But if, after they calm down, they still want to sue, and there's any possibility of winning, and they know that it's going to cost, then well, of course, I'll give it my best shot.

''But when it's absolutely hopeless I say so. I have to. And I have to refuse the case. That's how I do business. Tory simply had to accept it when I explained to him that this was not a case he could win, and this was a case I was not prepared to fight for him.''

He smiled. ''You know Tory. Do you think he would have paid my fees after I spent time and money fighting a case we were bound to lose?''

''What did he say? Did he accept it, that he couldn't take Kieran to court?''

''Not at first,'' Rob said. ''But we went at it a bit, and eventually he seemed to get the idea.''

''How did he take it?''

''Just as you'd expect. He told me he'd get a lawyer who had more balls, that he'd fly down to Vancouver to find the best, and that obviously I was only good for the small-town stuff.''

I felt hurt for Rob. I could accept Tory's meanness more easily when it was directed at me than when it was directed at Rob. I could feel myself flushing.

''Don't let it get to you,'' Rob said gently. ''People like Tory Barton always know where to stick the knife. They specialize in going after what they sense are your weak points. But Tory tended to miss the mark with me. A remark like that might have hurt me when I was younger, but believe me, I've heard worse. It just rolls right off me now. No, *that's* not what's got me upset. It was worrying about what had really happened with that accident."

We talked a while longer, and then Rob called the police, right from the kitchen phone. He said he knew a few people there, and it would be easier for him. I sat at the kitchen table, smoking, watching him, but only listening from time to time. I was thinking about Tory Barton, and what kind of man he was, and what he had done. I was finally accepting the truth about it; and it wasn't easy. From the bits of conversation I did take in, I could tell that Rob was getting his point across. The police would reopen the matter of Kieran's death.

And I was responsible for that. I started to use the word "fault", to think "that's my fault" but I stopped myself. When I looked back on the events since the coroner's inquest I was surprised to realize that I was not sorry about what had happened. I knew, and somehow it made me feel good knowing it, that I could not have done anything else than what I had done and that it had been the right thing to do. The fact that Rob MacNally felt the same way was a help, but it wasn't the whole story.

Now that Tory Barton has gone, the garden, under its new owners is slowly growing wilder and more ordinary. I can enjoy looking at it to my heart's content. Even though it has lost some of its strange seductive magic, but I find it, if possible, even more beautiful. I take a little responsibility for that, for the garden's new beauty. Maybe that's why living here now, in the big old house, with the kids and the dog doesn't seem as hard as it used to.

Dame Millicent's Revenge

TIM HEALD

Born in Dorchester, Dorset, England, Timothy Villiers Heald earned a B.A. (Honours) in modern history from Balliol College, Oxford, in 1965, going on to a career in journalism. He wrote the "Atticus" column in the Sunday Times, *London, from 1965 to 1967 and has been feature editor of* Town *magazine, feature writer with the* Daily Express, *and as a freelance writer has contributed to* Punch, *the* Spectator, *and the* New Statesman. *His first mystery novel,* Unbecoming Habits, *appeared in 1973 and introduced detective Simon Bognor, an investigative agent with the British Board of Trade. Bognor, of whom Heald says: "He smokes, drinks, and takes no exercise", has bumbled effectually through six more novels:* Blue Blood Will Out *(1974),* Deadline *(1975),* Let Sleeping Dogs Die *(1976),* Just Desserts *(1979),* Murder at Moose Jaw *(1981), and* A Small Masterpiece *(1982). Heald has also written the biographies of both Prince Charles* (H.R.H.: The Man Who Will Be King, *with Mayo Mohs in 1979) and the hero of "The Avengers", John Steed* (John Steed: An Authorized Biography *in 1977).*

DAME MILLICENT LISKEARD of Rose Cottage, Brambledene Parva, Wiltshire, was a creature of habit. Ever since school she had begun her day with five minutes of toe-touching and knees-bending which she referred to with a smile as her "physical jerks"; she then did the *Times* crossword; and only when the crossword was complete (quarter of an hour on a bad day) did she take breakfast. Breakfast was two slices of wholemeal bread lightly singed and topped with a thin spread of English butter and a thicker layer of her sister Gwendolyn's Oxford marmalade made from a secret recipe handed down via their uncle the Archdeacon. It was ever thus and would continue to be so, for when you have reached a certain age and are universally acknowledged as the world's leading authority on newts you do not lightly change the habits of a lifetime. "Not bloody likely," riposted the Dame, when her sister Gwendolyn suggested she switch from butter to something with a little less cholesterol, "Margarine wouldn't melt in my mouth."

It was a dank, green English summer morning and Dame Millicent was half way through her second slice of toast and a tiresomely dyspeptic book review by Woodrow Wyatt when there was a knock at the front door followed by the inimitable greeting call of her good friend and neighbour Colonel Freddie Barrington-Potter, otherwise known as "Pukka Chukka".

"Hello there!" he brayed. "Anyone at home?"

"In the morning room," she called back. "Come and have a

cuppa char." She drank Lapsang Souchong which the Colonel called "gnat's pee".

"Don't mind if I do," he replied, adding as he always did on these occasions, "I've brought my own bag." The kettle was simmering on the lower of the Aga cooker's two burners, so it took little time to brew a small pot of very strong Lyons' Indian tea and lace it liberally with milk and sugar. Only then did the Colonel emerge to face the woman they called "The Last of the Great Detectives". He Watson, she Holmes.

"Seen the *Times*?" he enquired, dangerously.

"In a manner of speaking." She was always loath to commit herself without good cause.

He glared. "Obviously not," she said. "They've led the paper with some absolutely putrid story about the Dodo."

The Dame put down her toast very carefully and turned to the newspaper. She folded away the disagreeable little book review and went to the front page which she read, frowning. Based almost entirely on a variety of unnamed sources in various shadowy reaches of British intelligence it told how Sir Arlington Dodderidge, Fellow of All Souls' College, Oxford, had been the most treacherous traitor of them all. Apparently he made Blunt look like a sharp instrument. Thousands of British agents had gone to their deaths because of what Sir Arlington, the incredibly secret head of a British department so secret that even now its identity could not be revealed, had told the Russians, the Chinese, the Bulgars, and even the Albanians. He had, according to the unnamed sources, been spilling the beans to anyone who chose to listen.

"Bilge," said Dame Millicent, when she had finished. "A tissue of lies from beginning to end. Only 'tissue' is altogether too flimsy a word. I don't know what that paper is coming to."

"It's the yellow perils," said the Colonel morosely. The paper had recently been acquired by a man from Hong Kong.

"Extremely fishy." Dame Millicent took a bite of toast. "It all appears to be based on this forthcoming book by someone called Perkins."

"Does it?" The Colonel was suffering from brain-fag. He was not at his best in the mornings and was beginning to feel he had overdone it.

"Of course it does, noodle. Listen, it's in the second paragraph, 'In his new book, *The Nth Man*, Gavin Perkins, a leading authority on the world's intelligence services, reveals that . . .' and so on and so forth, blah blah blah!"

"Ah," said the Colonel, brightening, "so it's just a publicity stunt!"

"Not *just* a publicity stunt. But still, in a sense a publicity stunt. It doesn't make it any less damaging. Typical of that sort of creep to wait until the Dodo's dead before maligning him."

The Dodo had died only two years before. The Dame and the Colonel had been to the funeral, an ill-attended affair which was only to be expected. The Dodo had been ninety-six. He had outlived nearly all his contemporaries. The Colonel and the Dame had been among his most junior acolytes.

"You don't suppose"—Pukka Chukka stared wearily into his thick dark tea—"you don't suppose there's anything in it? I mean I did always rather wonder about the Dodo and sex. He never married after all."

Dame Millicent stared disbelievingly at her old friend. "How on earth could you possibly *wonder* about the Dodo and sex?" she enquired. "*Everyone* knew the Dodo was as bent as a corkscrew, but when it came to his job he was as straight as a die."

The Colonel seemed rather taken aback by this pronouncement, running his finger around the inside of his collar, avoiding the Dame's eyes and turning pink.

The Dame smiled tolerantly. "Didn't he ever make a pass at you in the gents'?" she asked fondly.

"Millicent! Really!" The Colonel was quite upset. As the Dame frequently reminded him, he was, when it came to sex, "an awful noodle". There had once been a Mrs. Barrington-Potter and between them they had produced two sons, now grown up. Unfortunately the Colonel's wife had passed away in that same sad incident which had cost him his left eye somewhere north of Rawalpindi and that, as far as sex was concerned, was that. Ever since, he had remained celibate in thought, word, and most certainly deed.

"I sometimes wonder," said Dame Millicent, "if your knowledge of homosexuality is any greater than Queen Victoria's of lesbianism."

"It's what long-haired Johnnies in School House used to get up to behind the pavilion," he said, sourly.

"I understand it's quite popular in the Brigade of Guards." The Dame chuckled.

"Exactly!" As far as he was concerned she had proved his point. He himself had served most of his career with an impeccably heterosexual if not very aristocratic county regiment of light infantry.

"In any case," said the Dame, "I have to tell you that our friend the Dodo was a raging queen. In fact, if you did but know it, many of your best friends have been raging queens. It's just that you never noticed."

"I've never held a man's colour or religion against him," said the Colonel. "You know that."

"Nor sex?"

"Nor sex."

"Well at least we agree about that. And I take it that we are also agreed that the Dodo's reputation should not be tarnished by some pipsqueak twerp of an author who wants to make a fast buck out of a piece of cheap sensationalism."

"My sentiments precisely." The Colonel felt on surer ground. Personal loyalty was one of his strong suits.

"In that case take your tea back home while we titivate and get out the Alvis. We're going in to Salisbury. To the bank."

"To the bank? Whatever for? They'll cash a cheque at the village shop. We surely don't. . . ." The Colonel was nonplussed but Dame Millicent shooed him out, telling him not to try to understand but simply to do as he was told. This he was quite happy to do. It often surprised her that dear Freddie should have once commanded a battalion of some eight hundred men. Women, especially women like her, were so much better suited to command.

It did not take her long to change into sensible Salisbury clothes: sensible two-piece grey flannel suit, sensible low-heeled walking shoes, sensible cultured pearls on a string, all given freshness with a sensible splash of sensible eau-de-cologne. To a casual observer she looked wonderfully ordinary and unthreatening. It was the perfect disguise.

She refused to tell Freddie why they were going to the bank. Instead she spent most of the half-hour drive explaining the morning's crossword clues to a disconsolate Colonel who seldom managed to finish the puzzle at all (but who, if the truth be told, did not really try). It was a simple drive and the Colonel drove with a soldier's easy superiority and disdainful disregard for other road users. Occasionally he would mutter "Bloody man!" or "Typical woman driver" when another car intruded on his progress, but essentially he behaved as if he were driving his jeep across North Africa in the direction of Rommel.

At the bank, the Dame asked to see the manager, and they were, gratifyingly, shown into his office within minutes. The manager had known her for many years and she was what was known as a "valued customer". Also, should the occasion demand, a decidedly difficult customer.

The Dame did not beat about the bush. Bush-beating was not in character.

"You have a letter for me from Sir Arlington Dodderidge," she said.

Colonel Barrington-Potter gave a start. "I say, old girl . . ." he began, but he was quelled by a frosty, silencing glance, a glance which never failed, no matter who the target.

"You should find it among my things," she said. "If my records are correct you will see that it was deposited on June 15th, 1951."

The manager nodded. "I'll attend to it at once," he said absenting himself with ingratiating nervousness. When he had shut the door behind him Freddie Barrington-Potter said, sharply,

"That's just after Burgess and Maclean defected to Moscow."

The Dame smiled. You had to hand it to Freddie. Whatever his failings he had a marvellous, if selective, memory of dates.

"Spot on," she said, "and your instincts are correct. There is a connection. The Dodo was deeply disturbed by the Maclean-Burgess business. He'd known them both, of course, though they were Cambridge men and he was at Oxford. You'll remember that it started a regular little witch-hunt. Everybody was suspected of being the third man or the fourth man or some such nonsense. The Dodo was suspected along with everyone else and for some reason he never explained he was desperately worried that something might happen to him. He was afraid that he'd be bumped off in such a way that it would look like suicide because of a guilty conscience. You know the sort of thing: the traitor who could no longer live with his treachery. There'd have been a note."

"But—" began the Colonel.

"Oh yes," she interrupted, "he lived to a ripe old age and died in bed. Whoever it was didn't dare attempt anything until now."

"But what's the point?"

"I very much hope," said the Dame, "that we are about to find out. If I'm correct then this is a posthumous revenge. None the less satisfying for being posthumous."

Presently the bank manager returned with an air of subdued and deferential triumph, as well as a yellow envelope covered in faded sepia scrawl. "I think this is what you asked for, Dame Millicent. If you'd oblige me by signing for it. . . ."

The Dame duly obliged but did not open it until they had regained the security of the Colonel's moth-eaten but serviceable old car. As he crashed the gears through the city centre she began to read the many pages of handwriting, delivering spoken summary as she went. It was in essence much as she had predicted.

"Strange," she said, "reading something written thirty years ago for the first time. Certainly takes you back. He was obviously fearfully upset by the Maclean–Burgess thing. But he doesn't seem to mention Philby or Blunt. There's a whole lot of stuff here about a woman called Dolores da Silva. . . . Oh, I remember Dolores. Ravishing Goanese girl who was supposed to have seduced Stalin though, of course, oh now hang on a jiffy, this is interesting . . . the Dodo seems to think she actually did have an affair with Molotov. I don't believe that but still you never know. Ah, I see. She was originally working for us. In fact she was one of the Dodo's operators; but then it seems the Dodo suspected she'd switched allegiance and instigated enquiries. There's a lot of boring stuff here about Tito and the partisans in Yugoslavia. I'm going to skip that and come back if it's really relevant."

They were out of the town centre now, passing through a ribbon development put up in the thirties, a grubby brick finger stretching out into the lush green countryside. The Alvis began to pick up speed.

"Forgive me," the Colonel was wary, anxious not to appear foolish, "I don't see where this chap Perkins comes into it."

"Nor do I, yet." The Dame was frowning over the inky old scrawl. "I wish he'd used a typewriter," she said. "He always did have the most ghastly handwriting. Aha! I see. Would you believe it? Dolores seduced one of the Dodo's boyfriends. What a hoot! Not good for security. I do see why he was worried though. It seems that he found out for certain that she was working for the other side at almost exactly the moment that she made off with his fancy man. Dear, oh dear, what a web we weave."

"So what did he do?" Colonel Barrington-Potter passed a tractor and trailor, cutting in sharply to avoid an oncoming Land Rover at which he swore absent-mindedly and without rancour.

"I'm coming to that." She squinted at the paper. "He seems to have fired her but not turned her in. One reason he gives is that the boat had been rocked enough already. Another scandal so soon after Burgess and Maclean would be bad for national morale. The Americans would have cut us off completely. The other thing is that the ex-boyfriend came to see him and because the Dodo was fond of him *et cetera et cetera*. He doesn't say that the boyfriend threatened to make his homosexuality public but it's implicit. Anyway boyfriend was apparently appeased but not Dolores. Dolores insisted she was innocent and that the whole thing was a put-up job."

The Colonel turned off the main road on to a lane with high, flowery banks. It was impossible to see oncoming traffic more than twenty yards ahead but this in no way interfered with his speed which remained constant. He did, however, blow an occasional fruity raspberry on the horn.

"Could she have been right?" he asked with a chivalrous respect for the weaker sex. "Dodo couldn't have made a mistake, could he?"

The Dame was turning over some photocopies pinned to the main text of the Dodo's screed. "I don't think so," she said, "the evidence looks pretty damning. These are copies of notes Dolores passed to the Russians. Also there's a photo of her talking in some park to none other than our old friend Dmitri Smirnov."

"That bastard!" said the Colonel.

"Precisely. I'm afraid there's not much doubt about it. Dolores was in it up to her neck."

"Then she should have been thoroughly grateful to the Dodo for not turning her in. He could have had her hanged."

"Well life's not like that, is it?"

The Colonel said he supposed not.

The rest of the journey passed in silence. Both of them were alone with thoughts of espionage and counter-espionage, of double agents and triple crosses, the true nature of loyalty, of patriotism, of friendship, and much else besides. Once home the Colonel said he would walk the dogs. The Dame told him she had some telephone calls to make.

They lunched together at the Cat and Fiddle, Brambledene's village pub. The Dame, ordering a schooner of dry sherry, was in a state of some excitement. The Colonel blew froth off his pint of bitter and asked why.

"Because I've put the cat among the pigeons that's why! I've had words with Sigmund Fortescue who runs Albatross Books. Perkins is one of their authors, and Sigmund is a friend of friends. Put the fear of God into him and also winkled Perkins' phone number out of him. Spoke to Perkins and, after a few well-chosen words from me, he's coming down here on the five o'clock train. We'll dine here and I'll book him a room. But on no account are you to meet his train. After what he's said about the Dodo he can pay for his own taxicab. I thought I asked for dry sherry. This stuff is perfectly foul. If they can't do better than this I shall have a gin."

A friendly argument ensued between mine host, one Albert, about the quality of the sherry, and they ordered two ploughman's lunches.

"What did Mr. Perkins have to say for himself ?" asked the Colonel.

"Not a lot. He seemed surprised that I should have any special knowledge of the matter. Said he knew I was a world authority on newts but had no idea I knew about anything else. Which sounds rather offensive. I don't think he meant it to. He seemed quite agreeable but not unduly bright. Only a boy really, according to Sigmund, and got a first at university which has done him no good whatever. Thinks he has all the answers."

"I know the type," said the Colonel morosely.

It was not altogether an unpainful encounter. Perkins was a man in his early thirties and green corduroy. He was slight and sallow.

"Touch of the tar brush," thought the Colonel so unforgiveably that he did not even whisper it to his friend, the Dame.

Somehow they avoided coming to the matter under discussion until dinner was finished and they were on to coffee, cheroots, and port. Some people never mixed business with pleasure. The English, for whom food was seldom a pleasure, nevertheless considered it bad form to mix it with business.

"I take it your mother is dead," said the Dame unexpectedly.

Mr. Perkins seemed as surprised as Colonel Barrington-Potter.

"My parents were both killed in a car accident three years ago. Why do you ask?"

The Dame sucked on her small cigar and said, "Mr. Perkins, please may I be frank?"

"I should like that very much indeed."

"Mr. Perkins," the Dame leaned forward and smiled not altogether endearingly, "I'm afraid you may not altogether like what I have to say. Before I say it, are you prepared to withdraw the allegations you have made about Sir Arlington Dodderidge?"

"Of course not."

The Dame sighed. "Then I have no alternative. It's clear to me that your book is based almost entirely on published sources. The single exception to this is the evidence in your mother's papers. She is the sole source for your infamous allegations."

Perkins had gone very white. "I was alerted by what I found in my mother's papers," he conceded, slowly, "but it all stands up. I'm convinced it's true."

"Your mother disliked Sir Arlington very much," said the Dame, quietly. "He dismissed her because he discovered that she was—not to put too fine a point on it—working for the other side."

"That's a lie," said Perkins.

The Colonel's eyes darted incredulously from one to the other, like the umpire at a tennis match. He was extremely uncertain about what was taking place.

"I can prove it," said the Dame in a voice you could have frozen daiquiris with, "and will." Saying which she reached under the table and produced from a capacious handbag photostats of the documents which had been included with the Dodo's letter. "These," she continued, "may well be upsetting, but I think you will find them conclusive. Your mother was certainly not Sir Arlington's victim. Rather the reverse. And I am sure you will see that if it were shown that the sole or even the primary source of your allegations about him came from a proven traitress, then. . . ."

"If that were so," said Perkins, first signs of doubt creeping into his voice, "then why didn't Sir Arlington turn her in?"

The Dame smiled tolerantly. "Because, dear boy, Sir Arlington was a gentleman."

Later, over a nightcap at Rose Cottage, the Colonel said, "So, you think that's the last we'll hear of that?"

The Dame said yes.

"How did you know Dolores was his mother?" The Colonel sniffed at his whisky.

"Guesswork. She was the most likely source and he looked dusky. Could have been wrong but worth a try." She seemed surprisingly gloomy for someone who had so speedily solved a problem and prevented further insult to an old dead friend.

"You didn't mention that his father was a boyfriend of the Dodo's."

"There was no need. It would have been pure sadism. Bad enough for the boy to discover his mother was a traitress. Too much to discover his father was a queer. All in the same evening."

"Quite." The Colonel frowned. "Dashed clever of the Dodo to have put together all that evidence. Fast too. I didn't realize he was such a hot-shot operator."

The Dame sighed. "That's what bothers me. The more I think about it, the more I realize that those photostats and the picture could only have come from one source."

The Colonel put down his glass and stared at her.

"You don't mean?"

"I'm afraid I do." The Dame dabbed at a smudge of mascara below one eye. "I should have remembered. He had a preference for good-looking men as well. And it's the only way the Dodo could have put together that weight of evidence so quickly. I'm afraid, dear Noodle, that perhaps our hero, Sir Arlington, may have been twice bent. Not that we should say anything. But it does seem as if his relationship with a certain Russian may have been closer than desirable."

Colonel Freddie Barrington-Potter took a deep draught of Scotch.

"Good grief!" he said, "that bastard Smirnov!"

Wish You Were Here

FRANK JONES

Frank Jones is a columnist for the Toronto Star. *He has won a national news award for reporting, a Southam fellowship, and is a former Ottawa Bureau chief and London, England Bureau chief for the Toronto* Star.

Born in 1937 in Luton, England, he is married and has six children. Wish You Were Here *is based on an anecdote his sister-in-law told him which she claimed was true.*

THEY WERE WALKING towards the car when Dorothy noticed him. "Isn't he darling, Norah," she said stopping and pointing. On the way home from Norah's cottage they had made their usual stop at the doughnut shop and, coming out, Dorothy's eye had been caught by an object in the garden centre next door.

"Kinda cute," her friend agreed. "If you like that sort of thing."

"But I do," said Dorothy. "And I know exactly the place for him. You know that spot alongside the irises in the rockery—sort of an arbour?"

Norah nodded.

"Well, can't you just see him perched there? Come on, Norah. Let's see how much they want."

The sign said "Van Houten", and it wasn't hard to place the ruddy-faced man taking off his leather gloves as a Dutchman. "Can I help you ladies?" The rolling L-sound was a dead giveaway.

"I was interested in that gnome," said Dorothy. "How much are you asking?"

"He's a cute little rascal, isn't he," said the nurseryman. "Well, he's marked at twenty-five dollars." He seemed to be thinking. "Look, I'll tell you what happened. I sold him once already, but the people brought him back for credit. Didn't suit their garden, I guess. I'll let you have him for twenty dollars."

"Do you really want it?" Norah asked in an undertone. "Don't you think it's a bit, well, corny?"

Dorothy walked around the gnome, admiring the red and white toadstool on which he sat and the mischievous expression on his face. "Yes," she said at last. "Yes, I really want him. Norah, you don't mind, do you, if we put him in the trunk? Will you put him in the back of the car for us?" she asked the nurseryman.

When they got to Dorothy's place, Norah went to give her a hand lifting the gnome. "Wait, I'll get the wheelbarrow. He's heavier than I thought," said Dorothy. They trundled him across the lawn and then, bracing their feet against the rocks, lifted him into position.

"Doesn't he look just perfect there?" Dorothy bubbled. "As if the spot had just been waiting for him."

"Not bad," said Norah.

"Ted, when he was alive, never liked ornamental things in the garden, but now there's only myself to please. No," she said, putting her hand on Norah's arm, "I'll put the wheelbarrow away later. Come inside and I'll put the kettle on for tea."

When Norah had gone home, Dorothy went out again and swivelled the gnome until his lop-sided grin was directed towards the living-room picture window. "There, Mr. Gnome, now I'll be able to enjoy you winter and summer," she said. The gnome, one eye half-closed in the beginnings of a wink, seemed to be agreeing with her.

"He sure looks cute, Mrs. Graham." She gave a start and turned around. It was only Norman, the mailman, standing there with his empty bag, but she felt her cheeks flush at the thought that he might have heard her talking to herself.

"Just puts a nice finishing touch to the garden," he said, flicking back the lick of hair that always got behind his glasses. Norman was only in his mid-twenties, but he took an almost fatherly interest in the older people on his route. If he didn't see one of his customers for a couple of days, he'd make a point of knocking to make sure everything was all right.

"That's just what I thought," said Dorothy gratefully. "The spot seems made for him."

She had her housecoat on and was having breakfast in the kitchen next morning when the doorbell rang. Through the window at the side door she could see it was Norman, and she wondered idly who would be sending her a registered letter this time of year.

"Morning, Mrs. Graham," he said. "Thought I better tell you —them kids have been up to mischief again. Look what they did to your dwarf."

"Gnome, Norman," she said, stepping out onto the porch. The gnome had been tipped from his perch and was lying face-down among the Sweet William.

"I'll put it up again for you," he said, resting his bag on the steps. "Maybe it was those Allen boys." He and Dorothy had talked before about the random incidents of petty vandalism that seemed to plague the neighbourhood in cycles. "For sale" signs would be pulled up in the night and stuck in front of other houses, lawn chairs would be tipped over, and flowerbeds trampled. Dorothy realized it wasn't fair to blame the Allen boys, but sometimes when they went down the street shouting obscenities with their friends and hitting every road sign they passed, it was hard to believe they were not behind the mischief.

"Well, thank you, Norman. It was very kind of you," she said as he picked up his bag after righting the gnome.

After breakfast she took a damp cloth out to the garden and wiped away the earth staining the gnome's face. "There you are, old fellow," she said. "Feel better now?" He smiled his slightly conspiratorial smile.

For a couple of days nothing more happened. Then one morning when she went to the window she was surprised to see that he had been pushed over again. "This is too much!" she said furiously. "Too much! I'm going to put a stop to it right now."

She put on her shoes and, not even bothering to lift the gnome up again, strode up the street to the slightly run-down bungalow where the Allens lived. Old yellowed newspapers clung to the fence and a tired-looking dog rolled off the step and sniffed Dorothy's leg half-heartedly.

"Look, Mrs. Allen," she said when the pasty, somewhat overweight woman she knew only by sight opened the door, "I don't want to make any trouble, but I'm afraid those boys of yours have been causing damage in my garden."

"My boys?" She grabbed the elastic of her underwear and yanked it up under her stained yellow dress.

"Yes," Dorothy went on. "Someone keeps pushing over my garden ornament, and I'm sure they know something about it."

"My boys, eh? Well, let me tell you something, you snoopy old bat. My Tom's gone out to Calgary to visit his uncle, and Fred's working up north with the forestry. So don't be so bloody quick to blame people what ain't done nothin'." And she slammed the door.

Dorothy stood for a moment at a loss. Her face was hot with embarrassment as she turned and walked down the path, not daring to turn around in case Mrs. Allen was watching her from the window.

Next morning the gnome was gone. At first Dorothy thought he must be concealed among the clump of daylilies at the foot of the rockery, but when she went out to the garden there was no sign of him. This time her anger was mixed with other feelings. She was a little bit afraid, she realized. She looked up and down the empty street, but no curtain moved. Most of the people were at work. She went inside, found the number she kept handy by the phone, and called the police.

"We'll get someone around as soon as we can," said the police operator when she explained there'd been a robbery. He didn't seem to be giving it very high priority. She made herself a cup of coffee and noticed that her hand was shaking as she poured it. She drew the living-room curtains half-way to. When a car pulled up outside she was relieved to see it was Norah, and then she remembered that her friend was leaving that afternoon to visit her sister in Charlottetown and had said she would drop by to say goodbye.

"What a dirty trick!" Norah said when Dorothy told her what

had happened, and they went to look at the empty spot where the gnome had stood. A few moments later a young policeman arrived, but he seemed to lose interest when Dorothy explained that it was a garden ornament that had been stolen. "Okay, ma'am," he said, taking out his notebook with a resigned air. "Let's get the particulars."

As he was going out of the door afterwards, he stopped. "Frankly, ma'am, I wouldn't get my hopes up about seeing your gnome again. There's been a lot of vandalism going on, and it's probably kids who've chucked it somewhere now."

"Norah," said Dorothy after closing the door, "would you help me? That's exactly what I was thinking before you arrived. That maybe some kids threw the gnome down the ravine. I know I won't be able to sleep tonight for wondering. But down there's not a place I'd dare to go on my own."

"Well . . ." said her friend looking at her watch. "If we're not too long, because I have to do some things before I catch my plane."

The two women went cautiously down the steep stairs that an over-optimistic parks department had sign-posted "Nature Trail". "Booze Trail" is more like it, Dorothy thought to herself as they picked their way past the beer bottles discarded by teenagers and the empty wine bottles left by the decrepit men in bulging raincoats whom she had seen emerging from the ravine.

"It's just that I'd feel better knowing," said Dorothy as they reached the viaduct. "Even if he's smashed into fragments by now."

Pigeons rattled up noisily at their approach, and as they probed the undergrowth, a man lying on a pile of newspapers startled them by suddenly snorting in his sleep.

"Just don't let this affair get to you," Norah said after they had climbed panting back up the steps. "Look, I'll tell you what we'll do. Next time you come to the cottage, after I get back, we'll go into that garden centre and see if they've got another one."

Back home, Dorothy put on a cheerful front as Norah started her car. "Have a safe trip, dear," she said. "Don't make too much of a pig of yourself at those lobster suppers!"

Walking up the path she couldn't help looking sadly at the vacant spot in the rockery. It became a routine every morning for her. First thing she'd pull back the living-room curtains, half-expecting to see him back there. Darn it, she missed him, just as if he'd been a person. She'd shrug it off and after breakfast get out her gardening gloves and tools and busy herself with the weeding.

The first postcard arrived the following Wednesday. Finding it in the box, she assumed it was from Norah. But instead of a picture of Prince Edward Island, it had a photograph of the Rockies. It was postmarked Calgary, and the message, in a neat, round, almost childish hand, said, "Dear Dorothy, Having a great time. Saw a rodeo yesterday. Wild! Love, Mr. Gnome."

She sat down on the chair in the hallway. Her heart was racing. A trick. It had to be a trick. But who would go to such lengths to scare her?

Two days later there was another postcard in the box, this time from Vancouver. She didn't even bother looking at the picture. "Dearest Dorothy," said the message. "What a wonderful city! You really should see it. Just spectacular! See you soon, Mr. Gnome." The handwriting was the same. Angrily she tore it into pieces until her fingers hurt trying to reduce it to smaller and smaller scraps. She took them into the living room, put them in the fireplace and, lighting a match, watched the blue flame dance until the little heap was reduced to ashes.

She didn't tell Norman about it, but each morning she watched for him to come, sometimes giving him a cheerful greeting then anxiously going through her mail. To her relief no more cards arrived, except one from Norah. A week went by and she was beginning to forget the whole thing, when one morning a card with a foreign stamp turned up in the mailbox. Without even reading the caption she recognized the picture as that of the flying full wings of the Sydney Opera House.

"Dear Dorothy," she read. "Here I am in Sydney. Never

thought I'd make it this far. Australians super-friendly. Love, Mr. Gnome." She walked unsteadily into the dining room, got out the bottle of brandy, and poured herself some in a wine glass. Australian brandy, she noticed with a tiny shudder. Now she knew for certain there would be more cards.

The next one arrived a couple of days later. "Norman!" she called as he walked across the lawn towards next door. "Would you mind coming here a minute?"

"What's the matter, Mrs. Graham?" he said, flicking back his hair. "You look pretty shaken. Bad news?"

"Well, it's not that. But would you mind reading this card for me?"

He gave her a funny look. "Sure, Mrs. Graham. If you want me to." Maybe her eyes were playing up.

"Dear, dear Dorothy," he read in a monotone. "Please don't worry, but I'm laid up with some sort of bug. I'll keep you posted. Love, Mr. Gnome." Norman shook his head. "That's what it says, Mrs. Graham. Funny sort of message. Why is it signed like that?"

She asked him if he wouldn't mind coming inside and, sitting at the kitchen table, she showed him the first card she'd received.

"Look, Mrs. Graham, I don't know who would do a rotten thing like that, but what you've got to do is pay no mind to it. You hear me? It's just someone trying to scare you, eh? Well, don't think about it." He slung his bag over his shoulder as he got up to go. "This is what I'll do. I'll keep an eye open and if any more cards come like that, I'll knock and give it to you so you don't get a scare, like. I mean finding it in the box."

That night Dorothy had a strange, mixed-up dream in which she looked outside and the gnome had come back. Only when she looked again it wasn't the gnome at all, but Ted who was sitting in the middle of the rockery in his pyjamas. "Come on inside, Ted. You'll catch your death," she called. "I can't, Dorothy," he replied. "I'm too ill. Help me, please!" Then he got smaller and smaller, and his voice became squeaky until she could no longer hear or see him.

In the morning Norman met her at the door looking worried.

"Fact is, Mrs. Graham, there's another card," he said, handing it to her. It was another view of Sydney. She turned it over quickly. "Dorothy," it said, the handwriting spidery and sprawling now. "So ill. Miss you." The signature was almost illegible, but she knew well enough what it said.

"This really is beyond a joke," she said, leaning her head against the doorpost. "Norman, I think I'm going to call the police about it."

It was an older officer who came this time. She told him her story and showed him the postcards, except for the one she'd burned. "I can see how you'd be upset, ma'am," he said in a kindly voice. "It's a very unpleasant thing to have happen. Is there anyone you can think of who has a grudge against you?"

She couldn't, and finally he left with the same sort of reassurances Norman had given her. "If anything unusual happens, if you see any strangers hanging about the street, anything like that, you just be sure and call us," he said.

Norman looked almost shamefaced when he brought her the postcard next day. "I've read it. I suppose I shouldn't have. But you mustn't get upset," he said handing it to her. "Would you like me to stay while you read it?"

She shook her head. "I'll be okay. Thanks, Norman," she said, and took the card with her other mail into the kitchen. She sat down dully at the table and studied the picture of Sydney harbour for several moments before turning the card over. "Dorothy. Doc says operation my only hope. Pray for me. Feel so bad." The writing trailed off and this time there was no signature. She felt her eyes stinging. She took off her glasses, and put her head down on her arms. "Oh, please," she sobbed. "Leave me alone. Whoever you are."

She worked in the garden most of the day to distract herself then went out to dinner at the little French restaurant that had just opened at the shopping mall. Coming home, she turned on the television and then, unusual for her, watched not only the eleven o'clock news, but a late movie that didn't end until one. Even then she couldn't sleep when she finally went to bed, so she turned on the light and read a biography of Catherine the Great. It wasn't until three in the morning that her eyes drooped and she reached out sleepily to turn off the bedside light. It seemed as if she hadn't been asleep more than a few minutes when the phone rang. The red glow of the clock radio told her it was 5:14 a.m. Dorothy grabbed her robe from the foot of the bed and, bumping her shoulder on the door, stumbled down the hallway to the phone table.

"Yes, hello," she said.

"Is that Mrs. Dorothy Graham?" It was a male voice, official-sounding and faintly bored.

"Yes, who's calling?"

"This is CNCP Telecommunications. We have a telegram for you. Shall I read it to you?"

"Yes, yes. But just a minute please while I turn the light on. I'll get a pen."

It was unlike Dorothy not to be home at breakfast. Norah let the phone ring a few more times then put down the receiver. She had thought of calling the night before but it had been rather late when she had arrived home from the airport, so she'd waited until the morning. Perhaps Dorothy had taken ill. Norah got her handbag from the bedroom, picked up the car keys from the mantelpiece, and went out to the garage.

She passed the ambulance as it pulled out of Dorothy's street. It didn't seem to be rushing, and there was no siren. Probably dropping someone off, coming home from hospital, Norah thought.

As she walked up the path she was surprised to see a young man in a mailman's uniform sitting on the steps with his head in his hands. "Where's Mrs. Graham?" she asked.

He looked up startled. "They just took her away. Are you Mrs. Graham's friend, the one that was in P.E.I.?"

Norah nodded. "She told me about you," he said. "I'm Norman."

"Well, where on earth did they take her?" she said sharply. "What's the matter?"

"It's terrible really," he said, almost as if he hadn't heard her. "I found her, see. I had another one of those cards for her and I knocked on the door but she didn't come. Well, like, I looked in the window and I could see her lying there on the living-room floor. Right in front of the big window. She wasn't moving, eh? So, well, I went round the back and smashed open the window.

"She just looked sort of blue. I gave her mouth-to-mouth," he went on quickly. "I tried everything, but it wasn't no good. So I called the ambulance. She was gone."

Norah steadied herself against the wall. "Gone?"

"You look pretty shook up. You better come inside and sit down," said Norman. "I'm not feeling too good myself."

They went around to the back, and Norman showed her where he'd broken the window and put in his hand to open the back door. Norah walked through the empty rooms then back to the kitchen where Norman was making them instant coffee.

"I figure the postcards must have had something to do with it," he said. "That was a dirty trick."

"What postcards?"

"Didn't she write to you about them?" He looked around the kitchen then reached up on the shelf above the sink. "Here they are. Someone took her gnome then started sending her postcards from all over. They're signed 'Mr. Gnome'. Pretty weird, eh?"

Norah read the cards then laid them out on the table in front of her. "This one came only today," said Norman, pulling another card from his pocket and handing it to her. The picture was of Adelaide. "Dear Dorothy. Just here for a couple of days before returning Sydney. Beautiful spot. Love, Mr. Gnome," the message read.

Norah compared the datemarks. "It must have been held up. It was written before some of the later ones," she said. Norman had put his cup in the sink. "Anyway, I better get back to work. I'm way behind."

"Look Norman," said Norah, making up her mind. "This is all pretty fishy. I think we should call the police. How do we know something didn't happen here last night? You carry on with your route, but I'll stay here for the police. Where can they reach you if they need to?"

"I'll give you my number at home as well as my work number," he said, pulling a red pen out of the holder in his shirt pocket. He looked around for a piece of paper, then pulled over one of the postcards and wrote in an empty space. "See, that's my name, Norman Stannard," he said, handing her the card. "Bye now."

Norah went into the hall to phone, the card still in her hand. As she dialled her eye caught a message scribbled on the pad by the phone. "The gnome died today," it said.

She put the receiver back. Her heart was pounding. She looked at the card in her hand. "Beautiful spot," she read. Something tickled at the back of her brain. Two things trying to come together. She looked at the card again, at the round, childish handwriting. Then she noticed. The writing in which the name and phone numbers had been written above the address.

She got up and went to the front window. Norman, his bag slung over his shoulder, was walking down the street. She could hear him whistling. The tiny hairs on the back of her hands tingled. She knew someone was watching her. She didn't know how it was that she hadn't noticed before: the gnome was back in his old place. His smile had the same insolence she had noticed when she had first seen him at the nursery.

Hard Luck Joey

ELAINE SLATER

Elaine Slater, a graduate of Columbia University, is a professional designer as well as a writer. Her short mystery stories have appeared in Ellery Queen's Mystery Magazine *and several have been anthologized. More recently, she has written three published textbooks and one unpublished mystery novel and is presently involved in producing a resource directory for the Canadian professional designer.*

Elaine Slater lives in Toronto with her husband.

JOEY LIKED TO think of himself as a businessman—a sort of Wall Street broker or something of the sort. Of course, he didn't exactly work on Wall Street; he was a packer at the Skye Grade Meat Packing Company, but he was the local bookie's agent and he collected the illegal bets of all the guys in the plant. When their bets paid off, he felt like a maker of millionaires, a customer's man at Shmerril, Lobe & Ralston, giving inside tips on the market. When the bets didn't pay off—as usually they didn't—well, he would tell the guys that was the luck of the game. That was the way capitalism worked: you risked your money and you win or you lose. Simple as that.

But lately things had been going badly for Joey. It was as if the market went down a few points every day. Not that the guys weren't betting—they were, more than ever. But he was having terrible problems in his personal life and he couldn't seem to get himself out of the box. When he was a kid, everyone—even his Ma—had called him Hard Luck Joey. For a while he thought he'd escaped that moniker, but now it was back with him again.

It all started when Carol came into the Skye Grade as a file clerk. She was pert and pretty and all the guys eyed her even though the word was out she was married. That didn't seem to bother her and it sure didn't bother Joey, not with his fish of a wife, and soon he and Carol were spending more and more time together. It turned out she hated her husband but he was nuts about her and the real jealous type, so they had to be very careful. As for Joey's wife, it was nag, nag, nag all the time, so he could kill her. I mean, *really* kill her.

Well, the seed was there and as far as Joey was concerned it was his wife's fault, not his. So when he heard from the bookie who listened to his tale of woe about a "contract" guy who could arrange an accident for his wife, something like a shotgun blast in the head, Joey didn't hesitate too long. He didn't fill the triggerman in about Carol, only about his fish of a dumb-broad wife, and owing to his friendship with the bookie, Joey got a cut rate.

True, when he met the contract man Joey almost backed out, but he was afraid to look chicken. That man was as cold as steel and twice as hard, with hooded eyes, and mean, I mean *mean*!

It was all arranged for Wednesday when his wife would get back from her job about 5:00, arriving on foot at their crumby house—she was a sloppy housekeeper and he couldn't stand gardening or repairs. The gunman wouldn't have to get too close. He could wait across the street behind a bunch of bushes in the weed-strewn, garbage-laden empty lot, shoot, and beat it. Joey was planning to get home a little late that night, stopping for a few beers on the way home as he used to do before he met Carol.

But then when everything was arranged so beautifully, it began to be Hard Luck Joey all over again.

Get this. On Wednesday morning—*Wednesday*—his wife plops into the kitchen where he's grabbing off a cup of coffee and she's got a suitcase in her hands.

"Joey," she says, "I don't know how you're gonna take this, but me and Eddie—well, we gotta do our thing. So long, Joey."

So long, Joey. Before he could open his mouth to say, "But you can't—I've arranged everything for tonight," she was gone and he was left gaping.

That was bad right? Real unlucky, right? But listen to this. It turned out his bookie was out of town and of course Joey didn't know the contract man's name or where to reach him, so he couldn't head him off. Joey felt sick to his stomach. He was in over his head. He decided not to go to work that day, to call in sick. Joey, the big Wall Street broker, had run into a drop in the market and didn't know how to handle it.

He hung around the house all day in his undershorts, drinking beer and switching stations on the TV. He figured around 5:00 or so he'd go out and call off the action in the dirty lot across the street.

At 5:00 he switched off the soap opera he'd been watching and went into the bedroom to step into his trousers.

Just as he was putting the first leg in, the whole house was shaken by a blast of gunfire.

My God, he thought dumbly, the fish musta changed her mind and come home just when she coulda saved me some bucks by running off with Eddie!

Joey got into his trousers and ran outside prepared to look plenty shocked for the neighbours. He did a good job, too, only he wan't acting. It was Carol who was lying dead on his doorstep. Neighbours said she had come running up the street as if she were frightened out of her skin. And now she was lying dead and not a bush stirred across the street.

Hard Luck Joey became the centre of attention on his block. No one knew of his affair with Carol. He had called in sick and they all thought, since she and Joey worked in the same place, she was coming to tell him the boss was sore or something like that. The police didn't suspect a thing and Joey told them his wife had just gone away on a visit—uh—to her mother and her sister who lived in a trailer camp somewhere down in Florida. He expected her back, he said, any day.

And then, the very next day, the fish did come back, suitcase and all. She'd read about the awful gunning and felt bad for Joey, she said. He sure musta got scared, and gee, he'd stayed home sick all day—she'd read about it in the papers. She'd no idea he cared like that about her. So she told Eddie goodbye. "I belong with my Joey."

So here he was, Joey brooded as he stared out the window at the lot across the street, right back where he started, only his chick was dead and he was stuck for the rest of his life with the dumb fish he'd married.

He was Hard Luck Joey, all right.

But Joey didn't realize just *how* Hard Luck he was. As he walked down the street to find solace in a few beers, he saw the bushes move over there in the windless night. In another moment he would know why Carol had been so afraid of her husband.

An Evening at the Opera

ANNA SANDOR & BILL GOUGH

Anna Sandor was born in Budapest, Hungary, and left there in a hail of bullets in 1957. Her numerous television writing credits include over thirty episodes of "The King of Kensington"; *the television adaptation of the novel,* A Population Of One; *and many episodes of the mystery series "Seeing Things", co-written with Bill Gough. Her latest effort is the C.B.C. television movie,* Charlie Grant's War. *Ms. Sandor's proudest achievement to date is Rachel Alice Sandor-Gough, born in January 1984.*

Bill Gough grew up in Newfoundland and now works in Toronto as a television writer and producer. Among his many production credits is the award-winning C.B.C. television movie War Brides. *His most recent project as a producer is the television adaptation of Howard Engel's* The Suicide Murders. *Aside from his television work, Gough is an accomplished songwriter and poet. His first novel,* Maud's House, *appears this year.*

Overture

FOG SWIRLED AROUND the stone blocks of Cabot Tower and spilled down into the narrow, craggy harbour. Gulls mewed and clawed their way towards the ocean. As the foghorn wailed, sheets of water splashed across the taxi's windshield. Springtime had come to St. John's.

The weather didn't bother Alex Laszlo one bit. He'd been in Newfoundland long enough to know what to expect when April lurched in. Humming "Musetta's Waltz", he deftly manoeuvred his taxi around the potholes of Water Street, his mind drifting back to the first time he had heard *La Bohème*. He was so engrossed in the beautiful melody that he didn't even notice the nattily dressed couple he showered with rain water. It was only when he glanced in his rear-view mirror that he caught sight of the muddy twosome shaking their fists and mouthing curses at him. Alex felt sorry for them because they were forced to curse in a language so unsuited to it. Now if only they had known some Hungarian!

But sorry as he felt for them and their language, Alex had only one thought . . . *La Bohème*. *La Bohème* had come to the Arts and Culture Centre and Pavarotti was singing!

The parking lot was full, so Alex blithely double-parked and ran through the rain, his coat draped European-style over his shoulders and his ever-present cigarette hissing in the wind. Looking at the line-up he decided that he was capable of killing for a ticket.

Act One

Before Alex had to do anything drastic he became aware of a sound not unlike escaping steam. He looked towards the hiss and caught sight of Doc McCurdy, the beribboned and red-nosed commissionaire. His index finger lifted to his lips, Doc was beckoning Alex to him with a wild wave of his free hand. It looked like Doc was about to order another bottle of bootleg pinkie and Alex was in no mood to head for New Gower Street in search of illicit booze. Still, he left the line-up and went over to the small cubbyhole that the commissionaire called his office.

Doc tilted towards him and the faint odour of a condemned distillery escaped his pursed lips.

"I have no time to get you booze, Doc. I'm here for a ticket."

"I got 'um."

"You have a ticket?"

"Right, Alex. They're scarcer than hen's teeth, but I got one."

"And who is this ticket for, my friend?"

"Old Mawmouth was one that asked me to spell him, and he with one stick of a yaffle saved up for the biggoty ones. But I said, 'Sure as I squeezed more water out of my mitts than you sailed over, the ticket's not for some gommil in a monkey suit!' No sir. It's for you, Uncle Alex!"

Alex grabbed Doc and bestowed a rapid series of kisses on both cheeks, being very careful not to breathe in. He was surprised at the ticket and at being called "Uncle" by a man who was old enough to be his grandfather. But as he had enough trouble unravelling even the bland English that passed as Canadian standard, he didn't attempt to follow the vivid leanings and leapings of the poetry of the spoken Newfoundland tongue. In return he unleashed a torrent of Hungarian that complimented Doc and all the Newfoundland loins that laboured to produce such a perfect work of art. Thanks over, Alex rushed into the theatre.

As the lights began to dim Alex gave his smouldering stub of a cigarette to an usher and raced towards his seat. He eased his way past the tuxedoed, moneyed audience and settled into an obscure seat near the wall. He knew it wasn't front row centre —but he was here for the music, not the view. Alex relaxed and slipped off his leather windbreaker. Memories of the first time he saw *La Bohème* swept over him. The look of the great velvet curtain as it trembled just before rising in the Budapest Opera House, the rustle of candy wrappings as overweight ladies smacked their lips and got in one last crinkle before the performance, the way young women flirted with coquettish eyes over half-open programmes, the way garlic smelled. . . . Garlic! Alex was brought back to reality by an overpowering stench of garlic that floated from the fat man next to him. Not only did he smell of garlic but he had fallen asleep at the exact second the curtain rose to reveal a wondrously crafted set. Snow seemed to whirl around the grey-looking garret windows. The lights were down just enough so the flames from the manuscript reflected on Rodolfo's face. Alex settled back and awaited the arrival of the philosopher and the musician.

What arrived however were giant snores that joined Rodolfo and echoed around the Arts and Culture Centre. Alex jammed his elbow into the sleeping hulk next to him and the snoring stopped for a while. Puccini's glorious melodies worked their magic to transport Alex back to his youth.

Act Two

All through the evening there was a fight between Alex's memories, the great performance that was unfolding on stage, and the on-again off-again (nudged with elbow blows from Alex) snores that drifted to him on clouds of garlic.

It wasn't until the final moments of the opera as Mimi lay

dying and Alex felt the tears run down his face that the snoring stopped, even the garlic odour seemed to lessen. The curtain descended and the entire audience rose as one to its feet. Well, almost the entire audience. The fat man stayed put. This was the last straw for Alex. He grabbed the fat man by the lapels and tugged. But he didn't get up. Instead his body gradually tipped forward and sideways, until in clear sight was his own huge hand wrapped around the handle of a knife. The knife was imbedded deep in his heart, and as he fell it shifted, allowing blood to pour down the front of his dress shirt. A woman began to scream and people moved quickly away. Alex leaned over to help the man, but as soon as he touched him again he knew it was no use. He'd seen a lot of dead bodies in the war and in the revolution and this one was no different. Alex pulled out the knife and absent-mindedly waved it around as he moved back slowly and looked for something to wipe the blood off. A woman in the row in front saw the blood staining Alex's hands and began screaming "He's the murderer!"

Alex chuckled at the absurdity, but his smile looked more like a smirk to the patrons of the opera. More people took up the chant and as the cheering died down and silence started to spread, even Pavarotti himself stared at Alex.

Act Three

The director of the Centre was looking very uncomfortable. Not only had there been a murder in his jealously protected domain but the man who seemed to be the murderer was sitting at his desk and flicking ashes all over the "Thank You For Not Smoking" sign. Adrian O'Dea seemed to many people who knew him to care more about the building itself than he did about the people in it. One usher later swore that she heard him mutter after the murder, "Thank goodness the carpets are red."

Now Adrian leaned in the door of his office and cleared his throat in a delicate manner that should have conveyed to any civilized person that it was time to leave. However, Inspector

John Newman was not a civilized man. He'd grown up in the rough and tumble world of the Battery, fishing and fighting until he ended up in the police force much in the same way that a flipped coin will land heads instead of tails. Sometimes he regretted the way the coin had landed. Had he taken to crime instead of police work he was sure he'd have been just as good at that and a great deal richer. However, the coin had landed the way it had, so the Inspector decided to get on with his work which, at the moment, was interrogating Alex Laszlo. But there was one thing in the way—Adrian O'Dea. Inspector Newman looked at the director of the Arts and Culture Centre, smiled at him, and slammed the door firmly in his face. Constable Joe Byrne who was taking the official notes looked nervous but knew enough to conceal it.

With the door shut the Inspector turned back to a calmly smoking Laszlo.

"So, Alex why don't you confess and have done with it. We can then give that sculpin back his office and tell everyone to go home. Just explain to the little constable why you killed the fat man and we can wrap it all up."

"If I had killed the fat man would I have done it in front of two thousand witnesses? Besides, his own hand was on the knife. He killed himself."

"No one I've ever seen in my life would get all dressed up go to the opera and knife himself."

"Any man who could sleep through *La Bohème* is capable of anything."

Inspector Newman laughed. "I could sleep through *La Bohème*."

"My point exactly!"

This time Newman laughed even harder. He paced around the room almost sweeping from the wall dozens of different drawings of the Arts and Culture Centre, the main decorating motif in the office. Most of the drawings were clean and sparse —there were even the original blueprints for the building sealed in glass and surrounded by an icy blue metal frame. This was a tidy, cold world. In one corner, however, was a wonderfully designed ship. It was in full sail and the big jib held the wind of a storm that splashed grey along the putty forming the artificial ocean. To look at this ship was to taste the sea.

Alex looked at the inspector who had stopped in his pacing long enough to wipe some dust from the display case that held the ship.

"The boat is good."

"It's not a boat, it's a schooner."

"Whatever you call it. That is one of the finest things you ever built."

"Don't butter me up, you feeble excuse for a refugee."

"All that is long over."

"I don't think so." The inspector paced towards Alex. He stopped and leaned over him. The constable licked his pencil.

"I don't think so, because here's what I have. The man was Hungarian. . . . You're Hungarian."

"You're a Newfoundlander. The constable is a Newfoundlander. That doesn't mean you're going to kill him."

The constable laughed. Inspector Newman made a move towards him, but stopped short of actually doing him in because he felt honour bound to disprove Alex's statement.

"How do you know he was Hungarian?"

"He had a wallet. His name is full of bloody sz's all over the place, and he has. . . . Why am I telling you this?"

"Because we have a long-standing professional relationship!"

"Just because I arrest you every so often doesn't mean that we're friends."

"Of course it does! Each of us performs a service for the community. Can that young man go away?. . . . I cannot talk freely with him in here."

Newman nodded wearily and Constable Joe Byrne took the chance to slip out and get a beer. The door opened and shut again on the worried expression of Adrian O'Dea.

"Thank you, Inspector. As I was saying . . . each of us performs a service. I provide bootleg for the honest citizens of the city and you try and arrest me on behalf of the hypocritical citizens of the city."

Inspector Newman seemed to have stopped listening to Alex. He moved over to the glass case that held the schooner he'd made with such loving care during hours spent in his basement workshop. Everything in his workshop had its place and there was a place for everything. Drawers held tiny anchors and small pullies that worked and little wooden barrels that he'd made another winter. Selling his intricately carved creations brought in the money he needed to continue his hobby. Now as he stared, his schooner looked like a prisoner in this office, gone ashore on the shoals of bureaucracy. The inspector wondered if he should ever have sold it. He thought he heard someone talking to him and blinked his way out of the memory to see Alex looking at him.

"I was saying, Inspector, that it was a shame such a work of art as that boat had to end up in this asshole's office. Why don't we steal it?"

"I can't steal it. I'm a policeman."

"The perfect cover. Also, I will swear on my grandmother's grave that you didn't take it. Shall we go?"

"Alex, it tempts me . . . but I will probably have to arrest you tonight and that will ruin all our plans."

"Inspector, you have one small problem. You have to prove I murdered the fat man."

"I've got fifty witnesses——"

"Who can only say that they saw me with blood on my hands."

"You pulled the knife out afterwards."

"Where I come from if you see someone with a knife in him, you pull it out."

"Alex, I go a lot on hunches. And I have a hunch about this. We've got this guy who sits next to you and ends up dead. Half of the gentry of the province is at the performance. I know they didn't do it because they were in their best clothes and there was a chance of getting spattered with blood. I've done some checking up and found out that the deceased came over from Hungary about the same time as you. Also, you are a criminal."

"I am not a criminal. I have been arrested many times and acquitted every time. I am not a criminal; I am a victim of police harassment."

"Your prints were on the knife."

"I pulled the knife out. Of course my prints were on it!"

"There was blood on your hands."

"The man had a knife in him, Inspector. What I want to know is whose knife was in his chest?"

"His own. His initials were carved in the handle."

"So what we have is a man is killed with his own knife. No one sees the stabbing, but his prints are on the handle in a manner showing he pushed the knife in himself."

"I didn't say that."

"You also did not deny it, my friend, and I have the advantage of knowing I did not kill him. Don't forget, I arrived at the theatre at the last moment and received a ticket I did not know I was going to receive! That is the final point, unless you believe in total coincidence. How could I know I would end up next to my supposed victim?"

"That's what I can't figure. I can see how you might get his knife. I can see how you could stab him when no one was looking and then press his own hand around the handle to make it look like he did the job. But—and it's the only reason you're not in the clink—I can't figure out how you knew you'd be sitting next to him."

"Perhaps if I were not a foreigner you wouldn't have to spend time wondering such things."

The inspector glared at him.

"What the hell does that mean?"

Alex looked quietly at him. He sat on the edge of the desk and poured himself a glass of water from the director's silver thermos.

"You've known me for a long time now, Inspector. You know a little bit about my past. After what I went through in the camps do you think that I'd kill a perfect stranger? To end up locked away for the rest of my life? Never to see a sky that wasn't walled, never to be free?"

The inspector looked very closely at Alex. It was the first time they had even come near the subject of what this strange little man had been through in the war. Alex's cheeks flushed as he paced around, looking angrier and angrier. He stopped and gave the inspector a fierce look. The inspector decided that just this once Alex Laszlo was telling the truth. He turned and walked away towards the door. Just before he opened it he heard the unmistakable sound of a glass cutter on glass. He looked back at Alex who was cutting a hole in the glass prison that held his boat. Alex winked at the inspector.

"I always carry a glass cutter for good luck. It's a custom of my people."

The inspector walked out the door.

Act Four

It was near 3:00 a.m., and the inspector was trying to ease himself into bed without creaking the springs enough to wake his wife. The wind was up even more and howled as it drilled rain against the window panes. He had almost made it into bed when the doorbell rang. Cursing and stamping his way down the stairs, he ignored the calls of his wife wanting to know what was going on. After a struggle he opened the door and was almost knocked back inside by a gust of wind. The porch light's beam hit the edge of the steps where a pool of water had collected. There, shaking in the strong sou'westerly, her sails full and proud, rocked his little schooner the *Rachel-Alice*. He picked her up and shielding her from the wind moved back inside the house. As the door closed the inspector smiled. Now he knew what it would have felt like if the coin had landed on the other side. It didn't feel bad at all. He moved towards his workshop. Some of the rigging had been damaged by the storm and he knew he really should fix it before the night ended.

Finale

Alex was home. And there waiting for him was Mariska who had always waited. She looked more beautiful than ever.

"Alex, I worried so. Were you selling your bootleg booze, my darling?"

"No."

"Thank God."

"This time I was being questioned—"

But she interrupted him as there were more important things to discuss.

"Did you get to see *La Bohème*? I suppose there were no tickets."

"There was one."

"Alex, you should have told me right away. Now, sit down before the soup is cold. But tell me between sips. From the beginning to the end exactly what it was like."

She sat at the table and rested her chin in her hands. The kitchen light caught the gold that still streaked her hair and Alex remembered the first time he had ever seen her. It was at her father's house when he had gone there to study Talmud. He had taken a moment to go into the kitchen for a drink of water and found her there hunched over the table, reading. She had looked up at him from her book and his life had changed.

"Alex, pay attention. Tell me about tonight. Tell me about *La Bohème* . . . every moment."

"The opera was wonderful. Pavarotti was magnificent."

"Of course. I want details."

"The details are of different things. I sat in my seat and I smelled garlic from the man next to me. He was fat and he was asleep."

"What do I care of these things?"

"And he was Tamas Szekely."

"He could not have been. Not that pig. Till the day I die I will never forget his smile as he rounded up the whole village to send us to the camps. Anya, Apa, Janos . . . everyone. How is it possible you could have sat next to him?"

"Because one day somebody had to and I drew the ticket. When I recognized him I knew I had to act. There are so few of us left. Then I remembered that knife he always used to carry in his inside pocket—the initialled knife with the ivory handle that he was so proud of. I gambled that it was still in an inside pocket and I won."

"He's dead?"

"Yes."

"Good. I never thought I could say 'good' about taking another human's life. But for that one . . ."

She watched Alex as he finished his soup.

"You killed him in front of all the people?"

"Yes."

"And your fingerprints are on the knife?"

He nodded.

"Then the police will be here any minute!"

"No they won't."

"Why?"

"Because this was a murder of coincidence and we can thank God that North Americans do not believe in coincidence."

Mariska looked at Alex and thought of the coincidences in their lives. She recalled that moment many years ago when she just happened to be reading in the kitchen and Alex just happened to want a drink of water. She thought of the end of the war when she believed she would never see him again, and how she just happened to take the north road instead of the east. There, coming around a corner, was Alex.

Mariska reached out and touched his cheek as she remembered what had happened to all her family and what Alex had done tonight to avenge that horror.

She spoke quietly.

"It wasn't coincidence. It was fate."

She poured Alex more soup. For a while neither said anything. They just sat there together, enough in love to sit in silence. Mariska got up and went over to the stack of records. She picked up one, cherished over the years, and put it on. The old record hissed and crackled out "Musetta's Waltz." Alex and Mariska moved closer together. They held hands as they remembered the days when they were young. He reached over and clicked off the light. The music filled the dark, and he held Mariska as she cried and as she remembered.

Death on Horseback

JOHN BALLEM

John Ballem, Q.C., *is a Calgary lawyer and author. His writings include a textbook on oil and gas law and six novels, the most recent of which is* The Marigot Run, *a thriller set in the Caribbean, which was released earlier in 1984 in Canada and the United States. An expert horseman, he has been a television host and commentator for numerous horse shows.*

AT FIRST IT was just a distant drumming; a faint discordant note in the still peace of the summer afternoon. Then it swelled into the unmistakable, blood-chilling thunder of a runaway horse. In the stable yard Hal Innes paused in the act of saddling his thoroughbred jumper and stared in the direction of the main gate. A bay horse, his hooves striking sparks as he slipped and almost fell on the concrete culvert, careened off the highway and galloped up the road that led to the stables. Maddened by the saddle that had slipped underneath his belly, he was drenched with sweat and his eyes rolled back in terror at the dread human burden he dragged with him.

The pounding hoofbeats brought a female groom dashing out of the main barn. Hal thrust his thoroughbred's reins at her and went to try to intercept the runaway. He groaned with anguish when he recognized the bay. It was Sundancer—Vicki Bennett's three-day-event horse. Sundancer belonged here at Green Fields and would be frantic to reach the safety of his own stall. If he dragged Vicki over the barn's stone doorsill, the blow would kill her for sure. Hal sprinted for the stable door and slammed it shut just as the horse charged into the yard. For a moment it seemed as if he would crash headlong into the door, but he skidded to a halt and stood with heaving sides, the wild look gradually fading from his eyes now that he was back in familiar surroundings.

Moving with extreme care and making reassuring noises, Hal reached for the broken reins. Someone came over to hold the gelding's head, and he bent over the fallen rider. Vicki's riding boot was jammed into the stirrup, and it took a considerable effort to free it. A small crowd of riders and stable hands gathered around, and Mike Dawes, the manager of Green Fields, called out, "Don't move her. I phoned for an ambulance."

Kneeling beside Vicki's motionless figure, his fingers vainly searching for a pulse at the base of her slender throat, Hal realized with sickening certainty that she was gone. The back of her head was a soft, pulpy mess where it had been stove in on her hellish journey. Her riding clothes were ripped to shreds, and the leg that had been hung up in the stirrup was wrenched completely out of its hip socket. Gazing down at the battered remains of what had been a vibrant and attractive young woman, a woman who had been in his arms only a few nights before, Hal did his best to convince himself that she would have been mercifully unconscious from the moment she fell off the horse.

En route to the hospital, the ambulance turned on its flashing lights but didn't bother to use the siren; its passenger was beyond all aid. The doctor on duty in Emergency, a young smooth-faced Oriental, briskly pronounced her d.o.a. and made a pencilled notation on his clipboard. Hal had known she was dead right from the first but still the official confirmation hit him with numbing force. It was the bitterness in Mike Dawes' voice that snapped Hal out of his daze. The stable manager was saying, "You get to tell her parents. You were her latest boyfriend."

Which really burns your ass, thought Hal, but when he saw how torn up Mike looked, he swallowed his anger and agreed to perform the unpleasant task. In the last couple of months, since he and Vicki had started dating, he had seen quite a bit of her parents. A rising young lawyer, Vicki had her own apartment in town, but her attachment to the family ranch was strong and more often than not, Hal found himself eating Sunday supper at the Bar J.

The Bennett spread covered two and a half sections of rolling foothill country, traversed by a small creek that watered the Bar J Herefords. The bottom had fallen out of the cattle market in recent years and the lack of funds was just beginning to make itself felt. The big barn should have been repainted last year; the Ford pickup in the yard was several years past its prime—little things like that. But the oil well, its "Christmas tree" of pipes and valves poking above the ground in the west pasture, would change all that. It had gone on stream just last month and an elated Stan Starchuk, whose fledgling oil company had drilled the well, had gleefully told Hal that it was producing more than a hundred barrels a day. The Bennetts' royalties would quickly free them from the ups and downs of the cattle market.

As Hal had feared, Vicki's mother was alone in the house. Her husband was haying in a field on the other side of the creek. At Hal's request, she raised him on the mobile and told him to return home immediately.

"It's Vicki, isn't it?" she asked as she switched off. "She's had a fall."

"I think we had better wait until Mr. Bennett gets here," Hal said gently.

"She's not dead, is she?" Mrs. Bennett whispered and let out a small shriek at the stricken look on his face. She fell back into a kitchen chair and stared blankly ahead, blinking away the tears that welled from her eyes. The clatter of the farm truck pulling into the yard roused her and she ran to her husband as he opened the screen door. "Vicki's dead," she sobbed. "Our daughter is dead."

Hal stayed with the grieving couple while they prepared to drive in to the hospital. "You liked her, didn't you, Hal?" asked Mrs. Bennett with a wistful little smile as he helped her into the family sedan.

"Yes. Very much." That was perfectly true, even if it didn't go as far as Mrs. Bennett might think. He and Vicki had worked out a mutually satisfactory relationship—no strings, just enjoyment of each other's company, and great sex. She was ambitious and independent, determined to carve out a glittering legal career for herself, and he was committed, for the next few years at least, to leading the life of a penniless horse-show bum.

A blue and white RCMP cruiser was parked outside the Green Fields office, and Hal pulled his rusted-out Toyota in beside it. The police probably investigated all accidental deaths as a matter of course; even so, he was mildly surprised to find Sergeant Steinoff himself in the office talking with Mike Dawes. Steinoff was the officer in charge of the High River detachment, and you wouldn't expect him to be carrying out a routine accident enquiry like this one—unless Steinoff figured there might be a connection with the poisoning incident. That would explain it, Hal told himself as he shook hands warmly with the Mountie. He had seen a lot of the sergeant when they were trying to solve the mystery behind the poisoning of King Cotton, and he had come to like and respect the policeman. Especially when he had refused to lay a charge against Wendy Miller even though everyone was convinced she was the culprit.

"You can't charge a person on suspicion alone," Steinoff had told Mike Dawes when the manager pressed him to prosecute Wendy and put an end to the rumours that were swirling around Green Fields. "We don't have a shred of hard evidence. If we could establish that she had purchased strychnine, I'd book her like a shot. But all we've got is some kind of weirdo motive"—here he had paused to look askance at Hal before continuing—"and the fact that she acts and looks guilty. It's just not good enough. I'm not going to ruin a young girl's life without something more to go on than that."

Now there was an appraising look in Steinoff's rather alarming light hazel eyes as he asked Hal, "I understand you and Ms. Bennett were good friends."

"We were."

"She was an expert rider?"

"One of the best. She placed second in the cross-country at Chinook just last week."

"A dangerous sport. Do you have any idea where she might have fallen?"

"There are some cross-country fences over by the lake that she used for schooling. That's probably where it happened."

"Right." The Mountie got to his feet. "Maybe you wouldn't mind showing me this place?"

"What the hell gives?" Dawes demanded as Steinoff and Hal headed out the door. "You trying to give the stables a bad name? A rider falls off her horse and gets dragged. It happens."

"I'm sure it's an accidental death," the sergeant said placatingly. "And that's the way I'm treating it. But it's standard procedure to inspect the site of a fatal accident."

The jumps had been set up along a trail winding through a grove of poplars bordering a "lake" that was little more than a big prairie slough. A scolding magpie flitted through the branches above them as Hal and the sergeant examined the area around each jump. But the hard-packed ground, churned with countless hoofprints, and the weathered solid logs of the big oxers and triple spreads had nothing to tell them.

On the way back to where the cruiser was parked they stumbled across Vicki's riding helmet, lying on its side in a stubble field. "Would you look at that," said Steinoff as he bent down to pick it up. "The chin strap's torn clean in two."

Hal fingered the strap with distaste. "It's so rotted it's coming apart at the seams. No damn wonder it broke." He turned it over. The inside was encrusted with ancient dried sweat. "This isn't Vicki's style at all."

Driving back to the stables, he finally broached what was on his mind. "Isn't it a little unusual for the head of a detachment to be investigating an accidental death?"

"Hell, I'm just a working policeman," grinned Steinoff. "But, you're right. It was the Green Fields connection that caught my attention. Plus the fact that I had heard talk about you and Vicki Bennett. So when I got the phone call from the hospital, I thought to myself, oh, oh, here we go again."

"Well, now we know how it happened. She came off over a jump and got caught up in the stirrup when the horse bolted. Like Dawes says, it happens. So you can relax."

"I guess so." The Mountie eased off the gas pedal as they overtook a group of horseback riders trotting along the road allowance in single file. "Damn it, we both know it was the Miller girl who poisoned that grey horse. Was she around this afternoon?"

"Wendy? She's always around. If she's not hanging about the stables, she's off riding somewhere by herself." Hal shot a sideways glance at Steinoff. "Hey, I thought you had closed the file on that one."

"You know what they say about the Mounties always getting their man . . . or woman," replied Steinoff with an unconvincing laugh. "I've got to admit it still bothers me. It's not such a big jump from killing animals to killing people. Especially when the same motive is present."

"Now just what the hell do you mean by that?" demanded Hal with a puzzled stare.

"Think about it for a minute. You had something going with Vicki. Right?" Hal gave a curt nod of acknowledgment and Steinoff waved his hand as if his point had been made. "A valuable horse got poisoned for less than that."

Hal winced at the memory of King Cotton lying lifeless in his stall. It would have been child's play for anyone to feed him strychnine mixed in with a handful of oats. But why? Hal still found it hard to accept the popular theory that Wendy Miller had done it in a jealous rage because he had stopped riding her horse when King Cotton had been offered to him. Her horse had a lot of natural jumping ability, but he was too erratic to ever be a top contender in the show ring.

"Speaking of motive, how did Mike Dawes feel about you and Vicki? I understand those two were an item before you came along."

Hal stared at the Mountie incredulously. "You really keep in touch with what goes on at Green Fields, don't you?" He shook his head in mild exasperation. "It's true, he and Vicki did have a brief fling a while back, but people don't go off the deep end over something like that." Steinoff looked sceptical and Hal said flatly, "Anyway, you can forget about Mike. He was at the stables when it happened. He was the one who called the ambulance, in fact."

The cruiser passed under the Green Fields sign over the main gate and drove slowly up the same road that Vicki had been dragged over. In a corral outside a shedrow of stables, a groom led a bay horse around in slow circles.

"Good. They're cooling Sundancer out," approved Hal. "I'll go over and have a look at him."

"Hang on, I'll come with you." Steinoff parked the Plymouth in front of the office and got out.

Hal ran his hand expertly down the gelding's legs. There was a little heat in the off fore but a rubdown with liniment should take care of that. He straightened up and pointed to an ugly-looking scrape on Sundancer's fetlock. "That will be where the reins wrapped themselves around his leg. It's a wonder he didn't go down before they broke."

"I might as well take a look at those reins while I'm here," said Steinoff, adding with a shrug when Hal looked at him, "Just doing my job."

Like everything else at Green Fields, the tack room was spacious and well appointed. Rows of leather saddles gleamed on their racks and well-oiled bridles hung on the wall beside them. Someone had put Vicki's battered gear back in its usual place. While Steinoff inspected the severed reins, Hal tugged at the saddle's stirrup leathers.

"These things are supposed to release," he grunted. "If they had, she wouldn't have been dragged." Placing his left hand on the pommel, he pulled even harder but nothing happened. "The safety release must have jammed." Frowning, he lifted the leather skirt. "The bar shouldn't be up like that." He pointed to a small steel bar where the stirrup leather was attached to the saddle. "It should be level, like this." He reached out with his index finger and tried to push it down but it refused to budge. "Damn you, Vicki, I thought you had more sense," he muttered and lifted the skirt on the other side of the saddle. That safety bar was also in the upright position but it snapped down easily when he pushed it.

Steinoff poked at the release. "It's jammed in so tight it's digging right into the leather." He straightened up. "You're the expert. What do you make of it?"

Hal shrugged. "Probably nothing. A lot of riders get careless about the release and never think of checking it. Some even ride with the bars up so they won't lose a stirrup over a fence. Vicki could have been one of those. She was a very gutsy rider."

"Yeah." Steinoff lifted the saddle from the rack. "I think I'll have the lab take a look at this to see if they can come up . . ." A small gasp from the doorway kept him from completing the sentence. Wendy Miller, her arms filled with a bulky German saddle, was staring at the policeman with wide, terror-stricken eyes. Then there was a loud clump as she dropped the saddle and fled.

Hal gazed around the luxurious interior of Stan's new Mercedes coupe with open admiration. "So this is how the other half lives. How does it feel to be a budding oil tycoon?"

"Like a dream come true," Starchuk replied with an unabashed enthusiasm that brought a faint smile to Hal's face. It was good to see someone getting exactly what he wanted out of life. Vicki's funeral, held in a country church that was too small to accommodate the crowd of mourners, was just over. Hal had arrived with a delegation from Green Fields but had sat with Stan during the service. Now the two men were driving together to the Bar J where Vicki's parents would be at home to those who wished to call. The Bennetts had gone ahead in the funeral home's limousine, and Stan was driving slowly to give them time to get ready to greet their guests.

"That Mountie buddy of yours was at the funeral," said Stan. "Out of uniform, and sitting in the very last row."

"I know. I talked to him briefly while you were getting the car. I don't think he's completely satisfied that Vicki's death was accidental."

"What seems to be bugging him?"

"Nothing he can put his hands on, that's for sure. He had an autopsy done, but it didn't prove anything one way or the other.

Apparently her head injuries were compatible with either being dragged over rocky ground or being bashed with the well-known 'blunt instrument'. The safety release on her saddle was jammed tight, as I told you before. Steinoff thinks it was done deliberately, but again he can't prove it—there are no marks of pliers or anything like that. He figures the killer could have used a cloth to prevent the pliers from scratching the metal."

"Sounds pretty thin to me."

"Likewise. If it weren't for Wendy Miller, I'm sure the idea of murder would never have occurred to him."

"Wendy Miller? That dippy little teenager who's got the hots for you?" Stan's expression grew thoughtful. "You know, I wouldn't put anything past that girl. She's as flakey as they come. There's not much doubt that she was the one who poisoned King Cotton, is there?"

"I guess we'll never know," muttered Hal, fiddling with the air-conditioning controls so he wouldn't have to look at Stan. The fact was that he did know. He had known since last Sunday when a tearful Wendy, frantic because she realized Steinoff suspected her of murdering Vicki, had sought him out at the stable and confessed to poisoning the horse. She looked so abjectly miserable that Hal found himself promising not to tell anyone. "Unless," he had warned her sternly, "it turns out that you had something to do with Vicki's death."

"I didn't! I swear it."

Hal switched the fan to "low" and leaned back in the passenger seat. "Anyway, she claims to have had absolutely nothing to do with what happened to Vicki."

"Do you believe her?" Starchuk was visibly relieved that Hal was no longer messing about with his precious new car.

"Yeah. I think I do."

"Which means it was an accident."

"I'd be a lot happier with that explanation if it weren't for the chin strap."

"Chin strap?" Starchuk looked baffled and Hal told him about the strap being so badly frayed that it came apart, leaving Vicki's head unprotected.

Stan was unimpressed. "Hell, who looks at their chin strap anyway?" he asked with a shrug.

They were on Bar J lands now and the oil well was coming into view. A freshly painted sign proclaimed it to be Star Oil 11-8. "How about that!" Stan crowed. "You're looking at the cornerstone of the Starchuk oil empire!"

"It must give you a real rush, knowing it's pumping out that lovely black oil day and night and that it's all yours."

"It's not quite all mine. I wish it was. But I farmed-in the lease." Stan glanced questioningly at Hal. 'You know what I'm talking about?"

"I think so. You drill a well at your cost to earn an interest."

"Bang on. We'll make an oilman out of you yet. I own it fifty-fifty with the oil company that held the lease from the Bennetts. And of course there's the royalty that's paid to Mr. and Mrs. Bennett. But there's more than enough to go round and I can use the revenue as collateral to raise money from the bank. Whenever you get fed up with the horse-show circuit, there'll be a place for you at Star Oil."

"Hey, I may take you up on that!"

Mrs. Bennett's face brightened when she saw Hal and Stan standing in the entry. They were two of her favourites, and both had been good friends of Vicki. Recently, of course, Hal had become much more than a friend and who knew where that might have led if. . . . She swallowed the lump in her throat and asked both young men to remain behind after the crush of people had left so they could have "a little chat".

"Sit down. Sit down," Mr. Bennett boomed hospitably when the last guest had departed. "I'll fix us a drink."

"We can't stay too long," Hal murmured. "You two must be exhausted."

But it was obvious that Vicki's parents wanted to talk about their daughter. Soon all four of them were exchanging reminiscences about her riding exploits, her love of fun, and her law career. "She would have gone right to the top," asserted Hal.

"She had all the ambition in the world, and she'd tackle any kind of case."

"That's right," her father chuckled. "But I think she was beginning to zero in on petroleum law as her specialty. The last little while she was really hitting the books on the subject. Isn't that right, Jean?" he asked his wife who nodded fond agreement. "Why, she even had me dig out that lease of yours, Stan, and she pored over every word of it. Went through it with a fine-tooth comb, as they say."

"Is that a fact?" The oilman tried to sound casual but there was a telltale rasp in his voice. Hal stole a quick glance at his friend. Stan's nostrils were pinched, and there were blotches of white under his even tan. What the hell was wrong with him?

The two men took their leave shortly afterward. On the long drive back to Calgary Hal talked about Vicki but his thoughts were on that little scene in the Bennett living room.

The next day Hal presented himself at the Bar J, asking to see the lease. "I think Vicki has it in town," Mr. Bennett told him. "I have a key to her apartment, and I'd be happy to go in with you if you think it's important."

"If you wouldn't mind, I'd appreciate it, Mr. Bennett."

The lease was in the middle drawer of Vicki's desk. The two-page document was headed "Petroleum and Natural Gas Lease" and the closely printed words were so much gibberish to Hal. But they wouldn't be gibberish to Clint Rogers, a lawyer and amateur rider who specialized in petroleum law.

"I'd like to borrow this and have a friend of mine look at it."

"Help yourself." The older man looked troubled. "If there's anything wrong with that lease, you tell Stan we'll give him a new one for free. Mrs. Bennett and me are mighty fond of that boy."

"I'll tell him. Meanwhile, don't mention this to anyone. Okay?"

The first thing Hal did was to go to a commercial copier and have a photocopy of the lease made. Then he took a felt pen and carefully blanked out all the names and the land description so there would be no way of identifying the property. That done, he phoned Rogers to ask for an appointment. The lawyer, a great fan of Hal's, promised to make time to see him late that same afternoon.

"I'm not sure I can afford your fancy fees," said Hal as he settled into a chair in front of the lawyer's desk. "But I really do need an expert opinion on a petroleum lease."

The lawyer grinned. "You've never billed me for all the riding tips you've given me. It was your suggestion to ride the mare on a snaffle that won the lightweight hunter class for me up at Red Deer. This one's on the house. What have you got?"

Hal handed over the photocopy of the lease. The lawyer scanned it with the eager interest of an archaeologist examining the Dead Sea Scrolls. "It's past its primary term," he announced, adding when he saw the puzzled look on Hal's face, "It was for a primary term of three years and that expired on May 7th of this year. However, it will continue in force if there's production." He glanced across the desk at Hal. "Is it producing oil or gas?"

"Oil. Barrels of the stuff."

"Hmm. That should be okay then." The lawyer's eyes travelled down the page. "Now that's interesting." Once again he looked at Hal. "Do you know when the well was drilled?"

"Not exactly. Sometime in the last couple of months, I guess."

"Before the 7th of May?"

"I just don't know. It makes a difference, I take it?"

"You better believe it. This lease is the type that doesn't permit you to drill over the primary term. You have to have a well completed and on production before the end of the three years or you lose the lease." Rogers' finger tapped the space where Hal had inked out the land description. "I can get the exact date from the Conservation Board but I'll need the location and the name of the well."

Hal read off the land description from his copy of the lease and told Rogers the well had been drilled by Star Oil.

"Okay. That should do it. Why don't you come around just before lunch? I should know the answer by then."

"It's not worth the paper it's written on," the lawyer declared. "Drilling commenced on April 29th, and the rig wasn't released until the 21st of May—two weeks after the primary term had expired. I don't know whether that's good or bad news as far as you're concerned, but that's the way it is."

"It's pretty frightening news, if you want the truth. What happens to the oil now?"

"It belongs to whoever owns the minerals rights."

The Bennetts were multi-millionaires and didn't even know it. Hal cleared a throat that had gone suddenly dry. "One more question. Would an ordinary lawyer, not a specialist like yourself, be able to figure this out?"

"If something made him suspicious, he could work it out with the aid of a textbook. Where did this lawyer graduate from?"

Hal figured there was no point in telling him the lawyer was a she. "The University of Calgary."

"In that case, the answer to your question is definitely yes. They're heavy on oil and gas law. I lecture up there myself from time to time."

After he left the lawyer's office Hal drove out to the Foothills Riding Academy, a few kilometres west of Green Fields on Highway 22X. The Foothills stable specialized in western riding, and Stan went out there occasionally to hire a foolproof quarter horse for a quiet ride in the country. But they hadn't seen Stan for a couple of weeks. It was a setback to Hal's theory, but by no means a fatal one. Stan could easily have walked down to the lake from the highway and waited for Vicki to come along.

Back at Green Fields, Hal agonized over what he had found out before finally deciding that he had no choice but to bring Steinoff into it.

"This had better be good, old buddy." Starchuk slammed the door of the Mercedes with a force that made Hal wince. "I had to cut short a meeting with a drilling contractor to drive out here."

"We can talk in the tack room." Hal led the way across the stableyard where Vicki's lifeless body had lain—could it have been only six days ago? He was shocked by Starchuk's haggard appearance; the man looked like a sleepless wreck.

"Your lease is no good," Hal said bluntly, "and you've known it all along."

Stan's mouth worked, but no words came out. He staggered back, sending one of the saddles crashing to the floor.

"Vicki knew it, too. That's why you killed her."

Stan didn't seem to hear him. He had the look of a man who sees the abyss opening before him.

"You didn't have to kill her, you know. The Bennetts would have given you a new lease. They *like* you. How do you like that for irony?"

"Kill Vicki?" A look of bewilderment replaced the dismay on Stan's face. "I didn't kill anybody." He shook his head as if to free himself of an accusation that was too ridiculous for further discussion. "I'm finished before I even got started," he was mumbling to himself. "Everything depended on that well." He paused and looked at Hal with a sudden gleam of hope. "Did I hear you say the Bennetts would give me a new lease? Do you really think they would?"

"I wouldn't know," replied Hal indifferently. He felt like a fool. He had been so sure, and yet all he had accomplished was to forfeit Stan's friendship. He had known Stan for years and if there was one thing the exuberant oilman was not, that was an actor. It had been Stan's notorious inability to disguise his feelings that Hal had been counting on when he decided to stage the confrontation scene. Stan's reaction was that of a man overwhelmed by the financial disaster that had befallen him, not that of a man guilty of murder. Hal made no attempt to detain him as the agitated oilman scurried away.

"Good try, but no cigar." Steinoff stepped out of the adjoining small room where the waxes and leather polishes were left. "Hey, where are you going?"

"To call the Bennetts and warn them not to sign anything."

The pay phone was on the porch outside the main office. In the middle of telling Mrs. Bennett that she and her husband were not to sign any papers until he had a chance to talk to them, Hal happened to glance through the window and intercept a venomous look from Mike Dawes. The stable manager immediately lowered his gaze and pretended to study a show catalogue on his desk, but it was too late to hide the hatred burning from his eyes. Hal had always known that he and Mike had never been what you would call bosom buddies but he had never suspected anything like this. Could it be that Mike had been building a dream world around himself and Vicki that had come crashing down when Hal made a play for her?

Shaken, Hal hastily completed his call and headed back to the tack room to rejoin Steinoff. A horse was acting up in the nearby paddock. Big Bounce, a pretty fair jumper, galloped straight at the fence only to slide to a halt with his chest almost touching the rails. Funny how even the most experienced jumping horses would never take a fence on their own. Without a rider to urge them on, they would go around even the lowest obstacles. Hal stood stock still for a moment, then strode rapidly across the yard.

"I know how Mike could have killed Vicki and still got back here in time," he announced.

Steinoff looked as if he might have had enough of Hal's theories for one day, but he gave a small resigned sigh and muttered, "Let's have it."

"Sundancer would have to take the long way home, following the road. Dragging that weight he would have no choice, and besides horses don't jump on their own. If you were on a jumper you could take a straight line across the fields and cut off at least two kilometres. And don't forget that Sundancer would be slowed down by dragging Vicki. Let's assume Mike met up with Vicki in the woods. Nothing would be more natural then for them to dismount and have a visit. He kills her by smashing in her head with something like a hammer or a wrench that he's brought with him. He jams her leg into the stirrup, rigs the safety bar so it won't release, and loosens the girth so the saddle will slip and spook the horse. Then he turns Sundancer loose, starts him off with a slap on the rump, and races him home, dropping Vicki's helmet on the way. If he took one of the horses from the back pasture, he could strip off the tack, stash it somewhere, and be in his office in time to call the ambulance. And,'' Hal added as an afterthought, ''he would know enough to switch chin straps.''

''What if he was seen?''

''Not likely in the first place. Not at that time of day and coming up the back way. And nobody would think anything of it, in any case. The stable manager out for a cross country gallop, that's all.''

''Mr. Dawes was riding Stormy Lee at 1:30 that afternoon. I saw him.'' The wispy voice floated down from somewhere above them, making both men jump. Wendy's plaintive face was peering down through a partly open trapdoor.

''Don't do that to me, Wendy,'' Hal said with a shaky laugh. He caught her as she swung herself down and lowered her to the floor. She stared up in trepidation at the tall Mountie. ''I didn't figure it was important. He was just riding along the road.''

''In what direction, Wendy?'' Hal asked gently. ''Towards the lake?''

She nodded gravely and he said, ''The timing is right. He'd be on his way to intercept her. You didn't happen to see him holding a chin strap in his hand, did you?''

''Naw. I only saw him from far away.''

Steinoff surveyed his prospective chief witness gloomily.

''You're sure it was Mr. Dawes you saw?''

''Yes, sir. Positive. I was kinda surprised to see him riding Stormy Lee. He belongs to one of the private boarders who's away for the summer.''

''This Stormy Lee is a jumper, I take it?''

''Jumps like a bloody deer. Stands back at his fences and flies,'' Hal informed him. ''Ideal for the purpose.''

Hal turned back to Wendy; nothing at Green Fields escaped

the sharp gaze of the lonely little waif. "Vicki was kinda particular about her tack, wasn't she?"

"She sure was. She kept everything squeaky clean and oiled. I remember her telling me once that in three-day-eventing your life could depend on your equipment."

"So you wouldn't expect her to use a grungy old chin strap, half rotted through, would you?"

"Never," she replied firmly. "Not Vicki."

"Enough?" Hal asked the Mountie.

"Enough for me to take Mr. Dawes down to the station and ask him to 'assist us in our investigation,' as we police call it." Steinoff paused, then added grimly, "And he can start by explaining why he told me he had been doing paperwork in his office ever since lunch that day."

To Court Disaster

ELAINE MATLOW

Elaine Matlow lives in Toronto with her husband and two children. She was born in Toronto, graduated in English from the University of Toronto, has a master's degree in education, and has taught English, Theatre Arts, and English as a Second Language in Toronto, England, and Israel. She is presently teaching E.S.L. at a Toronto high school and is working on a novel featuring a charming, funny woman detective. This is her first story.

WHEN I WAS approached by John Jeffrey Edwards to do a week's work for two million dollars, I hardly hesitated. The body bothered me, not the risk.

I have always been a risk-taker. At forty-three my risk-taking had landed me in a genuine mid-life crisis. No vague feeling of life gone awry or life slipping away for me; instead, a full knowledge that life had gone awry, and that I had done it to myself. I had often wondered in the last few years at which point things became irretrievable, at which point could I have made a different decision and saved myself. My mother didn't help matters by frequently reminding me, or herself, that I had started out with such promise, had been thought of as a golden boy in high school and university. Now, I have two ex-wives, a child who has changed his name to Dev Singh and wears a white turban, a best friend who is wary of me because of a one-afternoon stand with his wife that I'm guessing she told him about, and, the *pièce de résistance*, a disbarment from the Law Society of Upper Canada. On that November day when this all started, I had, as well, too many debts and was unable to indulge my taste for very high living.

That grim, grimy November day was a nice example of pathetic fallacy for the way I felt about my life. I felt finished, totally lacking in confidence, and unable to do any of the things I enjoyed. Unfortunately, the things I enjoyed were those best things of life that are very far from being free, things like alpine skiing or Caribbean scuba diving or eating at places like Michel

Guérard's Les Prés d'Eugénie. I couldn't even afford a membership at the downtown "Y" at that time. And I hated my old bachelor apartment on Spadina Road. It was clear to me and I'm sure to everyone who still knew me that I was a failure.

But with two million dollars I'd be able to buy my life back again. I would be able to play the stocks, travel, live in a nice place, and get some respect as a survivor who hadn't gone down with his troubles. Best of all, I could buy myself an island on Stoney Lake where I had spent my summers as a boy before my father left and build a cottage there. And then I could pay off and kiss off my ex-wives and my prospective ex-creditors.

Edwards himself phoned that afternoon and asked if he could come to my apartment that evening at 8:00 p.m. He explained that he had an interesting proposition for me, and that our mutual acquaintance, Joe Stevens, had suggested me as the perfect man for the job. I knew Joe from a not exactly illegal and not exactly successful deal that I had gone into with him and a few other guys after my disbarment.

I told Edwards to come over for a drink. At precisely 8:00 p.m. he arrived at the building, buzzed me on the intercom, and came up to an apartment that had never seen better days.

He was a large man in his mid-fifties, very well-dressed in a custom-tailored, understated way. He had that air of power, parochialism, and wealth that attends small-town Ontario big shots. He was a multi-millionaire from a town called Edwardsville, no less, which is provincially famous as the home of McNairn's potato chips and Gruber's boots and skates. But in the town itself, as I was to find, the name Edwards carried the most weight.

I gave us both some Bell's whisky, which I usually hoarded for the worst depressions. Edwards told me the story which led to his offer of two million dollars for a week's work.

He had been charged with trafficking in narcotics to as much of western Ontario as he could organize. It was said that he dealt exclusively in cocaine. He told me that P.L. Wardinger, the no-lose defence lawyer he had imported from Toronto to defend him, couldn't see how Edwards could possibly escape a jail sentence. So Edwards had let Wardinger go. But Wardinger had left with a throw-away remark which had pointed Edwards towards me. Wardinger had said that Edwards' only hope would be if he owned his own judge.

Well, Edwards did own the one county court judge in Edwardsville, in a manner of speaking. Hugh Macpherson had been his best friend since birth. His family was one of the few acceptable to the Edwards in the town, I gathered, and the only acceptable family that produced a male of his own age. They had gone to Upper Canada College and to Queen's University together. Edwards had got him his appointment to the Bench when the Conservatives were in power federally. Edwards thought that Macpherson would probably do anything for him. Only the judicial system didn't allow friendship to mix with justice. And, if a principal in a court case was known at all well to a judge, another judge had to try the case. Since there was only one county court judge in Edwardsville, a Toronto judge would have to be sent there on circuit duty to try the case, and Macpherson would go to Toronto to do a stint during Edwards' trial. Even Edwards didn't think he could buy the unknown Toronto judge. So he was proposing to buy me.

He had already set up the operation. He had hired a not too bright hard-drinking lawyer from the town who would know nothing of the Toronto judges and who could be controlled. He had arranged with some of his drug-dealing colleagues to have two available henchmen kidnap the Toronto judge, keep him drugged in some hideout for the duration of the trial, and then arrange a fatal car accident near Toronto so that the Toronto police would be involved and not the police in Avon County where Edwardsville was. The Avon police might naturally be puzzled by seeing a different dead judge from the live one who had presided over their court. At any rate, Edwards assured me that everything was or would be arranged. All I had to do was drive into Edwardsville in that poor bugger's car, stay at whichever of the two hotels his secretary had booked for him

(Edwards could find that out easily), and then go to court and dispense some phony justice.

A very interesting and well-paid little job. I felt enormous excitement, a few qualms, and a few fears. I told Edwards that I was worried about people recognizing me, either in Edwardsville, or afterwards. He asked me if I had ever in my life run into anyone from Edwardsville before. I hadn't. I was almost certainly going to know no one as myself while I was there.

"But what if someone from Edwardsville recognizes me a year from now, say, and wonders why I'm not dead," I continued, worrying aloud.

"You put a sad look on your face and explain that your cousin, whom you've always resembled and who was a great guy, was the judge who was killed. Anyway, you can change your hairstyle or something afterwards."

"There's another possible problem," I went on. "What if the guy's wife calls him in Edwardsville?"

"That could be awkward. But the trial doesn't have to last for more than a few days. You don't call her, of course, and leave a message with the desk that you don't want to be disturbed by anyone. Tell them to take all messages and hold them for you. They can think you had a fight with your wife before you left, if they think anything. And she'll think you're terribly busy even if she wonders about it. The wife won't be a problem. Maybe there won't even be a wife."

"Oh, those guys all have wives. The establishment tends to behave in an established manner. But what you're saying makes sense. And if the job didn't have a few risks it wouldn't be worth that kind of money to you."

He agreed, and I wanted the job, all right. So I put my fears from my mind. I put the death of the unknown judge from my mind, too. It was like that game we played in university. We would ask each other questions such as: If you could kill an unknown person on another continent for a million dollars by pressing a button for one second, and never suffer any consequences, would you do it? In university, most of us thought we wouldn't.

I was well suited for the job by more than my healthy nerves or my sick scruples. When I was still a promising young man I was one of the three students chosen out of my bar-admission course of four hundred students to spend a year as clerk to the Chief Justice. During that year I sat through trials, drafted judgements for the judges, researched points of law, and acted as a sounding board for their lordships during cases. That experience, coupled with my years in the courtroom as a litigation lawyer, gave me a pretty good knowledge of how a judge conducts himself. I decided to read over some drug cases in back issues of *Canadian Criminal Cases* to familiarize myself again with some points of law and also with judicial jargon.

Then I decided that I would change my looks before the trial so that I could go back to looking like myself afterwards. I ate a lot, things I didn't even like, like rich desserts, and stopped exercising so that I began to look sloppy and out of shape. I slouched. I grew a moustache which turned out to be red even though my hair is light brown. I wore my glasses instead of the usual contacts. I had my hair cut much shorter directly before the trial. And when I eventually left for Edwardsville, I packed only my conservative clothes.

I drove west from Toronto to Joe Stevens' place in the Caledon Hills. The judge was to be kept there. I left my car in the double garage and got into his car. It was a green 1978 Volvo and had the usual CCJ (County Court Judge) licence plates. It also had a kid's red woollen glove on the back seat, one of those gloves with a different little face and yellow woollen hair on each finger and the thumb. Before I drove away, I took the glove and put it in the trunk so I wouldn't have to look at it. Then I got back into the driver's seat and drove to the only alternative to the Valhalla Inn in Edwardsville. The judge had been booked there. The hotel's vintage was somewhere between 1900 and 1920 with lots of dark wood, stained and leaded glass windows, and faded charm. There was a dining room, too. I told the young man at the desk who I was, Judge Stirling, and asked not to be disturbed by anyone at all, including my wife, while I was there. Let them think what they might.

I'm lucky to be able to sleep well under any circumstances. So the disturbing excitement didn't hit me until the next morning. I dressed in my grey flannel suit and took the judge's green velvet robe bag downstairs with me. It contained his black and white striped trousers, a white shirt with a wing collar and legal tabs, a vest coat, and his black robe with purple trim. An obvious possible snag we hadn't considered was the possibility that the judge was a totally different size and shape from me. But, in fact, he was almost the same size as I am as I ascertained with relief as soon as I had got to the hotel room the evening before. That morning I wondered if there were any more obvious snags we had left unconsidered.

I wanted to have breakfast in a room full of people so I picked up a Toronto *Globe and Mail* and ate in the hotel dining room. I couldn't read much of the *Globe.* I was going to impersonate a judge that day. Actually I already was impersonating a judge; people were busy giving me covert glances from various parts of the dining room.

I took a cab over to the courthouse. It was a moderately ugly 1950s building which housed the Provincial Court, the Supreme Court, the County Court, and the Registry Office, separated by just a short distance from the county jail. It didn't look like a real courthouse to me, either because it was so different from the one in Toronto or because I thought of it as a stage set for my performance.

I went in and was directed with a lot of bowing and scraping to the judge's chambers adjacent to the courtroom. I hung up my grey suit in the closet and put on my borrowed finery. Then I waited for my cue. The sheriff's deputy came to the chambers and said, "Whenever you're ready, Your Honour."

The courtroom was large and square. I sat on the usual bench on a raised platform and felt unexpectedly comfortable there. I was protected by my image. I so represented position, authority, and, possibly, justice to those assembled in that room that they were concerned only with how they might impress or affect me. Certainly no one would dream of questioning my credentials. I remembered my own feelings towards judges, especially in my earliest years in the law. I thought of them in the same way as I had my teachers in elementary school: that is, as suprahuman beings whom I felt it necessary to please, and who had no existence in my mind beyond the time I was with them.

I listened carefully that morning and made copious notes in a notebook. Every once in a while I asked a pertinent question. The whole thing was easy for me, and I was doing fine. I was also enjoying myself. I hoped that Edwards appreciated what a class act he had hired.

The sheriff took me out to lunch that first day at the Valhalla Inn. He was a nervous man with almost no chin who talked incessantly. Most of his conversation was highly improper for a sheriff to a presiding judge. He went on about what a great guy Edwards was, and how he was sure that Edwards couldn't be guilty. Not the sort of guy who supported every charity in town, Edwards had just last year donated a whole new wing to the town hospital. I let him talk, ate my hamburger, and thanked him for lunch. He had wasted a lunch on me. I had already been bought.

The rest of the three-day trial continued without a hitch, and so did the rest of the scam. It worried me that Stirling's wife phoned a few times. Obviously I couldn't return her calls, and I wondered if she wondered if anything was wrong. Well, she may have wondered, but nothing ever came of it. I gave judgement with ingenious plausibility at the end of the trial, drove to Joe Stevens' place, drove my own car home, and started drinking the Bell's.

It was in the *Globe* that night. I was drunk by that time but I made it to the box a block away which carried the first edition. At the bottom of the front page was a short report of the "accident" under the headline: JUDGE DIES IN CAR CRASH. I kept drinking for several weeks.

But I emerged to question whether justice existed anywhere, because my life became very sweet after that time. There wasn't a day I didn't enjoy with that conscious appreciation of those who have made a comeback from a prolonged depression.

Of all the pleasures in my life, the summer house I had built on my quickly purchased island on Stoney Lake gave me the most gratification. I had it winterized and went up there often. The lake didn't freeze over in the winter, so there was always access to my island. And the Millbanks on the mainland kept up a kind of boat and general store service throughout the year. During the summer, I had found a local woman who was willing to clean for me twice a week, and she was pursuaded to come once a week during the rest of the year. I often invited friends to stay, some new ones and some I'd had the confidence to rediscover once I had some money.

Even my son came for a week in August. I suspect he had to get permission from his cult leader; I know for a fact that he had to get permission from the leader before he could see a movie. But he came, and we found a way of being together. He loved sailing, we had some swimming races, he cooked me some gourmet vegetarian meals, and I found that he was just as angry as I was at the greedy bastards who are polluting our air and ruining our country. I liked being with him, and he liked being with me for the first time in years. I was hardly even embarrassed at going over to the Millbanks with a son who wore a T-shirt over his bathing suit which read "Follow a Spiritual Path" and a white turban.

Yes, I was happy that summer and happy during the autumn and winter. I had fun investing my money, spending time at the island house, having my condo at St. Clair and Avenue Road redone, and skiing as much as I could. Whenever I thought of Judge Stirling, or his wife, or the kid of the red glove, I forced myself not to, turned my mind to the off position, and thought about anything else.

One of the things I thought about was doing some good with my money. I gave a lot to various charities, joined the board of The Public Against Pollution, became a Big Brother to a Laotian kid who had managed to get here with his family only to have his father die of a heart attack after they arrived.

I gave the most money and the most time to ecological

organizations. One of these organizations, the Against Acid Rain Coalition, gave a benefit dinner in May, a hundred-dollar-a-plate dinner at the Sheraton with the Canadian ambassador to Washington as the guest speaker.

At first I was just going to send in my hundred dollars. The money was to be used to send lobbyists to Washington. I didn't like the idea of a dull dinner with hundreds of strangers. But then the president of the cottagers' association of Stoney Lake phoned me and talked me into going. They were going to keep aside a few tables for our cottagers' association, and I wanted to meet some more of my neighbours. It was a community that I wanted to be part of.

I arrived early and didn't see anyone I knew from Stoney Lake, just a lawyer from my pre-disbarment days who pretended he didn't know me. I got myself a scotch. And then I saw her.

Except for the odd pick-up, I had been avoiding women for the last three or four years. Perhaps that made me more vulnerable. There isn't a precise equivalent in English for what the French call *coup de foudre* and the Italians call *innamoramento.* I looked at a face which was the most satisfactory face I had ever seen and she looked at me and we both kept looking. I felt a shot of an almost forgotten emotion. A rush of pure joy moved me towards her.

I took a risk.

"Let's forget the dinner," I addressed her. "We've already given our money to the still-living fish. Will you have dinner with me somewhere alone?"

Perhaps she was a risk-taker too.

"I'd love to," she smiled. A lightbulb shone behind her face.

"Do you have a cottage?" I asked. It was the most common reason for wanting to come to this dinner.

"Yes, we've had a cottage in Muskoka for many years. I was up there with my children for a month this summer."

"Did you see the effects of acid rain this summer?" I noted with relief that she had said, "*I* was up there. . . ." Not we.

After I had asked her for dinner, I had noticed that she was wearing a wedding ring. But she had to be divorced or separated. I hoped.

She told me about the polluted water and dying trees in Muskoka. While she was talking I watched her face with total pleasure, happy to be able to look at her and talk to her. I interrupted her with an unusual lack of finesse, for me, based on an unusual amount of real feeling.

"I haven't wanted to go out to dinner with a woman for a long time," I ventured.

"It's been a long time since I've wanted to go out to dinner with a man too," she replied.

"How come?" I asked.

"There have been reasons. I'll tell you later. At any rate, it has been a season for lying fallow."

"O.K. I'll ask you later. Where would you like to go for dinner?"

"Il Posto, if you like it."

"It's my favourite restaurant in Toronto."

I took her arm and with neatly manoeuvred gallantry swept her out of the bar area. As we were coming off the escalator to head for the front door I saw the sheriff of Edwardsville standing in front of me with a woman I assumed to be his wife. He was staring at me in horror.

"My God, Judge Stirling, I thought you were dead!"

I stared at him for a few seconds, trying to will myself to respond naturally. I had to explain to him about being Judge Stirling's cousin.

"This must be your wife," he babbled on. "Are you Mrs. Stirling?"

She was looking at me with a darkened face and an expression that was very different than the one she had had for me a few moments ago. It was a look of savage surmise.

"Yes," she answered slowly. "Yes, I am Mrs. Stirling." She was still looking at me. "Judge Stirling's wife."

The Girl in the White Dress

TONY ASPLER

Tony Aspler, one of the founding members of the Crime Writers of Canada, acted as the association's first Chairman from 1982 to 1984. He has written five novels: The Streets of Askelon *(1972),* One of My Marionettes *(1973),* Chain Reaction *(1978),* The Scorpion Sanction *(1980), and* The Music Wars *(1982), the last three with Gordon Pape. He is also a wine writer, contributing a weekly column to the* Toronto Star, *and is the author of* Vintage Canada.

A SILVER-DOLLAR SUN shone out of a blue sky on the abandoned summer hotel. A light wind banged a shutter against its peeling facade. The grass, which had grown unchecked for years, brushed against rotting timbers and threatened to engulf the only access route to what had once been Ontario's most fashionable summer resort.

The hotel itself was a three-storey building of wood built on a promontory overlooking Lake Ontario. It stood above limestone cliffs honeycombed with caves. Below it the water—blue as a young girl's ribbon—stretched away into a white haze which, on a clearer day, would have been visible as the shoreline of New York State on the other side of the lake.

Even in decay the summer hotel had a stately dignity which suggested the grandeur of former days when it had been the magnet for wealthy Torontonians escaping the city's heat in July and August and for vacationing Americans.

The main building was shaped like an "E" without the middle bar. Connected to it by a covered walkway was a dance pavilion whose walls could be raised on hot summer nights, several guest cottages, and a gatehouse which commanded the only road into the grounds.

On that afternoon the sound of the grasshoppers humming in the long grass and the banging of the shutter were drowned by the arrival of a two-tone Lincoln convertible which pulled up in front of the hotel dragging a trailer of dust behind it. The car was observed by an old man at the window of the gatehouse as he squinted myopically through a broken pane.

The old man watched as the driver opened the car door and stood surveying the ruined hotel. The sun flashed on gold cufflinks and dust settled on the alligator shoes. The man wiped perspiration from his forehead with a silk handkerchief.

"Mr. Kinnear," the stranger called out. The only reply was the electric whine of the grasshoppers and the sigh of the wind through the grass. "Is anyone there?"

Garratt Kinnear grunted to himself and moved away from the window. He pulled at the straps of his denim overalls. Another one had come. Why didn't they leave him alone? He coughed and spat on the floor.

The man had his back to him as he shuffled out into the sunlight. He shielded his eyes against the reflected light off the lake. Why did they keep coming?

"What d'you want?"

The man turned, startled at the sound of his voice.

"Are you Kinnear?" he asked, moving around the car to get a better look at the old man.

"Who wants him?"

"The name's Armitage. President of Armitage Developments." He took a card from his breast pocket with a flourish and handed it to Kinnear who did not take it.

"I made an offer for the property. I want to look around."

The man gestured towards the hotel. Garratt Kinnear's features twitched as if he were listening to a voice in his head and not to the man.

"You hearing me, old man?"

"Don't know nothin' about that. Nobody told me."

"I talked with the Ministry."

"I'm only the caretaker. Get someone else." He turned away and rubbed a sneakered foot into the dirt as if he was stubbing out a cigarette.

"I haven't got all day, Kinnear. Just open the place up."

"What you goin' to do with it?"

"If I decide to buy it, I'll tear it down and build a motel complex." The man took his wallet from his inside pocket and ostentatiously riffled through the bills inside.

"Motel you say," repeated Kinnear, rubbing his hands down his denims. Armitage took out a $10 bill and stuffed it into the old man's hand. Kinnear accepted it without pleasure and shuffled towards the front door.

"Wasn't always like this," he said. "Used to be the best summer place along the bay, maybe in the whole of Prince Edward County."

Inside it smelled of dank earth and fungus. The man looked at the ruins of what was once the hotel's reception area. The desk was a few splintered boards. To the left was a dining room. In the centre was a rusty fountain long since devoid of water.

"How long's it been like this?" asked Armitage.

"Been closed these ten years. I look after the place," said Kinnear, gazing at the ceiling.

"So I see. They pay you, do they?"

"Pay?"

"How do you live, old man?"

"Pension. And visitors like you."

Armitage took a notebook from his pocket and with a small silver pencil began to make notes.

"What are you writin'?" demanded the old man.

"Estimates," replied Armitage. "For demolition."

Garratt Kinnear pushed a loose floorboard out of his path and spat again.

"What's up there?" asked Armitage.

"Guest rooms," he replied.

"Let's take a look."

Kinnear followed the businessman to the foot of the stairs. The oak timbers creaked under their weight as they moved. Motes of dust danced in the shafts of sunlight that filtered through the boarded-up windows.

"Are these stairs safe?" asked Armitage. "They look like they should have been condemned years ago."

"You won't find a better view of the lake. They all used to like it. I can show you the comments in the guest book," said Kinnear.

Armitage placed a tentative foot on the bottom step.

"How long have you worked here?"

"Man and boy," said Kinnear. "1928. The view from the third floor's best."

"You sure it's safe?"

"Used to be up and down those stairs a hundred times a day till my heart went funny on me," said the old man. He leaned against the balustrade and nodded encouragingly at Armitage who began to move slowly up the stairs.

"Every summer they used to come here. All the fine people in their fancy carriages and motorcars. Mr. Brock, he was the owner then. Garratt, he said, your job is to wait on tables and carry the luggage. Take the lady's bags up to room fourteen. Nice leather luggage it was. Smelled as sweet as hay. And the ladies all in white."

"The view's fine," Armitage called down from the second-floor landing.

"It's better from the top," Kinnear shouted up. "Over that elm out back."

He listened to the creaking of the floorboards above as Armitage moved up to the third floor.

"Every Sunday they had a corn roast on the rocks. Can you see the rocks? And picnics. I helped spread their tablecloths on the grass. And they danced in the pavilion. There was always dancing. Can you hear the music, Mr. Armitage?"

Suddenly there was a loud splintering sound of dry, rotten wood giving way. Then a crash as Armitage fell through the stairwell. Garratt Kinnear heard him scream as he fell three stories and the sickening thud as his body hit the rocks below the ground floor. The old man nodded his head and walked out into the afternoon sunshine once more. The sound of a jazz band playing "Maple Leaf Rag" echoed in his head and he thought of the girl in the white dress he had seen nearly fifty years ago. . . .

Clara Powell and her eighteen-year-old daughter, Angela, stepped off the train at Picton Station, accompanied by eleven pieces of luggage for their summer vacation. They looked around for the transportation the hotel had promised. Eventually, an awkward young man approached them, tipped his cap, and introduced himself as Garratt Kinnear. The open, horse-drawn carriage was ready. He would load their luggage and drive them to the hotel.

The young man could not take his eyes off Angela Powell, the most beautiful girl he had ever seen. On the ten-mile journey to the hotel he listened to the conversation between mother and daughter, glancing in the side mirrors to see the girl.

"I've been coming here for the last seven years, Mother," pouted Angela. "Why can't we go somewhere exciting, like New Orleans?"

"This is your father's busy time, Angela. In the winter we can go south together as a family."

When they arrived at the hotel Garratt Kinnear helped the two women down from the carriage. Sam Brock, the son of the owner, was at the desk when they checked in. Kinnear noticed the looks that passed between Angela and the young man. Their exchange of glances did not escape her mother either.

Sam Brock came out from behind the desk and took the suitcases Garratt Kinnear was holding.

"You've certainly got taller since last year, young Brock," said Clara Powell. "I take it we have the same suite as always."

"Sure thing, ma'am. If you'd like to follow me."

"I'd rather you had nothing to do with that young man, Angela," said Clara, once they had closed the door of their room and taken off their travelling hats. "He's in trade and trade is vulgar. I'm sure you'll meet some very nice young men here. More fitting. Now I suggest you have a little nap after your journey."

"I'm not tired, Mother. I think I'll read by the lake."

Garratt Kinnear watched her as she walked across the croquet lawn and settled herself on a flat rock overlooking the lake. Her pale dress spread out about her, foaming like milk. The sun seemed to shine just for her. There was no one on the desk to see him leave so he took a parasol out to the girl, moving quickly among the croquet players, oblivious to the pock and click of mallet on ball.

"Thought you might need this," he said gruffly, trying to cover his confusion. But she refused it, laughing. The blue of the lake was in her eyes and the butter of the sun in her hair.

At dinner that night all heads turned as Clara and Angela Powell entered the dining room and took their seats at a table by the fountain. But no eyes were more rivetted on the girl than those of Garratt Kinnear from his station by the kitchen door. When he cleared the dishes from their table he accidentally dropped a knife in Angela's lap. Her mother admonished him for his clumsiness but the girl just smiled at him and dabbed at her dress with her napkin.

"You better not be getting any ideas about that girl at table five," said Sam Brock in the kitchen. "I'm taking her to the dance tonight." Garratt Kinnear watched through the service window as Sam Brock approached the table. He saw Angela smile up at the young man and the expression of distaste on her mother's face. And he saw Sam wink at the girl over her mother's shoulder.

That night Angela called out softly to her mother to see if she was sleeping. When she got no reply she slipped quietly out of bed and put her dress on. Carrying her shoes she tiptoed over the creaking boards and closed the door gently behind her.

Sam Brock was waiting for her under the trees outside the dance pavilion. The music of a five-piece band reverberated off the marble floor and rolled out across the lawn towards the lake. A line of Chinese lanterns strung between the trees defined the gardens which ended abruptly at the cliff edge. Angela Powell held her hands out to Sam Brock, and they drew each other close as they moved onto the dance floor.

"You've grown up a lot since last summer," said Sam.

"You wouldn't think so to listen to my mother," replied Angela.

As the young couple swayed to the syncopated rhythm, their bodies flush, a sweet warm wind blew off the lake. More guests had joined them on the dance floor and Sam Brock glanced around. Standing by a pillar, watching them, was Garratt Kinnear.

"How about a walk?" suggested Sam.

They strolled hand in hand until they were past the boundary of the lanterns. A path led to the top of the cliff, illuminated by the light of the moon in a cloudless sky. They could hear the sound of the music but the hotel was hidden from them by the rising sand dunes. In the silvery distance of the lake the lamps of the night fishermen glowed like fireflies above the still water.

Sam Brock stopped and pulled Angela to him. He kissed her on the lips and the young girl responded. He began to feel her breasts through her dress. Alarmed by the pressure of his hands and frightened by her own response, Angela pulled away from him.

"Please Sam. It's my first day."

"What about tomorrow then?'

Angela laughed, picked up her skirt, and ran back towards the hotel.

She crept back into her room and slid out of her dress and into bed. She lay awake listening to her mother's heavy breathing. Her eyes shone in the darkness, and she stared at the ceiling, composing in her mind what she would confide in her diary about Sam Brock. If the lights had been on she might have noticed a crack in the ceiling. In the attic above, Garratt Kinnear had his eye to it. He watched her for nearly an hour until she had fallen asleep.

"Where the hell have you been, Sam?" His father, Henry Brock, proprietor of the summer hotel, stood on a small dock in a cave below the limestone cliffs to the west of the hotel. A motor launch, weighed down to the gunwales with wooden crates, rolled on the gentle swell. "This is no time to be late. Is anyone standing watch up there?"

Henry Brock's voice echoed in the cave.

"The busboy, Kinnear. He's as thick as two planks but he's got the eyes of a cat."

"He better have. The U.S. Coast Guard's been swarming over the lake and so have the feds. Our people in Sodus Bay are expecting this lot tomorrow night, so I want you to check the manifest." He handed his son a list and left him to work.

Sam pulled back the tarpaulin and inspected the cases. When his father was out of earshot, he pried open one of the cases and removed a bottle of whisky, which he secreted away in his jacket pocket. When he had counted the cases and secured the tarpaulin once more, he climbed out of the cave to the ridge below the line of sand dunes. He covered the entrance with driftwood and felt his way up the path to the cliff top. There, silhouetted against the night sky, stood Garratt Kinnear staring dreamily out at the silvery water.

"Anyone come by?"

Kinnear shook his head.

"You'd better get some sleep then. You're up early tomorrow."

Sam Brock watched as the boy walked off, sure-footed in the darkness, in the direction of the hotel.

The next morning a stiffening breeze blew off the lake, pressing the women's skirts against their legs as they played croquet on the lawn. Garratt Kinnear knocked on the door of the Powells' bedroom. Once he was sure there was no one inside he let himself in with a pass key. His nostrils detected the faint odour of cologne. He picked up the pillow on Angela's unmade bed and held it to his face, inhaling its scent. Still clutching the pillow he moved over to the window and looked down. There was Angela, alone, half-heartedly striking croquet balls with a mallet.

"What are you doing with that pillow?" Clara Powell stood in the doorway, stern and suspicious.

Garratt Kinnear swung around to face her, eyes darting from left to right like a cornered animal.

"I was only—I was checking the beds," he stammered. "The maid asked me to check which rooms needed doing." He squeezed around the bed and moved towards the door. Clara Powell took the pillow from him as he passed her and threw it onto her daughter's bed.

"You can tell the maid she can make up the room after lunch. I'm going to take a nap," said Mrs. Powell, imperiously.

Garratt Kinnear took the back stairs to the kitchen and continued his vigil of Angela Powell from the tiny window above the plate racks. He saw Sam Brock walk out onto the croquet lawn and Angela's smile as he approached her.

"Good morning," said Sam. "Sleep well?"

"My mother snores," replied Angela with a grimace.

"Do you?" asked Sam.

"That's not a question you should ask a young lady," said Angela in mock reproof. "Why don't you take me for a walk instead."

"Where do you want to go?"

"My mother's lying down. Why don't we visit that old cave we used to play in when we were kids."

Sam frowned. "That's off limits to guests. It's too dangerous now. The limestone's eaten away."

"You're just saying that because you don't want to be alone with me," teased Angela. Picking up her skirts she ran off playfully in the direction of the cave. Sam called for her to stop but she kept running until he was forced to follow her. At first it was a game but when Angela realized that Sam was pursuing her in earnest she kept running through the reed-fringed dunes and up the path to the cliffs. She could hear Sam charging after her, calling for her, but she ran on until she found the entrance to the cave he had shown her years ago when they were children.

Angela scrambled down the narrow rock face that led into the cave. She could see a half-circle of light above the waterline and as her eyes became accustomed to the gloom she made out the lines of a motorboat and a small wooden dock. She stood on the shingle beach, breathing heavily as Sam called to her from the mouth of the cave above.

"I told you not to come here," said Sam, as he joined her by the boat. "You shouldn't have seen this."

"It's booze, isn't it, Sam? You're rum-running," exclaimed Angela, excitedly.

"Whisky," said Sam. "For the States." With a flourish he flung back the tarpaulin and Angela gasped at the quantity of liquor cases stacked underneath.

"When are you taking it across?"

"Tonight," said Sam. "If there's enough cloud."

"Oh Sam, let me come with you. I've never done anything exciting. Please Sam."

"Are you crazy? It's dangerous. There are patrol boats all over the lake. It's jail for me if I get caught."

"You won't get caught; you're too smart for that. You know this lake better than anyone. Please, take me with you."

Sam pulled her away towards the steps that led up to the dunes.

"It's not possible. So just forget you ever saw it, for my sake and yours. Now let's get out of here."

He held the young girl by the arm as he led her into the sunlight. Angela stopped and turned to him.

"What can I do to make you take me with you?" She kissed him on the lips and pulled him down on the sand beside her.

"Now. Are you going to take me along or not?" She laughed. He shook his head and again she kissed him. On the ridge above the young couple, concealed behind a clump of reeds, Garratt Kinnear observed their love-making. He saw Sam Brock's hands slip under the girl's white dress, and he could hear her sighs in the wind. Then Brock rolled over on top of her, spreading her legs. Angela cried out as he began to move above her. . . .

Tears of rage squeezed out of Garratt Kinnear's eyes. He kicked the sand under his feet and dug his teeth into his bottom lip until it bled. The groans of pleasure rang in his ears as he turned and rushed blindly back to the hotel.

"Chef's been looking for you," warned the maître d' as Kinnear ran into the pantry and closed the door behind him. In the darkness, amid the smell of potatoes and onions, Garratt Kinnear decided what he must do.

When the guests were at lunch and the hotel staff preoccupied in serving them, Kinnear made an anonymous phone call from the manager's office to the local police station. Sam Brock would be caught with a boatload of contraband liquor in the middle of the lake that night.

"Where have you been to get your dress in this condition?" demanded Clara Powell as mother and daughter readied themselves for the evening meal. Angela brushed her hair and smiled at her reflection in the mirror.

"Are you listening to me, young lady?"

"Yes, Mother. You were talking about my dress."

"Just look at it; it's ruined."

"It's only sand. I was climbing in the dunes."

"You're not a child any more, Angela," said Clara. "Kindly behave like a young lady. And hurry up and dress."

As they descended the staircase, Garratt Kinnear lingered at the foot. When Angela Powell approached she smiled at him, and as she passed, Kinnear pressed a note clumsily into her hand unseen by her mother. At the table Angela unfolded it, under cover of her serviette. Scrawled across it in large block capitals was the message: "I still love you."

Angela turned scarlet, realizing the implication of the note. The half-witted boy had spied on her. He had seen her in the dunes with Sam Brock. She glanced around the dining room, her face burning.

"What on earth is the matter with you, Angela? Are you having a hot flush?" demanded her mother.

"I want to go home!" hissed Angela.

"Are you ill? Is it too much sun?"

"I just want to go home. I hate it here."

"Kindly keep your voice down. People are looking." Clara Powell smiled at the neighbouring tables.

"I will not be treated like a child any more, Mother. I am not ill. I just want to go home."

"You will go to the room now. This instant, do you hear, missy. We will discuss it when I have had my dinner." Clara glared scornfully at her daughter, breathing heavily through her nostrils.

Angela rose from the table and threw down her serviette. Keeping her eyes fixed on the doorway she moved quickly past the fountain and out of the dining room into the hall. Garratt Kinnear stood by the serving door and watched her but she did not look at him. Her eyes were hot with tears as she ran up the stairs and into the bedroom.

When Clara Powell finished her dinner and had given herself sufficient time before she could follow her daughter, she too rose from the table. but when she knocked on the bedroom door to announce her presence there was no reply. The room was empty. Concerned, she retraced her steps downstairs.

"Have you seen my daughter?" she enquired of the girl behind the reception desk.

"No, ma'am," was the reply.

Clara opened the doors to the garden. The band had begun to play and the Chinese lanterns around the lawn were already illuminated, moving gently in the wind like candle flames. Shreds of cloud veiled the face of the moon.

Clara pulled her shawl about her shoulders and walked to the dance pavilion in search of her daughter.

In the cave below the cliffs, Sam Brock and his father were making final preparations for the whisky delivery.

"Now don't forget," whispered Henry Brock, "Their signal is two short flashes and two long ones. When you see it, cut your motor and drift in. They'll come and get you. Be sure and count the money in their presence. Don't let them hurry you. Understood?"

Sam nodded.

"Good luck, son. Get aboard and I'll cast you off."

Sam started the engine. In the confines of the cave it rang like a buzz saw. Slowly the heavily laden craft pulled away from the dock, through the cave mouth, and out onto the open lake. Sam glanced up at the sky. A bank of cloud had moved in and virtually obscured the moon as the forecast had promised. He kept his speed down to create as little wash as possible. Half a mile from shore he passed some night fishermen, their light boats identified with lamps on their prows.

Suddenly he heard a rustling behind him. The tarpaulin moved and Angela Powell appeared, smiling sheepishly at him. Sam hit the steering wheel in anger.

"What the hell are you doing here? This is no place for you. I told you."

"The only fun I have is when I'm with you," she pleaded.

"I'm going to turn back," said Sam, testily.

"No, please. I promise I won't be any trouble." She moved up the cramped deck towards him and held onto his arm.

"Then you've got to be absolutely quiet. And look out for any lights. We'll be on the American side of the border in a moment. If you see anything let me know."

Angela leaned her head against his shoulder and felt the wind in her face. She was with the man she loved and they had a mission.

"Do you hear anything?" whispered Sam.

Angela strained her ears. Faintly she discerned the throbbing of an engine. Sam pushed in the throttle and let the boat idle. The sound grew louder. A shaft of light sliced the darkness and moved over the water. A couple of hundred yards away a dark shape loomed out of the night and with it the sound of a loud-hailer: "This is the United States Coast Guard. Stop your engines and drop anchor. We are coming alongside."

Sam gunned the engine and turned the wheel a hundred and eighty degrees. "Hold on," he whispered frantically to Angela, "I'm going to make a run for it to our waters."

The motorboat heaved under the sudden thrust of power and roared off. The loud-hailer barked again: "Stop your engines or you will be fired upon."

Sam clutched the steering wheel and gritted his teeth, willing the boat to go faster.

A burst of machine-gun fire sizzled into the water in front of them. Angela clung to Sam, shaking with fear. Sam began to weave left and right as the Coast Guard vessel gained on them. The voice on the loud-hailer became more insistent. Then another burst of machine-gun fire. The shots smacked into the stern of the boat, igniting the fuel tank. The engine exploded and in seconds the vessel was a ball of flame.

The guests of the summer hotel gathered on the clifftop and watched in horror as a fire burned in the middle of the lake under the spotlight of the U.S. Coast Guard patrol boat.

Garratt Kinnear watched too from the attic of the hotel, nodding his head in grim satisfaction. He waited in the darkness for Angela Powell to return to her room so that he could watch her undress through the crack in the ceiling. . . .

The marble floor of the dance pavilion is cracked and splattered with wet leaves. The roof overhead has collapsed, leaving only a skeletal frame. The wind shudders through the long grass and whips it against the rotting timbers of the hall. The only presence is an old man in stained blue denim overalls — dancing to a half-forgotten melody that rings in his head.

Garratt Kinnear holds a remnant of material in his hands as he shuffles across the floor, accompanied by the sound of the wind and the lake water below the limestone cliffs.

"You're so beautiful in your white dress," he murmurs. "I'll protect you, don't you worry. You are my darling. I will never leave you. We will stay at the hotel forever. Just you and me, my love."